CAMBRIDGE LIBRARY COLLECTION

Books of enduring scholarly value

European History

This series includes accounts of historical events and movements by eye-witnesses and contemporaries, as well as landmark studies that assembled significant source materials or developed new historiographical methods. It covers the social and political history of continental Europe from the Renaissance to the end of the nineteenth century, and its broad range includes works on Russia and the Balkans, revolutionary France, the papacy and the inquisition, and the Venetian state archives.

Bibliotheca Anglo-Judaica

The pogroms in Russia following the assassination of Alexander II led many Jewish scholars in Europe to examine closely the history and culture of their people. In England, journalist and historian Lucien Wolf (1857–1930) and writer and folklorist Joseph Jacobs (1854–1916) were among those to write articles on the situation in Russia, and also on the wider history of European Judaism. In particular, they were both interested in the chequered history of the Jews in England, and following the successful Anglo-Jewish Historical Exhibition of 1887 (whose catalogue is also reissued in this series) they jointly compiled this important bibliography. Published in 1888, it was an attempt to list for the first time published works concerned with Judaism in England. Also including entries on manuscripts dating back to the reign of Henry III, this remains an essential resource for students of Anglo-Jewish history.

T0370871

Cambridge University Press has long been a pioneer in the reissuing of out-of-print titles from its own backlist, producing digital reprints of books that are still sought after by scholars and students but could not be reprinted economically using traditional technology. The Cambridge Library Collection extends this activity to a wider range of books which are still of importance to researchers and professionals, either for the source material they contain, or as landmarks in the history of their academic discipline.

Drawing from the world-renowned collections in the Cambridge University Library and other partner libraries, and guided by the advice of experts in each subject area, Cambridge University Press is using state-of-the-art scanning machines in its own Printing House to capture the content of each book selected for inclusion. The files are processed to give a consistently clear, crisp image, and the books finished to the high quality standard for which the Press is recognised around the world. The latest print-on-demand technology ensures that the books will remain available indefinitely, and that orders for single or multiple copies can quickly be supplied.

The Cambridge Library Collection brings back to life books of enduring scholarly value (including out-of-copyright works originally issued by other publishers) across a wide range of disciplines in the humanities and social sciences and in science and technology.

Bibliotheca Anglo-Judaica

*A Bibliographical Guide
to Anglo-Jewish History*

COMPILED BY JOSEPH JACOBS
AND LUCIEN WOLF

CAMBRIDGE
UNIVERSITY PRESS

CAMBRIDGE UNIVERSITY PRESS

Cambridge, New York, Melbourne, Madrid, Cape Town,
Singapore, São Paolo, Delhi, Mexico City

Published in the United States of America by Cambridge University Press, New York

www.cambridge.org
Information on this title: www.cambridge.org/9781108053747

© in this compilation Cambridge University Press 2013

This edition first published 1888
This digitally printed version 2013

ISBN 978-1-108-05374-7 Paperback

BIBLIOTHECA

ANGLO - JUDAICA.

Bibliotheca Anglo=Judaica.

A BIBLIOGRAPHICAL GUIDE

TO

ANGLO-JEWISH HISTORY.

COMPILED BY

JOSEPH JACOBS AND LUCIEN WOLF.

Publications of the Anglo=Jewish Historical Exhibition.
No. 3.

LONDON:
OFFICE OF THE "JEWISH CHRONICLE,"
2, FINSBURY SQUARE, E.C.

1888.

TABLE OF CONTENTS.

a 3

PREFACE.

In the following pages we have attempted to bring together the raw materials of the history of the Jews in England, hitherto scattered among many thousand volumes or tracts, but some day, we hope, to be properly digested and suitably presented in artistic form. Our aim has been to prepare the way for this consummation, by arranging our materials in such a way as to make them most easily available for the students of Anglo-Jewish history—if any such there be. We have accordingly classified the entries, and under each class we have arranged them alphabetically or chronologically, according as we considered either method of arrangement more suitable, letting uniformity give way to utility. As so much of the work is already arranged alphabetically, and so much else is anonymous, and as our immediate purpose is to subserve history rather than bibliography, an Index did not seem necessary.

We have prefixed to the lists of books some account of the MSS. containing information on Anglo-Jewish history. Here we have been working on almost entirely virgin soil, which was scarcely even touched by the investigations connected with the late Anglo Jewish Historical Exhibition. Where possible it has been our aim to give some short account of the contents of the various MSS., so that the student may judge whether it is worth consultation.

The bibliography itself is divided into three parts dealing respectively with the Pre-expulsion period up to 1290,

the Middle Age up to 1656, and the Modern period
down to the present day. In the former periods we have
endeavoured to collect every item of information that
we could come across in the original sources. In the
Pre-expulsion period this has involved a reference to
almost every work of importance, dealing with the general
history of England for that period. Hence we can only
profess to give those items which are given in the indexes to the Rolls Series and Record Commission publications, the chief county and town histories, and the
publications of the antiquarian societies which deal with
the period. In these cases the entries are taken directly
from the indexes in the volumes, which are unfortunately
often too meagre. At the same time many other items are
given, and in the case of the various series of Rolls published by the Record Commission (Nos. 129-135, 154-165),
the references have been obtained by searching out the
Jewish names from the indexes, which include considerably over 100,000 names. A few references are added
to modern historians of repute, and Holinshed's entries
have been given as a specimen of the Elizabethan
annalists, who cannot however be considered as original
authorities.   Lastly, care has been taken to give as
many references as could be found to the Jewish sources
for the period.   In a few cases where only a single piece
of information is contained in a volume we have given it
in full.*

We have been equally full in the entries relating to
the Middle-age of Anglo-Jewish history, between the

---

* The student may be reminded that the majority of the Papers
of the Anglo-Jewish Exhibition, as well as Mr. M. D. Davis's
edition of the *Shetaroth*, issued with this volume, deal with the
Pre-expulsion Period.

Expulsion and the Return. This period has till lately been regarded as a blank, but, as Mr. S. L. Lee was the first to show, and as our entries amply substantiate, there are a large number of scattered references to the existence of Jews in this period at all times from Edward II. to the Commonwealth.*

In the Modern period, since the return in 1656, we found it impossible to give facts scattered in isolated volumes, and our entries relate for the most part to books and pamphlets entirely devoted to various aspects of Anglo-Jewish history during this period. In two sections, however, those giving biographical details and information about communal organisation, we have departed from this rule, and have given every scrap of information we could collect on these subjects, which form the backbone of the recent history. Most of the works mentioned have passed under our eyes,† but in a few instances, the titles have been taken from bibliographical works. Where size and place of publication are not given, it should be understood that the book was published in London in octavo form. The date is at times omitted in sections arranged chronologically : in such cases it is the same as the preceding number.

The bibliography will probably be considered sufficiently extensive by most who consult it. Yet it includes only part of the materials we have collected, as in our opinion bearing on the subject. We have collected a very large number of entries on Christian

* A paper on this subject will be found in the volume of Papers issued with this work.

† A number of the rarest formerly belonged to the collection of the late Alfred Newman, now in the possession of Mr. Asher I. Myers. To these we have added the initials A.N. in brackets.

Rabbinic scholarship in England, on dramas,* novels, and poems written about Jews, on Belles Lettres written by English Jews and Jewesses, and on contributions to science and scholarship by English Jews, and on the "Anglo-Israel" craze, as well as details of Anglo-Jewish music. But these topics, though interesting in themselves, only indirectly throw light on Anglo-Jewish history, and would have unnecessarily increased the size of the book. Articles in periodicals dealing with Jewish subjects have been very fully given by Poole in his "Index to Periodical Literature," and it seemed scarcely worth while to print the few additions we could make.‡

Lastly, the pleasant task remains of thanking those who have kindly aided us in some of the sections. Dr. C. Gross has been enabled, by his unrivalled knowledge of English municipal records, to add the items given in Appendix to Part I. under his name. Mr. Lewis Emanuel has kindly revised the sections relating to the Acts of Parliament and leading cases, to which he has made many valuable additions. Dr. Friedlander has been good enough to check the Hebrew items. We would also like to record the services of Mr. Dunn, Reader to Messrs. Wertheimer and Lea and Co., whose care has prevented many mistakes from creeping into a work which has been produced rather hurriedly so as not to delay the series. This unavoidable haste must

* A tolerably complete list of these appeared in the "Era Almanac" for 1881.

† A few of the earliest and most interesting of these were exhibited at the British Museum during the late Exhibition (Cat., pp. 201-2).

‡ A number of medical and anthropological articles are given by Billings in his magnificent "Medical Bibliography," *sub voce* "Jews."

be our excuse for any lapses beyond those to which bibliographical works, even when produced under more favourable circumstances, are proverbially liable.

We have by this work done our best to enable the inquirer into Anglo-Jewish history to quote his sources accurately, and to fulfil the Rabbinic maxim, " Say a thing in the name of him who said it." We trust we shall not be considered presumptuous if we express a hope that we shall be spared the fate, too often dealt out to bibliographers, of not being quoted at all. In making this request we ask but a small reward for a great labour —a task which has, however, been lightened throughout by being a labour of love.

JOSEPH JACOBS.
LUCIEN WOLF.

NOTE.—By an inadvertence the numbers at the end of Part II., and at the beginning of Part III. overlap for seventeen items (280-296). If any of these are to be quoted they could be distinguished by a reference to the Part. In the section " Communal Organisation " some of the entries have no bibliographical references, as none could be obtained by the time fixed for passing the sheets for press.

MANUSCRIPT SOURCES OF ANGLO-JEWISH HISTORY.

BESIDES the extensive materials for Anglo-Jewish History that are given in the printed works catalogued in the present volume, there exists quite as much inedited in MS. form. Indeed, with regard to the period previous to 1656, the MS. sources largely exceed in bulk the matter that has already been printed. As these are gradually printed or calendared, references to English Jews are almost invariably found in them, leading to the conclusion that those MSS still inaccessible will be equally rich in new information. It was, however, obviously impossible to indicate all these sporadic references, and we confine ourselves in the following account to MSS. dealing entirely with details of Anglo-Jewish History.

The MSS. throwing light on the pre-Expulsion history of the Jews in this country are more than usually accessible to the student, being mainly concentrated in three repositories—the Public Record Office, the British Museum, and the Chapter House, Westminster. At the two former institutions the documents can always be seen; and at Westminster the Dean and Chapter have shown themselves willing to place their treasures at the disposal of a duly-qualified student, under proper restrictions and conditions. A short account of the various documents to be found at these institutions will be some guide as to their value and use.

A. PUBLIC RECORD OFFICE. (Rolls House, Chancery Lane.)—The Jewish MSS. at this store-house of English history are mainly comprised of three series of documents, termed respectively :—(1) " Exchequer of Receipt—Jews ; (2) " Exchequer of Pleas—Jews ;" and (3) " Memoranda of the Queen s Remembrancer—Jews," under which headings the various rolls are to be asked for. A short description of the first series, which gives the receipts of the Tallages for various years, was given by M. Schwab in the *Revue des études juives* (XI. 256, *seq*.), and need not here be repeated. It may however be remarked that in the Record Office the rolls are numbered consecutively from No. 85, so that 84 is to be added to the number given by M. Schwab.

The second series of plea rolls, recording cases tried before the Justices of the Jews, have never yet been calendared, and a list of the terms and years to which they apply may here be given :—

EXCHEQUER OF PLEAS—JEWS' ROLLS.

No.	Term.	Year.	Mem.	No.	Term.	Year.	Mem.
1	——	3-4 Hen. III.	Printed by Cole.	12	Hil.	1 Ed. L.	8
				13	Trin.	1 Ed. I.	10
				14	Trin.	1 Ed. I.	4
2	Easter	28 Hen. III.	4	15	Mich.	1-2 Ed. I.	11
3	Trin.	28 Hen. III.	7	16	Mich.	2-3 Ed. I.	12
4	Mich.	28-9 H. III.	6*	17	Trin.	2-3 Ed. I.	12
5	Easter	37 Hen. III.	1	18	Hil.	3 Ed. I.	11
6	——	37 Hen. III.	9	19	Easter	3 Ed. I.	10
7	——	50 Hen. III.	2	20	Trin.	3 Ed. I.	21 †
8	Trin.	51-52 H. III.	5	21	Mich.	3-4 Ed. I.	18
9	Easter	51 Hen. III.	2	22	Trin.	4 Ed. I.	16
10	Easter	54 Hen. III.	8	23	Easter	5 Ed. I.	12
11	Trin.	56 Hen. III.	4				

* Entry in Hebrew on last membrane relating to a debt of £27. Also contains tallage memoranda.

No.	Term.	Year.	Mem.	No.	Term.	Year.	Mem.
24	Trin.	5 Ed. I.	9	36	Easter	8 Ed. I.	10
25	Mich.	6 Ed. I.	14	37	Trin.	8 Ed. I.	10
26	Mich.	6 Ed. I.	9	38	Easter	9 Ed. I.	7
27	Hil.	6 Ed. I.	8	39	Trin.	9 Ed. I.	11
28	Easter	6 Ed. I.	5	40	Hil.	10 Ed. I.	9
29	Easter	6 Ed. I.	6	41	Mich.	10-11 Ed. I.	10
30	Trin.	6 Ed. I.	6	42	Hil.	11 Ed. I.	5
31	Mich.	7 Ed. I.	7	43	Easter	11 Ed. I.	9
32	Hil.	7 Ed. I.	4	44	Trin.	11 Ed. I.	5
33	Easter	7 Ed. I.	5	45	Trin.	12 Ed. I.	9
34	Trin.	7 Ed. I.	7	46	Mich.	12-13 Ed. I.	7
35	Hil.	8 Ed. I.	9	47	Trin.	14 Ed. I.	9

The whole legal history of the early Jews in England is written in these 381 membranes, which include the names of almost every Jew who existed in England in the reigns of Henry III. and Edward I., and record almost every transaction in which he was connected. The more interesting cases should be selected, and the names occurring in the remainder tabulated, if a solid foundation is to be made for the early history of the English Jews.

The third Jewish series at the Rolls House is more varied in its character than the other two, as may be judged from the following short calendar :—

MEMORANDA OF THE QUEEN'S REMEMBRANCER.—
JEWS' ROLLS.*

		Memb.
556.	1. Bonds, temp. Hen. II.	3
	2. Tallage 5,000 marcs, 5 Ric. I.	3
	3. Debts found in Cambridge archa, 8-24 Hen. III.	3
	4. List of Lincoln Jews, 1240, A.D.	11
	5. Bonds, 33-53 Hen. III.	14
	6. Chattels of Abraham of Berkhampstead, 34 Hen. III.	3
	7. Receipt of Tallage, 38 Hen. III.	1

* A fuller calendar will be found in the MS. descriptive 'i t of this series (vol. xxii.) at the Rolls House.

This series of rolls is peculiarly rich in information about the Expulsion, full particulars of the results of which can be obtained from 557, Nos. 9-23.

Besides these series, specially devoted to Jewish matters, isolated deeds occur in many of the other series, some of which may be here referred to :—

Inquisitio post mortem. 34 H. III. 50 Jacob Crispin.
      ,,   ,,   36 H. III. 49 Joce le Prestre.
Misc. Q.R. Misc.   10 Ed. I.   Inquisition into Jews' house
                                       at Oxford.
      ,,   ,,   Constable of Tower, 561-5. Transport of 1335
                          Jews to " Wytsond " at Expulsion at a charge
                          of 4d. per head [See D. K. Rep. xl. p. 474.]
Tower Misc. 74. List of grantees of houses at Expulsion.
   ,,   ,,   144. Jews' houses escheated to King, c. 5 Ed. I.
Chapter House. London Bag 14. Four *Shetaroth.*
      ,,   ,,   Box 43 Jews' Bonds.
Royal Letters, 4961-3. Correspondence about a Jewish physician.

Items relating to Jews occur, indeed, in all the great series of rolls, as can be judged from the references in the bibliography to those parts of the series already printed (Nos. 21-25, 129-135, 154-165).   It would be a huge task to go through the whole of these series to discover the Jewish items, but it may be anticipated that as the Pipe Rolls and other documents are printed, fresh accessions to our knowledge may be anticipated from these publications.

B. BRITISH MUSEUM.—A full list of the original charters relating to the Jews, in the British Museum, was given in the "Catalogue of the Anglo-Jewish Exhibition," pp. 183-188. Besides these a few transcripts occur as follows :—

Harl.   980. Notes on Presbyter Judæorum.
  ,,   1,709. Reference to Justices of Jews.
Lansd.   215. Excerpts from Tallage, 35 H. II.
  ,,   625. Grantees of Jews' houses at Expulsion.
Add.   4,363. Notes on Jews,
  ,,   4,542.   ,,   ,,   } Madox Collection.
  ,,   4,565.   ,,   ,,

Add. 24,509. Bonds [= Misc. Q.R. 556. 1.]
  ,,   24,510. Inquisition Abstract [= Misc. Q.R. 557, 12.]
  ,,   29,868. Three *Shetaroth* translated by E. Mendes da Costa.

C. WESTMINSTER ABBEY.—This collection consists of 489 rolls, some of several membranes, put together in sixteen bundles, and numbered in pencil at the back. It will be useful to present a list of these bundles, and a short indication of the documents they contain.

   I. [Nos. 140-157] Small Rolls of various kinds, four of them (140, 145, 147, 157) giving transactions of Norwich Jewish Exchequer day by day in the years 9-11, Hen. III.
  II. [182-210] Sales of Houses to Jews.
 III. [202-206] Writs to Cyrographers of Norwich, Nottingham, and Canterbury.
 IV. [158-169] Sales of Houses to Jews.
  V. [1-11], VI. [12-104], VII. [105-139] Hebrew *Shetaroth*, all now printed in Mr. M. D. Davis' edition.
VIII. [256-380] Writs of various kinds to the Cyrographers.
 IX. [211-255] Bonds to Jews.
  X. [381-391] Quittances by Jews to Christian Debtors.
 XI. [391-404], XII. [170-181] Writs issued by Justices of Jews.
XIII. [405-420], XIV. [421-424], XV. [425-439], XVI. [440-486*b*.] Bonds to Jews.

A small number of these deeds were selected by P. C. Webb, and published by him in 1753, in his *Question*, etc. (*see* No. 192); but the Norwich Daybook, in Bundle I., still awaits publication. Indeed, the larger proportion of the deeds relate to Norwich : of the 267 deeds contained in bundles I.-IV., VIII.-XII., no less than 94 relate to that town. The remainder are chiefly from Nottingham, Canterbury, and Colchester, and are probably the results of the " scrutiny " of the archa of these places at the "Starr Chamber" at Westminster.

Besides the deeds contained in these three institutions, there are a few others elsewhere, most of which have been described by the Historical MSS. Commission (*see* No. 75), among which the deeds at St. Paul's, in the Ninth Report, are the most important and interesting. Besides the Oxford Deeds referred to in the Fourth Report, others are given by Macray (No. 95, cf. *Revue* v. 248), and by Mr. Madan in his just issued *Rough Notes*, Nos. 326, 687. There are besides some documents belonging to the Corporations of London, Norwich, and Winchester, which have not yet been made accessible to the inquirer, but will shortly be made known through published calendars. Indeed, as the bibliography shows, there is scarcely any publication of original deeds relating to national or local history previous to 1290 that does not contain sporadic references to Jews.

The Records of the House of Converts in Chancery Lane supply a connecting link between the Expulsion in 1290 and the Re-settlement in 1656. These are contained in 177 Rolls at the Record Office, known by the title of "Miscellanea of the Queen's Remembrancer— Domus Conversorum," and extend from 5 Edw. III. to 5-6 Jac. I. They contain the accounts, year by year, of the Master of the House of Converts, and include the receipts of the Converts themselves. Some of the latter are signed in Hebrew (*vide* 2-3 Hen. IV.). Among the names which may be found of interest are Philip Ferdinandus (41 Eliz.), Eliz. Fardinando (5 Jac. I.), and Yehooda Menda (20 Eliz.). There does not appear to have been any convert between 6 Edw. VI. and 20 Eliz.

Of more general interest are the State Papers also in the Record Office. As far as these touch what we have

called in the following pages the "Middle Age" and
the "National Movement for the Return," they have
been exhaustively calendered; and transcripts of the
Indexes, giving all necessary indications for the student,
will be found under Nos. 209 and 293. These extracts
have been prepared in the light of the most recent
investigations, and they will be found to comprise
such new names in Anglo-Jewish history as Maria
Anthony de Verona, Mark Raphael, Carvajal, Coronel,
Casseres, &c. Some Hebraic names have been hypotheti-
cally included, as likely to lead the student to further dis-
coveries. The calendars of Domestic State Papers of the
years 1641-1649 have not yet been printed. It is highly
probable that they will be found to throw considerable
light on the history of the events which led up to the
return, and on the condition of the Marrano community which is believed to have existed in London
at this period. The minutes of the Privy Council
since 1542 also remain unprinted. These have, however, been searched—thanks to Mr. C. Lennox Peel—
and one Jewish reference relating to the fate of Jacob
Barnett (No. 220) has been found.* One of the printed
entries referred to at No. 208 speaks of an important
list of Jews, and an inventory of their estates, drawn up
in 1542, at the instance of the Privy Council. The book
containing these precious data has been sought for, but
unfortunately without success. The "Johnson MSS."
discovered at Hull (see Nos. 218a and 223), of which a few
still remain unprinted, contain curious references to Jews
during the Middle Age, and one describes a synagogue
established in Hull, about 1600, on the site of a still older

* This has since been printed at length in the "Anglo-Jewish
Historical Exhibition Papers," pp. 74-75.

Jewish house of worship. The genuineness of these documents has been strongly assailed, and is very doubtful.

The British Museum Collection of MSS. affords a few important contributions to the history of the Re-settlement. The two petitions of Manuel Martinez Dormido, *alias* David Abrabanel (*see* No. 958), presented to Cromwell in 1654, are to be found in the Egerton Collection (Add. MSS. Eng., 1049, fol. 6). One of these is a formal petition to Cromwell to allow the Jews to settle freely in England, and it bears a memorandum which illustrates the Protector's favourable view of the question. Another interesting MS. (Add. MSS., 4106, fol. 253), refers to certain negotiations between the Jews of Amsterdam and Charles II., then in exile at Bruges, and incidentally yields significant evidence on the question of the extent to which Menasseh ben Israel represented his Dutch co-religionists in his mission to England. The Museum also possesses a large number of the manuscripts of Emanuel Mendez da Costa (No. 943). One volume (Add. MSS., 29,867) is a commonplace book, in which are a few memoranda on Anglo-Jewish history. Another (Add. MSS., 29,868) consists of a collection of miscellaneous MSS., among which is a list of Jews (fols. 15 and 16), hitherto supposed to be "a list of the earliest Jewish settlers in this country."* A comparison of the document with the burial register of the Bevis Marks Synagogue conclusively proves that the date assigned to it is too early, and its importance much exaggerated. It refers to the "widow" of Antonio Ferdinando, *alias* Antonio Fernandez Carvajal (see No. 923), and it includes the name of Dormido. It must con-

* Picciotto : "Sketches of Anglo-Jewish History," pp. 32, 33.

sequently have been drawn up sometime between 1659 when Carvajal died and 1667 when Dormido died. From internal evidence it would appear to have been the work of a non-Jew, and, perhaps, had some connection with the threatened re-expulsion of the Jews soon after Charles II.'s accession to the Throne in 1660. The Restoration was by no means so happy an event for the Jews as has been represented. So far from Charles II. having been favourable to them,* there is abundant evidence that with the inauguration of his reign the Jews of London were again reduced to the secret worship which they had followed previous to the mission of Menasseh ben Israel. The London merchants, who had then exclaimed against the tolerance of Cromwell, seem to have expected that the "Merry Monarch" would reverse the policy of the Protector in that respect. So much is evident from a petition on the subject presented to the King by the Lord Mayor and Aldermen, in 1660, and the text of which is preserved in the Remembrancia of the City of London (vol. ix., 44).

For the later political history of the English Jews the archives of the London Committee of Deputies of British Jews will be found exceedingly valuable. The Board was founded in 1745 as a Committee of Diligence, to assist the progress of the Jewish Naturalisation Bill, introduced into the Irish House of Commons in that year. Its minutes and letter-books are intact from that date, and form a complete documentary history of the external relations of the Anglo-Jewish community for over a hundred and forty years. The Board took the lead in the struggle for Jewish emancipation; it caused measures, adapted to Jewish requirements, to be initi-

---

* Picciotto: "Sketches," pp. 30, 31.

ated in Parliament, and has been instrumental in obtaining the extension or modification of clauses in Acts affecting Jewish interests. It has also watched over and defended Jewish rights and privileges on every possible occasion. In assisting foreign oppressed communities, it was, during the presidency of the late Sir Moses Montefiore, and before the foundation of the Alliance Israélite Universelle, the leading Jewish body in the world. On all these subjects its records contain precious information. Of late years the Anglo-Jewish Association has shared with it, in amicable co-partnership, the conduct of foreign affairs. The minutes of the latter Society, and especially the reports of its Executive Committee—complete since 1871—offer copious data, not only on Anglo-Jewish history, but also on general Jewish history. In the library of the College at Ramsgate, established by the late Sir Moses Montefiore in memory of his wife, are some valuable letters and records relating to the foreign missions undertaken by that philanthropist on behalf of the Board of Deputies. These include the note-books kept by him during his travels in the East, and the original firman of the Sultan of Turkey, granting equal rights to Jews. The original decree, in the same sense, obtained from the Emperor of Morocco, in 1864, is to be found in the vestry-room of the Bevis Marks Synagogue. An important collection of documents relating to the emancipation struggle is in the possession of Sir Julian Goldsmid, Bart., M.P., whose grandfather, Sir Isaac Lyon Goldsmid was the leading figure in that crisis of Anglo-Jewish history. They are contained in two volumes, and consist principally of correspondence with Lord Holland, the Marquis of Lansdowne, the Duke of Wellington, Earl Grey, Sir Robert Peel, Lord Melbourne, Lord Denman,

Dean Milman, Lord Wynford, the Earl of Auckland, and other influential personages.

From the year 1664 the MSS. relating to the internal history of the community are fairly complete. The only important documents of an earlier date are the memoranda of leases of the first Jewish cemetery, founded in 1657, which have, however, been printed (see No. 296), and some accounts relating to repairs of the Synagogue in King Street, Aldgate. These are in the Bevis Marks Synagogue. It is curious that the earliest document bearing on the history of the Jews of Ireland also relates to their cemetery, being a deed of conveyance of the burial ground at the foot of Ballybough Bridge, Dublin. This is dated 1727, and is preserved at Dublin Castle. With one exception the Minute Books of the Spanish and Portuguese Congregation are intact from the year 1664. The first volume is an interesting record of the organisation and early struggles of the community. The missing volume (from 1698 to 1724) was in the possession of the late Isaac da Costa, of Amsterdam, and was sold in 1861 when his library was dispersed. In it is contained all that the historian will require to know with regard to the building of the Synagogue in Bevis Marks, the oldest Jewish house of worship in the country. The records of the other London synagogues are also in good preservation, and are full of information on the organisation and social condition of the community during the periods to which they relate. The same may be said of the archives of the Charitable and Educational Institutions, a list of which will be found on pp. 160-167. Of the provincial synagogues and societies we cannot speak with certainty. The records of several extinct communities

are known to have been lost or mislaid. It is to be
hoped that the present revived interest in Anglo-Jewish
History will result in some measure for the systematic
preservation of such records in the future.

For Anglo-Jewish Biography and Genealogy—two
branches of history which remain as yet unexplored—
the manuscript materials are abundant. Foremost among
them must be mentioned the Synagogue Registers of
Births, Marriages, and Deaths. These have been
admirably preserved, and, in the Bevis Marks Synagogue,
are fairly well indexed. One volume of marriage contracts was unfortunately destroyed some years ago when
a fire took place in the house of the Chacham (Chief
Rabbi), to whom it had been lent. The earliest Register of Burials dates from 1657. It is apparently not
the original register, but a careful copy of names and
dates made direct from the tombstones. Its genealogical value is inferior to that of the subsequent
volumes as the names are given in simple form
instead of in the genealogical form usual in such
registers. One of the Khetubah (Marriage Contract)
Books (1701-10) has the following curious title :—
" Registers of Marriages by the Right Rev. Father in
God, David Netto Archacynogue." An important register is the Alien Book, which contains the counterfoils
of certificates granted to Jewish aliens by the secretary of
the Bevis Marks Synagogue under the Act of 1803. It
records the origin of a large number of Anglo-Jewish
families ; and the frequent occurrence of the phrase,
" who fled from the Inquisition," invests it with mournful
interest.

Of actual pedigrees the only extensive collection will
be found mentioned in the Catalogue of the Anglo-

Jewish Historical Exhibition (p. 31, No. 762), where a list is given. They number about sixty, and have been compiled from Synagogue records, the archives of Heralds' College, family documents, &c. Some of them are very elaborate. One of the Montefiore family contains nearly 1000 names. The Beth Hamidrash contains a set of elaborate pedigrees of the English Chief Rabbis, prepared by Mr. N. L. D. Zimmer.

The Jewish genealogist may also be recommended to consult the following MS. collections :—

Private Acts of Parliament.
Petitions to Parliament.
Le Neve's Obituary, from 1658 to 1680 (Brit. Mus. Harl. MSS., 6404-6418).
Musgrave's Obituary (Brit. Mus. Add. MSS., 5727-5749).
Wills in the Probate Office.
Grants of Arms at Heralds' College.
Patents of Denization on the Patent Rolls at the Record Office.

The British Museum contains the following MSS. of Jewish biographical interest :—

Moses Hart: Petition to Geo. II., 1744 (Add. MSS. 23,819, fol. 63).
Abraham Israel: Contract with Charles II. for gold mines in Jamaica, 1662 (Add. MSS. Eg. 2551, fol. 152).
Antonio de Souza : (Add. MSS. 15,194, fols. 161, 183 and 15,199, fol. 245).
Antonio de Sousa, Commission to, 1660.   (Add MSS. 20,846, fol. 187.)
Emanuel Mendez da Costa: Letter to and from the Princess of Waldeck (Add. MSS. 15,943, fols. 126-127).
Emanuel Mendez da Costa: Minutes of the Royal Soc., and Soc. of Antiq., 1757-62 (Add. MSS. Eg. 2381).
Emanuel Mendez da Costa : Correspondence 1727-1787, 11 vols. (Add. MSS. 28,534-28,544).

David Mendez da Costa, Commissariat Officer in Germany: Letter and Memo. Book, 1757-1759 (Add. MSS. Eg. 2227).

Franz Van Schonenberg, Envoy to Spain and Portugal: Credentials to Pedro II., 1702. (Add. MSS. 28,945, fol. 353.)

Franz Van Schonenberg: Letter to Lord Portland, 1689. (Add. MSS. Eg. 1707, fol 45.)

Franz Van Schonenberg: Letters to Lords Manchester and Nottingham, 1702, 1703. (Add MSS. 29,590, folios 3, 40, 64, 66, 265.)

Solomon da Costa : Letters to J. Caryll, 1746. (Add. MSS. 28,330, fols. 323-324.)

Solomon da Costa, Letter to Sir N. H. Carew, 1748. (Add. MSS. 29,599, fol. 347.)

Collections of autograph letters, of substantial biographical value, are in the possession of Dr. Maurice Davis, Mr. Lewis Emanuel, Mr. C. K. Salaman, and Mr. C. I. de Sola, of Montreal. Details of these Collections may be found on pp. 26–30 of the Catalogue of the Anglo-Jewish Historical Exhibition (1887).

At the same Exhibition were shown some interesting literary MSS. of Solomon da Costa Athias (775-777), Rabbi Zebi Hirsch (779-782), Dr. Meyer Schomberg (783), Naphtali ben Abraham (786), Rabbi de Falk (787-789), Rabbi Tevle Schiff (791), Abraham ben Naphtali Tang (792 and 808), N. L. Benmohel (794-796), E. H. Lindo (802-3, 2142-2145, and 2146-2148), Grace Aguilar (804-806), and Michael Josephs (809-810). Particulars of these may be found in the Catalogue on referring to the numbers appended to their names. In the Montefiore College at Ramsgate are a few inedited MSS. of the late Lady Montefiore.

Bibliotheca Anglo=Judaica.

I.—PRE-EXPULSION PERIOD.

Cam. Soc.—*Camden Society Publications.*
E.H.S.—*English Historical Society.*
R.C.—*Record Commission.*
R.S.—*Rolls Series.*

1. ABRAHAM BEN MEIR IBN EZRA.—מורא ספר יסוד
Grundlage der Gottesverehrung in einer paraphras-
tischen Verdeutschung, von M. Creizenach. Frankfort a. M., 1840.

> First separate edition in 1529. Written in England in
> 1158. Some copies of Creizenach's edition were issued at
> Cambridge, with title page attributing German version to
> D. H. Oppenheim.

2. —— אגרת השבת.—Sabbath Epistle.
> First printed 1690. Best edition by Luzzato in *Kerem
> Chemed,* iv. 158. Written in England in 1158. Introduc-
> tion to, translated into Italian by Benedetti, *Canz. Sacro,* and
> in English by J. Jacobs, *Jewish Chron.,* Jan. 13, 1882.

2*a.* ACTA SANCTORUM. Edit. Bollandus, etc.
> ix., 586 : Mart. xxv : Willielmus de Norvico. [From
> Capgrave.]
> xxxiii. 494. Jul. xxvii. : Hugo puer Lincolniæ.
> lvi. 576. Oct. xix. S. Frideswida Oxoniæ.

3. ANCIENT LAWS OF ENGLAND.—Edit. Thorpe (R.C.),
1840.
> *Anglo-Saxon Laws.*
> All Jews under King's protection. Ed. C., 25.

B

Monumenta Ecclesiastica.
If a Christian woman fornicate with Jews, Th. P. xvi. 35.
If any one celebrate Easter with the Jews, Th. P. xxx. 4.
If any Christian accept unleavened bread, or any food
or drink from Jews, Th. P. xlii. 1.
If any Christian sell another to Jews, *ibid.* 3, Ecg. E. 150.
Mass not to be celebrated where Jews are buried, Th. P.
xlvii. 1.
That no Christian turn Jew, Ecg. E. 147, 150.

4. ANGLO-SAXON CHRONICLE, edit. Earle.   1865.
   1137. Martyrdom of William of Norwich, 263.
   [Sketch of Loddon Screen given on p. 371.]

5. ANNALES MONASTICI, edit. Luard, 1869.
                Annals of

Wi.—*Winchester.*	D.—*Dunstable.*
M.—*Margan.*	Be.—*Bermondsey.*
T.—*Tewkesbury.*	O.—*Ossory.*
Bu.—*Burton.*	W.—*T. Wykes.*
Wa.—*Waverley.*	Wo.—*Worcester.*

Miracle respecting a boy in 552, ii. 4 Wi.; Crime of in
766, ii. 157 Wa.; crucify a boy at Norwich in 1144, iv. 25 W.;
massacre of at coronation of Rich. I., i. 20, ii. 63, 246, iii.
25, iv. 42, 44, 386, M., Wi., Wa., D., O., W., Wo.;
pillaged and massacred by John in 1210, i. 29, ii. 81, 264,
iii. 32, 451, iv. 54, M., Wi., Wa., D., Be., O., W.; deacon
burnt at Oxford in 1222 for marrying a Jewess, ii. 296,
iii. 76, iv. 63, Wa., D., W.; contribution to Henry III. in
1225, ii. 301, Wa.; attack on and robbery of by Oxford
clerks in 1244, iv. 91, O., W.; ordered by Council of Lyons
to remit interest to crusaders, i. 269, Bu.; story of a Jew at
Toledo, iv. 437, Wo.; money borrowed of in 1249 by Richard
de Clare, i. 137, T.; inquiry into the chattels of those killed
in the diocese of Lichfield in 1254, i. 330, Bu.; same before
justices at Stafford in 1255, i. 338, Bu.; crucify Hugh of
Lincoln, i. 340, ii. 346, iv. 443, Bu., Wa. Wo.; execution
of eighteen in London in consequence, i. 346, ii. 348, Bu.,
Wa.; Dominicans try to save the rest, but fail, i. 346, 348,
Bu.; they are saved for a large sum by R. of Cornwall,
i. 348, 371, Bu.; how those who offend in ecclesiastical
causes are to be punished, 1258, i. 418, Bu.; complaints
against in the petitions of the barons at Oxford in 1258,
i. 442, Bu.; guardians of the Jewry appointed in 1258,
i. 451, Bu.; exchequers of, i. 478, Bu.; slaughter and
plunder of at Worcester in 1263, iv. 449, Wo.; slaughter in
London, 1263, ii. 101, iv. 141, 142, 450, Wi., W., Wo.;
slaughter in London by S. de Montfort, and in Canterbury
by G. de Clare, 1264, iv. 145, O.; slaughter by S. de

Montfort younger at Winchester, ii. 363, Wa.; slaughtered in Cambridgeshire by barons, ii. 371, Wa.; statutes against in 1269, iv. 221; statutes of Westminster against, respecting dress and money, ii. 119, 384, 385, iii. 265-6, iv. 265-6, 467-8, Wi., Wa., D., O., W., Wo.; hanged and imprisoned for clipping coin in 1278, ii. 390, iii. 279, 281, iv. 278, 279, 474, Wa., D., O., W., Wo.; imprisoned and fined in 1287, iv. 308-9, O., W.; insult to Sacrament by a Jew, who is burnt for it, iv. 503, Wo.; expelled England, ii. 409, iii. 361, 467, iv. 326, 503, 561, Wa., D., Be., O., Wo.: fr. Aquitaine, ii. 409, Wa.; ill-treatment at Cinque Ports, iv. 327, O.

Henry, a converted Jew, a papal letter to Dunstable Priory to provide for him, iii. 265, D.

James, settlement with Dunstable about Wadlow land, iii. 164 D.

Mossy, attempt of forgery on the Prior of Dunstable, iii. 66, D.

6. ARCHÆOLOGIA. [From Index to vols. i.-xxx.]

Their crucifixion of a child at Lincoln, i. 27, confirmed by records, 28.

No certain account of their appearing in England before Wm. I., vi. 163.

Their synagogues not built in a circular form, vi. 166, 172.

J. Caley, a memoir on their origin in England, viii. 389-405.

Wealth over-estimated in England in early times, xxviii. 224, 225.

Jews alone are licensed usurers, *ibid.*

6a. BACON, ROGER.—Opera Inedita, by J. S. Brewer (R. S.), 1859.

Pref. pp. lx., lxi., Jews helped to translate Arabic works.

7. BAKER, G.—History of County of Northampton, 1830.

Debts to, 152.

Lands pledged for, 351.

Reward for giving information of property of, 262.

8. BAKER, T.—History of College of St. John, Cambridge, edit. Mayor, 1869.

Settlement of, in Cambridge, 26.

Supposed site of their synagogue, 27.

Joceus, a Jew, owner of Bede's house in St. Sepulchre's parish, 27.

9. BANNISTER, J.—Jews in Cornwall, in *Journ. Roy. Inst. Corn.*, 1867.

Pp. 324—42.

See also P. Abrahams, "Curiosities of Judaism."

9a. BANNISTER, J.—Marazion, in *Notes and Queries*, xi. 456 (3rd series).

10. BAYLEY, J.—History of the Tower of London, 1830.
    1282, 600 for clipping in Tower, Clause 10, E. I., m. 5, in London 280 hanged, many more elsewhere, 279.

11. BIGLAND, R.—History of Gloucester, 1819.
    East Gate St. was formerly Jewry St.; on N. side remains of Jewish synagogue, 135.
    1169. Joce fined 100s.—1217. Committee of 24 townsmen appointed to watch over Jews, *ibid.*

12. BLOMEFIELD, F.—History of Norfolk, 1810.
    iii. 26-28, martyrdom of William of Norwich.
        64, Gul. de Norwich Justiciar of Jews, 1204.
    iv. 184, house of Abraham fil Deulecresse.
        510, Miryld filia Humfrey de Havile escheated her lands by marrying Jurnet the Jew, c. 1199.

13. BLUNT, J. E. —A History of the Establishment and Residence of the Jews in England: with an Inquiry into their Civil Disabilities. Lond., 1830.
    [A succinct résumé from Prynne, Madox, and Tovey.]

14. BOASE.—Oxford ("Historic Towns"), 1887.
    Jews, pp. 22, 32, 65, 68, 81.

15. BOND, E. A.—Extracts relating to Loans of Italian Merchants to Kings of England, in *Archæologia* xxviii.
    222-3 [wealth of Jews exaggerated], 224, 238, 242, 263, 264, 279, 280.

16. BRACTON.—De Legibus Angliæ, edit. Sir T. Twiss (R. S.), 1883.
    Jews capable of taking donation, i. 105.—Debt to a Jew, when interest shall not be paid, i. 481.—Jews excepted from a donation, i. 377.—Chattels of slain Jew to go to King, ii. 245.—May practise circumcision, ii. 464. [e.g.] Jew would lie if he said Christ was born of a virgin, as being against his intelligence, iv. 393.—Jew might impute to Jew [of essoins], v. 269.—Jews cannot have any property of their own, vi. 51, 57, and pp. xxiii.—xxviii.

17. —— Notebook, edit. F. W. Maitland, 1887.
    Nos. 169, 301, 581, 918, 456, 475, 1376, 1445, 1554, 1825.

18. BRAKELOND, JOCELIN DE.—Chronicon. (Cam. Soc.).
    2, 4, 8, 33, 106, 123.

19. BRAND, J.—History of Newcastle-on-Tyne, 1789.
    i. 359, Silver St., formerly Jewgate.
    ii. 140, expelled.

20. BURTON.—Chronica Monast. de Melsa, edit. E. A.
    Bond (R. S.), 1868.
    Transactions with, i. 133, 174, 306, 367, 374, 377; ii. 55,
    109, 116.
    Lands mortgaged to, i. 315; ii. 12, 115.—Search in the
    Jews' charter chest at York, i. 377.—Crucify a boy at
    Norwich, i. 138.—Crucify a boy at Gloucester, i. 210, 216.
    —Circumcise a boy at Norwich, i. 437.—Massacre of, *temp.*
    Rich. I., i. 243, 244.—Persecution of, 250 hanged in York
    Castle, i. 251.—Story of a Jew in Tewkesbury, ii. 134.—
    Punishment of Jewish money-clippers, ii. 163, 167.—Ex-
    pelled from France, ii. 248, 283, 318; from England, ii.
    251.—Miracle connected with Jews of Seville, iii. 153.—
    Massacre of, in Seville, iii.* 154.

21. CALENDAR OF DOCUMENTS.—Irish Series (R. S.).
    i. Justices for custody of Jews, Nos. 1291, 2079; ii. 473,
    526.

22. CALENDAR OF STATE PAPERS RELATING TO SCOT-
    LAND, vol. i., 1108—1272 (R. S.).
    No. 1211 [expelled from Newcastle, 1234], 1216 [York
    Jews].

23. CALENDARIUM GENEALOGICUM, edit. C. Roberts.
    20, 29, 33, 46, 50, 51, 95, 124, 131, 144, 158, 184, 259,
    301, 302, 312, 373, 467, 671.

24. CALENDARIUM INQUISITIONUM POST MORTEM, vol.
    i., edit. Lemon (R. C.), 1806.
    1, 5, 7, 11, 12, 42, 47, 70.

25. CALENDARIUM ROTULORUM CHARTARUM (R. C.).
    2, 5, 9, 10, 11, 20, 29, 40, 72, 98, 103, 110, 111.

26. CALEY, J.—Memoir on the Origin of the Jews in
    England, in *Archæologia*, viii. 389—495.

27. CAMBRENSIS, G.—Opera, edit. Dimock, vol. vii.,
    (R.S.), 1877.
    Legacy to converts to Judaism, in will of Hugh de Wells,
    227, vii.
    Abelard's retort upon a Jew objecting against Christian
    fate, the fact of churches being struck by lightning, vi. 95.—
    Witticism of a Jew travelling in company with a bishop and
    dean of Salop, vi. 146. [Peche (Peccati) and Dayville
    (Diabolus).]

28. CAPGRAVE.—Chronicle, edit. Hingeston (R. S.) 1858.
Jews accused of assisting certain lepers to poison wells, are burnt, 186.

29. —— Nova Legenda Angliæ, 1516.
Martyrdom of William of Norwich, *f.* cccix*.

30. CARTULARY OF ST. PETER'S, GLOUCESTER, edit. W. H. Hart (R.S.), 1867.
Jews, ii. 149, 179, 297-299.—Murder by, of a boy at Gloucester, i. 20, 21.
Slain Jews, chattels of, ii. 277.

31. CATALOGUE OF THE ANGLO-JEWISH EXHIBITION, 1887.
Sketch of pre-expulsion period, 1-4.
Relics of period shown at Exhibition, Albert Hall, 6-13.
Documents shown at Rolls Office, 175-8.
Documents shown at British Museum, 183-8.

32. CHRONICA MONASTERII S. ALBANI, edit. H. T. Riley (R.S.), 1869. (Walsingham, Gesta.)
i. 183, 193, 239, 401-406, 471.

32*a.* —— (Trokelowe and Blandford), 1866.
P. 57. Expulsion.

32*b.* —— (Walsingham, Historia), 1864.
Dispute between a Jew and a Christian settled by Ed. I., i. 28.—Punished for clipping coin, i. 18.—Expelled from Gascoigne, i. 30; from England, 31.—Enormities committed against by certain fanatics, i. 157.—Charge against of conspiring against Christians, i. 158.—Persecution of by Samaritans alluded to, i. 399.—Of Constance meet Pope Martin V., ii. 321.

33. CHRONICLES OF ED. I. and II., by Stubbs, 1883.
[Annales Londonienses et Paulini.]
Persecuted by John, i. 14.—Eighteen drawn at London on charge of crucifying boy at Lincoln, i. 48.—Persecution of at Cambridge, i. 71.—Suffer at Worcester in 1263, i. 61; at London in 1267, i. 78 ; in 1279, i. 88.—Hanged as money-clippers in London, i. 93.—Harno Hauteyn and Robert of Ludham, justices of, i. 95.—William Carleton and Henry de Bray, justices of, i. 95.—A new chest for Jewish bonds, i. 96.—All in London imprisoned in 1288, i. 97.—All banished from England in 1290, i. 99.—Petition to be recalled, i. 174, 269.—Persecuted in France in 1320, i. 289.—Massacred at Estella, i. 341.

34. CHRONICLES OF HEN. II. AND RIC. I., edit. Stubbs (R. S.), 1867. [Benedict of Peterborough.]

> Hen. II. allows them to have cemeteries, i. 182.
> They are forbidden to possess arms, i. 279.
> Riot against at Richard's coronation, ii. 84.
> Protected by proclamation, *ibid.*
> Persecution and self-immolation at York, ii. 107.

35. CHRONICLES OF STEPHEN, HEN. II., RIC. I., edit. Hewlett, 1885. [William of Newbury, q.v.]

> Jew converted prophesies concerning see of Lincoln, 154. Favour shown to by Hen. II., 280.—Richard forbids presence at coronation, 294.—Disobey, and a tumult arises, 295.—Massacre of Jews in London, 295-97.—At Lynn, 308, 309.—A Jewish physician murdered, 310.—Massacre at Stamford, 310-12.—Attempts at Lincoln fail, 312.—Massacre at York, 312-22.—Exiled from England, 574.

36. CHRONICLES OF RIC. I., edit. Stubbs (R. S.), 1864.

> Massacre of, 142.—Regulations for, 449.

38. CHRONICON PETROBURGENSE, edit. T. Stapleton (Cam. Soc.).

> Crucify St. William at Norwich, 2.
> „ a boy at Gloucester, 3.
> All seized by order of Ed. I., 26.
> Those convicted of clipping hanged, 29.

39. COGGESHALE, R.—Chronicon Anglicanum (R. S.).

> 12, 30, 27, 28, 191 [Incantation by a Jew].

40. COLE, H.—Documents Illustrative of English History in the 13th and 14th centuries (R. C.), 1845.

> [Pp. 285-332. Contains the first Jews' Plea Roll extant for the year 4 Hen. III.]

41. COLLINS, J. H.—Note on a Block of Jew's Tin, in *Journ. Roy. Inst. Corn.*, 1872, pp. 73, 74.

42. COOPER, C. H.—Annals of University and Town of Cambridge, vol. i., 1842.

> 1073. Jews settle here (said to be by Fuller).
> 1159. Donum of Jews.
> 1169. Fine paid by Jews.
> 1215. House of Hakin the Jew.
> 1224. King grants house of Benjamin the Jew to the town as a gaol. (Had been Jews' Synagogue, site of present

Guildhall, which includes churchyard, for in 1782 stone dug
up with מצבת ישראל. MS. Bowtell, iii. 490).
1241. Tallage of the Jews.
1266. Letter of protection for the Jews, bècause gentlemen of Ely had kidnapped some.

43. COOPER, W. D.—History of Winchelsea.
Expulsion of, 20.   Their hall now named Trojan's Hall,
in nineteenth quarter, 40, 113, 219, 234.

44. COTTON, BARTOLOMEUS, edit. Luard (R. S.)
Slaughter at Rouen, 54.
1144. Alleged crucifixion of William of Norwich, 67.
Persecuted at Ric. I.'s coronation, 83-84.
Persecuted by John, 99.
Obtain protection from Greg. IX., 118.
Of Lincoln crucify a boy, 132.
Clip coin, 157.
Crucify boy at Northampton, 159.
Banished the realm, 178.

45. COVENTRIA, WALTER DE.—Historia, edit., W. Stubbs
(R. S.), 1873.
Allowed to have cemeteries in England, i. 301.
Not to keep arms, 313.
Riot at Richard's accession, 375; and at York, 391.
Taxation of, ii. 73 [*Capitula* from Hoveden].
Are allowed to live in French towns, 163.
Persecuted in England, 1210, 203.

45a. CUNNINGHAM, W.—Growth of English History and
Commerce.   Camb., 1882.
68n, 105, 139, 142, 142n.

46. DAVIES, JOHN S.—History of Southampton, 1883.
456, In 1340, a house on West Quay is described as between "the Jews' house" and that of John Twyg.

47. DAVIES, R.—On the Mediæval Jews of York, in
Yorkshire Archæol. and Topog. Journ., vol. iii.,
pp. 147-197.

48. DAVIS, M.D.—The Mediæval Jews of Lincoln, in
Archæological Journal, xxxviii., p. 178 *seq.*
[Containing mass of details unfortunately without authorities. Mr. Davis has also written articles on the mediæval
Jews in the *Jewish World*, 1875, *Jewish Chronicle*, 1877
and 1887, *Norwich Argus*, 1877, *Nottingham Guardian*, 1877,
and Manchester *Jewish Record*, 1887.]

49. DEVIZES, RICHARD OF.—De Rebus gestis Ric. Primi (edit. E. H. S.).
    Massacre of, 1 ; story of a boy deceived by, 60 *seq.*
    60-62, [Jew goes through character of all towns, London, Canterbury, Rochester, Chichester, Oxford, Exonia, Bath- (onia), Wigorn. Cestria, Herefordia, Eboracum, Ely, Dun- elm (Durham), Northwic, Lincolnia, Bristollum, but recom- mends boy to go to Wintonia=Jerusalem of Jews.] Quoted by Pearson, *Hist. Maps*, 37.

50. DEVON, F.—Issues of the Exchequer (R. C.), 1837.
    Converted in time of Edw. III , 163.
    Jewry, London, 514.—St. Mary's Chapel in, 12.
    Converted, inquisition into chattels, 17. Land purchased for, 24.
    House of, 68, 73, 471. Archives inspected, and Debts enrolled, 81.
    Enabled to traffic with Christians, 242. Allowance to, 471.
    Roll of, 17 Hen. III., 506.—Fines of, 509. Church of, 514, 515.
    [Contains also fac-simile of caricature.]

51. DICETO, RANULF DE.—Opera Historica, edit. W. Stubbs (R.S.), 1876.
    Imprisoned in France, ii. 4 ; persecuted in England, 69, 75, 76.

52. DRAKE, F.—Eboracum.
    57, 94, 95, 96, 228, 253, 254, 265, 277, 322, App. pp. xiv., xv.

53. DUGDALE.—Monasticon, edit. Ellis, &c.
    Massacre at St. Edmund's Bury in 1189, iii. 104.
    Depositing money in Abbey as a bank, *ibid.*
    Maintenance of two Jewish converts imposed on the Abbey at Reading, iv. 31.

54. DUTHY, J.—Sketches of Hampshire, Appendix, 1839.
    Richard Tochir, Bishop of Winton, allowing Adam de Port to grant the manor of Abbotstow to a Jew in security for a loan.

55. EADMER.—Historia, edit. M. Rule (R. S.), 1884.
    Jews converted to Christianity, 99-101.

56. ECCLESIASTICAL DOCUMENTS, edit. J. Hunter (Cam. Soc.), Part II., No. vi. p. 60.
    Grant by John, Bishop of Norwich, to Ralph Roman of certain houses in Linne, which had belonged to Isaac, a Jew of Norwich, at the request of King John, A.D. 1214.

57. Eulogium, edit., F. S. Haydon (R. S.), 1863.
    Burnt at Northampton for conspiring to employ Greek
    fire to burn City of London, iii. 120.

58. Eyton, R. W.—Antiquities of Shropshire, 1860.
    i. 311; ii. 176; xi. 328.

58a. Fleta seu Commentarius Juris Anglicani.
    Edit. 1685.
    I., c. 20, p. 30.—Justices errant can have jurisdiction
    over custodians of Jews.
    I., c. 37, p. 54.—Contrahentes vero cum Judæis vel Ju-
    dæabus pecorantes et Sodomitæ in terra vivi confodiantur
    dum tamen capti per testimonium legale vel publice con-
    victi.

59. Fowler, J. T.—On certain "Starrs," or Jewish
    Documents, partly relating to Northallerton, in
    Yorkshire Archæol. and Topog. Journ., vol. iii.,
    pp. 55 to 63, with facsimiles.

60. Freeman, E. A.—English Towns and Districts, 1883.
    Jews of Lincoln and Aaron of Lincoln, 216.
    Aaron of Lincoln at St. Alban's, 261.

61. Freeman, E. A.—Norman Conquest (Index Vol.).
    Dealings of William Rufus with, v. 72.
    Not mentioned in England before his time, v. 858.
    Position under Karlings, *ibid.*
    Position in England; their houses, v. 819.
    Coming influenced by Norman Conquest, *ibid.*

62. Freeman, E. A.—The Reign of William Rufus,
    1882.
    Settle in England, 160.—Their position, *ibid.*
    Fabrond (Rufus), 161; compared with the Sicilian Sara-
    cens, *ibid.*
    Dispute between their Rabbis and English Bishops, *ibid.*
    Converts forced to apostatize by Rufus, i. 162, 164; ii. 504.

63. Fuller, T.—History of the University of Cam-
    bridge, 1840.
    Pp. 8, 21, 77.

64. Gervase of Canterbury, edit. Stubbs (R. S.), 1880.
    Minister to the Monks at Canterbury, i. 405.
    Taxed by Henry II., i. 422.
    Taxed by John in 1210, ii. 105.
    Persecution of in 1264, ii. 235.
    Banished by Edward I. in 1290, ii. 296.

64a. GLOUCESTER, ROBERT OF.—Metrical Chronicle, edit. W. A. Wright (R.S.)   1887.
    Lines 9909, 9920 [Massacre Ric. I.]; 11,936.

65. GOLDSCHMIDT, S.—Geschichte der Juden in England. 1ter Theil, xi. and xii. Jahrhundert, Berlin.   1886.
    [First published in Berliner's *Magazin*, 1885-6. Makes use of Rolls Series and Record Commission publications.]

66. GOULBURN, E. M. and H. SYMONDS.—The ancient sculptures in the roof of Norwich Cathedral.
    Ch. ix. St. William, the boy martyr of Norwich, pp. 101 *seq*. [Illustration, p. 83.]

67. GRAETZ, H.—Geschichte der Juden.
    vi. 168, 240-7 [Massacres under Ric. I.]; 414-6 [Ibn Ezra in England].
    vii. 11, 12, 120-3, 191-8 [Expulsion]; 463-6 [Conversion of a Dominican cause of expulsion].

68. GREEN, J. R.—Short History of English People (Macmillan), 1875.
    Relation with Wm. I., 83.
    Position in England at Conquest, *ibia*.
    Persecution, 198.
    Banished by Ed. I., 199.
    Restored by Cromwell, 573.
    [See also Oxford Medical School of J. at, 83.]

69. GROSSTESTE.—Epistolæ, edit. Luard (R. S.).
    On the proper treatment of Jews, 33-36.
    Christians not to consort with, 318.

70. GÜDEMANN, M.—Gesch. d. Erziehung der Juden in Frankreich.
    Image der Monde·translated into Hebrew by R. Hagin f. Deulacres [Neubauer], p. 86.
    Semag, law 65, ולעבור ים האי שקורין אינגילטיר"א דרך
    86, דרייפ"א רגילים לעבוו יום אחד כשיש להם רוח טוב.

71. HALLAM, HENRY.—Middle Ages (Murray), 1860.
    Wealth amassed and persecutions endured by, i. 209.
    Early celebrity as usurers, *ibid*, note[b].
    Final expulsion from France, i. 210 and note[d].
    Ordinances against them, i. 222.
    Exorbitant rates paid by them in England, ii. 320.
    Massacre of by Pastoureaux, iii. 297.
    Liability to maltreatment, iii. 305.
    Barbarous customs regarding them, *ibid*, note.
    Jew drowning story, iii. 366, note[n].
    Early money dealings, iii. 338.

Toleration vouchsafed to them, *ibid.*
Decline of their trade, iii. 339.
Addiction to coin clipping, iii. 369, note[t].

72. HARGROVE, W.—History of York (York), 1818.
Massacres of, i. 71-82.
Jewsbury, ii. 558.
Jewish Feasts, ii. 402.
Jewish Synagogue or Tabernacle, Walmgate, 292.
Jubbergate, ii. 386-8.
(On N. side of Jubbergate remains of several ancient
walls tradition states were formerly part of a Jewish Syna-
gogue now Unitarian Chapel.)
Clifford's Tower, 248-59 [with illustration and wood-cut].

73. HASTED, E.—History of Canterbury, 1801.
Confined in Castle, i. 61.
Where they dwelt, i. 126 [South side of High Street].
Houses in possession of Corporation, ii. 364.

74. HEMINGFORD, WALTER DE.—Chronicon, ed. H. C.
Hamilton (E. H. S.)
Massacre at coronation of Ric. I., i. 138-147.
Expelled by Ed. I., who receives one-fifteenth from laity
and one-tenth from clergy, ii. 20-22.

74*a.* HIGDEN.—Polychroncion, edit. Luard (R.S.) 1886.
viii. 40, 52, 82, 84, 88, 90, 208, 262, 270.

75. HISTORICAL MSS.—Commission Reports.
i. 96, Deeds at Westminster.
iv. 448, Mildegoda at Oxford ; 458, her seal, &c., &c. ;
387, Pardon for murder of Jew, temp. Ed. II.
vi. 576[b], Isaac of Wallingford.
viii. 319[a], 408[a].
ix. 1[b], 6[a], 14[a], 14[b], 22[a], 22[b], 45[b], 49[b], 50[b], 77[a]. [London].

75*a.* HOLINSHED, R.—" Chronicles." 1586.
A good Jew's Answer to William Rufus, 27, a 60, b 10.—
Stricken by a Christian, 118, b 50.—Hath his tooth drawn
out, 174, a 40.—At Tewkesbury falleth into a jakes, 252,
b 60.—Jews and Christians dispute, 27, b 20.—Burnt to
death, 119, a 10.--Suit to William Rufus against Jews become
Christians, 27, c 40.— Brought into this land by Duke
William, 15, a 10.—At Lincoln slain and spoiled, 272, a 20.
—Inhabiting London are slain for treason, 267, a 60.—Slain
at London and why, 263, b 40.—Accused and executed for
crucifying a child, 253, a 50.—Charged on pain of hanging
to pay Henry III. 8,000 marks, 252, a 10.—Robbed in
Oxford, 238, b 10.—Constrained to help Henry III. with
money, 242, b 30.—Released out of prison, 254, a 30.—

Meant to crucify a child in spite of Christ, 219, a 30.—Generally imprisoned throughout all England, 285, a 50.—Give
Henry III. the third part of all their moveables, 211, b 60.
—Indicted and punished for abusing the King's coins, 279,
b 30.—Crucify a child, 56, b 30.—Grievously taxed tor-
mented, and imprisoned, 174, a 30.—And when they buried
their dead, 101, b 20.—Appointed to enrol all their debts,
pledges, &c., 145, b 20.—Exceedingly hated and murthered,
121, b 50, 122 *all.*—Houses set on fire in London, 118, a 60.
—Beaten and abused by the people, 118, b 60.—Meant to
present King Richard with a rich gift, 118, b 40.

75*b*. HOUEDENE, ROGER DE.—Chronica, edit. Stubbs
(R. S.), 1871.
> Allowed to have cemeteries in England, ii. 137; under
> the protection of the King, 231; not to keep arms, 261;
> riots against at Richard's accession, iii. 12; and at York in
> 1190, 33, 34; taxation of, and measures taken to ensure the
> credit of, iii. 266; are allowed to live in French towns, iv.
> 118, 119.

76. HUME, A.—Sir Hugh of Lincoln, or an Examination of a curious Tradition respecting the Jews,
with a notice of the popular Poetry connected with
it. 8vo., 54 pp. 1849.

76*a*. HUNT, W.—Bristol ("Historic Towns"), 1886.
> The Bristol Jewry, pp. 27-30.

77. INGULPH.—Chronicon, edit. Gale, 1684.
> 9, Reference in charter [probably forgery].
> 111, 114, 115 (at Cambridge).

78. JEHUDA BEN ELIEZER.—מנחת יהודה Commentary on
Pentateuch, published with דעת זקנים, Livorno, 1783.
> [Contains references to English Rabbis, Aaron of
> קומובײרה (? Canterbury), Berachyah of Nicole, Benjamin
> of Canterbury, Elia Menachem, Jacob of Orleans, Joseph of
> Nicole.]

79. "JEWISH CHRONICLE."
> 1849, June 22. On early Anglo-Jewish Rabbis, by L.
> Dukes.
> 1859, Feb. 25. Letter of S. M. Drach, on Shetaroth.
> 1862, Aug. 22. Inquiry as to Jewry Hall (?), Leicester.
> 1877, July 6. Reference to article in "Norwich Argus."
> 1877, July 13. Reference to articles in "Nottingham
> Guardian" of July 7.
> 1877, July 13. Letter of M. D. Davis, suggesting search
> among Tosaphists for נורגיץ and for York under איוורגיק.
> 1877, July 20. Letter of S. Heilbron, calling attention to

passage in Shem Haggedolim on Tosaphoth גורני׳׳ץ, and
suggests should be גורגי׳׳ץ.
1882. Jews at Southampton, by S. L. Lee.
1883, Jan. 16. Domus Conversorum, by S. L. Lee.
1886, Nov. 9. "Aaron son of the Devil," by J. Jacobs.

80. "JEWISH WORLD."
    1873, April 18. Aaron of York.
    ,, Aug. 22. Jews at Exeter.
    ,, ,, 29. Starr.
    1874, May 1. Jewish tallies.
    ,, ,, 15. Jewish tragedy, 1220.
    ,, ,, 22. Starr of 1252.
    ,, June 26. Moses of Oxford.
    ,, Aug. 14. Jewish Receipt, 1182.

81. JOHNSON, R.—Ancient customs of City of Hereford, 1868.
    70-1, Splendid wedding of Jews. Swinfield at Bosbury
issued a veto. On expulsion their property, as fines and
forfeitures, fell to city. Ultimately portion of the confiscated
property was converted into an almshouse now known as St.
Gile's Hospital.

82. JOSEPH BEN JOSHUA COHEN.—Emek Habacha über-
setzt von Dr. M. Weiner, 1858.
    A.D. 810. German Jews fled to Spain and England, 8.
    A.D. 1190. York massacre, 36.
    A.D. 1241. *Emeute* in London, 41.
    A.D. 1358. Finally banished from England, 54.
    A.D. 1531. References to English Jews, 72.
    Heb. App. pp. 9 and 10. Massacres at London and York,
22 proselytes slain.

83. JOURNAL OF THE BRITISH ARCHÆOLOGICAL ASSOCIA-
TION.—Index i.-xxx., 1875.
    Jewry Wall at Leicester, Mr. Thompson on, vi. 393-402.
Treatment of in ancient deeds, xxii. 312.

84. KING, C. W.—Jewish seal found at Woodbridge, in
Suffolk, *Arch. Jour.*, xli. 168-170.

85. LAING, H.—Supplementary Catalogue of Scottish
Seals.
    No. 1294. Seal of Sampson b. Sampson found near
Duddingston.

86. LAURIÈRE, DE.—Ordonnances des rois de France
de la troisième race.
    i. 317, Writ of expulsion of Jews who had fled from
England in 1290.

87. LEICESTERSHIRE ARCHITECTURAL AND ARCHÆO-
LOGICAL SOCIETY'S TRANSACTIONS.
The Jews and the Jewry Wall, by James Thompson, iv.
48.
[Jewry Wall figured in vol. i. and mentioned in every vol.]

88. LELAND'S COLLECTIONS, edit. T. Hearne, 2nd
edition.
i. 148, 163, 229, 245, 247, 267, 456, 460, 475, 536.
ii. 209, 313, 402.

89. LIBER ALBUS, &c., edit. H. T. Riley, 1862.
(Vol. i.)—
Custom of threepence halfpenny charged on each Jewish
burial, Pref. p. l.
Jewry, 99.
Jews, violent death of certain, 74.
Jews, escheats and tenements of, 79.
Jews, chattels of slain, 80.
Jews, inquisition concerning the death of, 99.
Jews, ordinances as to, 590, 591.
Joce (Joseph), the Jew, death of, 99.
(Vol. iii.)—
The Jewry in London, 430.
[In vico qui vocatur "Colchirchstrate" in Parochia S.
Olavi in Judaismo.]

90. LIBER DE ANTIQUIS LEGIBUS.—Edit. Stapleton
(Cam. Soc.).
1, 16, 19, 23, 50, 62, 199, 234 *seq.*

91. LIFE OF SAINT HUGH OF LINCOLN.—Edit. Dimock
(R. S.), 1864.
Grief of Jews at his death, 373 [the bishop not the boy-
martyr].

91a. LIVERE DE REIS DE BRITTANIE.—Edit. J. Glover
(R. S.).
Crucify St. William of Norwich, 202-5.
Massacred at Norwich, 250.
Persecuted by John, 280.
Banished the realm, 308, 324.

92. LOFTIE, W. J.—History of London, 2nd edition.
i. 112, 114, 122, 145, 185, 196.
ii. Map in Appendix F. gives position of the Jewry
(hypothetical).

92A. —— London ("Historic Towns"). 1886.
Jews, pp. 98 *seq.*

93. LYTE, H. M.—The University of Oxford. 1886.
    P. 26 [Situation of Jewry and *Domus Conversorum*].
    41 [Riot in Jewry, 1244].
    44, Interest allowed to Jews.
    59, Charter of St. Frideswyde's Church.
    66, 67, The incident of the Cross.

94. MAPES, W.—De Nugis Curialium, ed. Wright (Cam.
    Soc.).
    Jews in France, 216. "Insolence of richest Jew in
    France," in seizing a cleric who had stoned his boy.

95. MACRAY, W. D.—Notes from the Muniments of
    Magdalen College, Oxon, 1882.

96. —— Chronicles of Carfax.
    Pp. 35-37, Jews at Oxford.

97. MADOX, T.—Formulare Anglicanum.
    P. xi. [Grant to Elyas l'Evesk], 77.

98. —— History of the Exchequer, 2nd edition. 1769.
    Pay the disme for recovery of Holy Land, 34 Hen. II.,
    i. 20 ; great outrage committed on, i. 21 ; Abraham, Jew of
    London, 28 Hen. II., i. 113, c. 2 ; Aaron of Lincoln, i. 191 ;
    exchequer, 221 ; how they enriched the crown by tallage,
    fines, and amerciaments, *ibid.* ; by way of tallage pay one-
    fourth of their chattels, 33 Hen. II., 222 ; are plundered of
    66,000 m. by John, an. 1210, 223 ; fined 20,000, 28 Hen. III.,
    224; and 60,000 more imposed, *ibid.* ; wives, children,
    lands, to be seized for payment, 229 ; paid fines for recovery
    of debts, 230 ; might not marry without king's licence, 228;
    Jews of London fined £2,000 for a manslaughter, 5 Steph.,
    229 ; exchequer and rolls or records, 231 ; Justiciars, 233;
    Custodes of Norman Jews, 5 John, 239 ; whether a Jew may
    take money of a Jew, 244 ; forger (falsonarii), *ibid.* ; Jewish
    wife entitled to her thirds, 247 ; money laws, 248 ; to have no
    schools [synagogues] 249 ; charter of liberties from Henry I.
    and John, 253 ; home for converted Jews, 259, 745 ; Bishops
    of Jews in E., 24 Hen. II., ii. 206; exchequer of Jews, ii. 276.
    [Has a special chapter on the Jewish Exchequer, full of
    facts.]

99. MALMESBURY, WILLIAM OF.—Gesta Rerum Anglo-
    rum. G. D. Hardy (E.H.S.). 1840.
    Jewish youth, anecdote of, 466.
    Jews of London brought over by Conqueror, 500, note [1].
    Encouraged by Wm. Rufus to hold a dispute with Bishops
    500, and note [1].
    Complain of unfair treatment in controversy, *ibid.*

100. MARGOLIOUTH, M.—The History of the Jews in England. 3 vols. 1851.

[First vol. contains pre-expulsion history entirely derived from Prynne, Tovey, and Blunt. Third vol. contains a few records from Prynne or Tovey.]

101. MARGOLIOUTH, MOSES.—Vestiges of the Historic Anglo-Hebrews in East Anglia. With Appendices and an apropos Essay. 1870.

[With sketch of Bodleian ewer on cover and in text. Reviewed by A. Neubauer in "Academy," 1870, p. 188.]

102. MEIR BEN ELIAS, of Norwich.—Hebräische Poesien des Meir ben Elias aus Norwich. Edit. A. Berliner. London. 1887.

[Only 25 copies printed from MS. in Vatican. One long poem and 15 smaller ones containing elaborate acrostic on author's name.]

103. MEIR OF ROTHENBURG.—Responses. Edit. Lemberg. 1860.

No. 160 [Sends decision on slaughtering meat to English Jews].
No. 246 [Refers to charge of clipping coin].

104. MICHEL, F.—Hugues de Lincoln. London, 1834.

[Contains Norman-French and other ballads on the supposed martyrdom of Hugh of Lincoln.]

105. —— Histoire de la Commerce de Bordeaux.

ii. 409-446, "Les juifs commerçants à Bordeaux," some from England mentioned.

106. MILNER, J.—History of Winchester, 1801.

Expelled from Winchester, i. 259.—Their Synagogue, ii. 180. [Trussil, now Gaol, Street, called the Jewry, where Synagogue was.]

107. MONUMENTA FRANCISCANA, edit. Brewer and Howlett. (R. S.)

i. 17, 18 ; ii. 143.

108. MOSES BEN ISAAC, of London.—The Sepher Hassoham, a Hebrew Grammar and Lexicon, edit. by G. W. Collins, M.A., Pt. I. 1883.

[Most important literary production of an English Jew before the Expulsion.]

109. MOSES BEN ISAAC, of London.—דרכי הנקוד. Frag-
mente aus der Punctuation-und Accentlehre der
hebräischen Sprache, angeblich von R. Mose, Punc-
tator. Edit. S. Frendsdorf. Hanover, 1847.

110. MÜLLER, MAX.—"Are there Jews in Cornwall?"
in Chips, vol. iii. 299-329.
    [First appeared in "Macm. Mag.," xv. 484-94.]

111. NEUBAUER, A.—Catalogue of Bodleian Hebrew
MSS.   1886.
    1311, 11d. אנשים לפני השופטים האי אשר נקרא היום
    אינגלאטירה (? printed)
    1547. MS. belonged to Tomaso Markenfeld from Eng-
    land [1563].
    781(2). 72.   R. Yose of Nicol Decision 69ᵇ R. Mose of
    London quoted.
    882. Quotations from R. Moses of London.
    1234(9). R. Joseph b. Jacob of Murel heard this comment
    from Abraham ibn Ezra in London.

112. NEUBAUER, A.—Hebrew Translation of "Image du
Monde" in Miscellanies of Soc. Heb. Lit., ii., pp.
158 seq.
    [Attributing it to Hagin fil. Deulecresse. First appeared
    in Romania.]

113. NEUBAUER [RENAN].—Les Rabbins Français.
    Exegetes.   Eleasar of Beaugenci is quoted by R. Moses
    of London (437).
    Jacob of Orleans, Jehuda, Sir Leon, Joseph Sir Morel,
    Salomon de Chateau, London, quoted by Isaac Halevi de
    Sens, 428.
    Also Berachyah Hanaqdan, Berachyah de Nicole, Jacob
    of Orleans, Joseph de Nicole.
    Moses Naqdan quotes Samuel Hanaqdan and Berachjah
    Hanaqdan, 484.
    Shneior quotes and excerpts Moses Naqdan, 487.
    "Image du Monde" (attributed to Hagin fil. Deulacret),
    502 seq.
    Suggests that Elias the Holy, of אובריוק, was of York
    (Eboracum), 742.

114. NEWBURY, WILLIAM OF.—Historia Rerum Anglicanum, edit. H. A. Hamilton (E. H. S.), 1856.
    Favoured by Hen. II., i. 282.—Excluded from Ric. I.'s
    coronation, ii. 2.
    Massacre of, in London, 3-6 ; at Lynn, 15, 16 ; at Stam-

ford, 17, 18 ; at Lincoln and York, 19-23 ; at York, 24-29 ; displeasure of King thereat, 29.

115. NORGATE, K.—England under the Anglian Kings, 1887.
> i. 27, 46, 53 ; ii. 289, 290, 486-9.
> [Also Jewries marked in maps of Lincoln, Winchester, Oxford, London.]

116. "NOTES AND QUERIES."
> *First Series :* Tewkesbury, xii. 195, 479 ; in Cornwall, v. 455.
> *Second :* Charged with crucifying, vii. 37, 261, 386, 479 ; Canterbury, viii. 243.—Halls named after, in Oxford, viii. 144.
> *Third :* In Cornwall, xi. 456.
> *Fifth :* In England, i. 397 ; ii. 12 ; iii. 177, 216.—In London, iv. 268 ; v. 30.
> *Sixth :* Exeter, c. 1233, x. 495 ; of Tewkesbury, ii. 52, 318 ; iii. 318.—Jewish converts' houses at Oxford and London, i. 352, 386.—Ancient conveyances to, vi. 106 ; vii. 24.

117. OLIPHANT, J. L. K.—Old and Middle English.
> *Giwerie* in *Ancien Riwle.* (1220.)
> *Iuhede* in *Cursor Mundi,* p. 250. (1290.)
> *Iudisskenn* and *Juden* in *Ormulum.*
> *Giwes* becomes *Geus* in Kentish Sermons. (O. E. Misc., p. 26.)
> *Iudeu* and *Juev* both occur in Philip de Thaun, 1120. (*Pop. Treat. on Science,* p. 124.)
> *Folc of Iudeus* and *Giwis.* (*Homilies,* 1160, p. 9.)

118. OXENDENE, JOHN OF.—Chronicles, edit. Ellis (R. S.), 1859.
> Apply to Pope for protection, 164.
> Forbidden to eat fish at Lent, 194.
> Crucify boy at Northampton, 254.

119. PARIS, MATTHEW.—Chronica Majora, edit. Luard. (R. S.), 1883.
> Passage through Red Sea, i. 11 ; wanderings in desert, *ibid.* ; numbering of, i. 12 ; stations in Desert, *ibid.* ; expelled from Rome by Claudius, i. 105 ; rise against Romans, i. 108 ; account of war, i. 109 ; dispersion of, i. 112 ; persecuted by Domitian, i. 116 ; rebel and are put down in 112, i. 119-121 ; lay waste Palestine, i. 123 ; reduced by Severus, 131 ; dispute with Pope Sylvester, 160 ; attempt to rebuild temple under Julian, 166 ; in Crete, discovered by a diabolic appearance in the shape of Moses, 180 ; a converted Jew, miracle with respect to in 552, 224 ; a Jew who tried to burn an image of the Saviour stoned in 560 ; a Jew per-

C 2

suades Jezid to issue an edict against images in 724, i. 330 ;
slaughter of at Mentz and Cologne, by the Crusaders, ii. 54 ;
at the coronation of Richard in spite of his prohibition,
ii. 350; their consequent persecution throughout England,
351 ; king gives them protection, *ibid.* ; attacks on, in
Norwich, Stamford, and St. Edmund's Bury in 1190 by
Crusaders, ii. 358 ; their dreadful fate in York, 359 ; robbery
of by the Chancellor W. Longchamp, ii. 381 ; seizure and
plunder of by John, ii. 528 ; especial torture of one at
Bristol, *ibid.* ; many fly the kingdom in 1210, ii. 531 ; provisions respecting debts to them in Magna Carta, 592 ;
deacon hanged by F. de Buarté at Oxford in 1222 for
becoming a Jew, iii. 71 ; forced to pay a third of their
property to Hen. III. in 1230, iii. 194; house for converted
Jews built in London by Hen. III., iii. 305 ; privileges
granted to, by Pope Gregory IX., iii. 309; forbidden to de-
mand usury from Crusaders, iii. 284, 312 ; deride the Christians in consequence of the Caursin usurers, iii. 331 ; great
slaughter of, in Spain, iii. 369; give money to Hen. III.,
and are protected, *ibid.* ; pillaged by Geoffrey the Templar
in 1239, iii. 543 ; pay a third of their property to the king,
ibid. ; homicide by, *ibid.* ; circumcise a boy at Norwich, iii.
543, iv. 30 ; their punishment, iv. 31 ; the Ten Tribes shut
up by Alexander in the Caspian mountains, iv. 77, 131 ; compelled to pay a heavy ransom in 1241, iv. 88 ; believe the
Tartars and Circassians to be the Ten Tribes, iv. 131 ; their
stratagem to assist the Tartars with arms, iv. 131-33 ; tor-
tured when this is discovered, iv. 133 ; pillaged by Henry III.
in 1243, iv. 260; again in 1244, iv. 373 ; the body of a boy
murdered by, found in London, iv. 377; buried in St. Paul's,
378 ; regulations as to debts due to them by Crusaders issued
by the Council of Lyons, iv. 459 ; the coinage clipped by
them, iv. 608, v. 16, 114, 136; impoverished by the King's
extortions in 1250, v. 114 ; crime of one Abraham, *ibid.* ;
accused by Abraham of treason, v. 115 ; their endeavours to
have him put to death, *ibid.* ; justices sent throughout England by Hen. III. to investigate their possessions, *ibid.* ;
their secrets revealed to the King's exactors by a Jew, v. 116 ;
extortions from by Hen. III. especially from one Aaron,
v. 136; their joy at the attacks on the Caursins, v. 246 ;
Philip Luwel takes bribes from, v. 261 ; pillaged by
Hen. III. in 1252, v. 274; the prelates bound to, v. 339;
their false accusations of justiciaries Robert de la Ile and P
Luwel, v. 345 ; banished by Louis IX. from France except-
ing under certain circumstances, v. 361 ; this caused by
words of the Saracens, v. 362 ; their place supplied by the
Caursins, *ibid.* ; their murmurs against the Caursins, v. 404;
less exacting money-lenders than the Caursins, v. 425 ;
demands of them by Richard of Cornwall for Hen. III , v.

441 ; speech of the high priest Elyas, *ibid.* ; not allowed to leave the kingdom, *ibid.* ; their small remaining substance pillaged, *ibid.* ; the money got from them by Hen. III. given to the Pope, v. 458 ; demands of Hen. III. from in 1255, v. 487 ; ask to be allowed to leave the country, *ibid.* ; sold by Hen. III. to Richard of Cornwall, v. 488 ; spared by Richard, *ibid.* ; at Lincoln steal and murder the boy Hugh, v. 516 ; all the Jews of England share in the guilt of this, v. 579 ; their punishment, *ibid.* ; those executed not lamented by the Caursins, *ibid.* ; the year 1253 a bloody year for them, v. 537 ; some of those condemned at Lincoln saved by the Franciscans, v. 546 ; some released from the Tower, v. 552 ; inquisitions respecting, in 1258, vi. 398.

School of, in London, v. 399.

The wandering, account of, iii. 161-163 ; v. 341.

Elyas Bishop, a Jew, the charter of St. Alban's to Richard of Oschey taken from, v. 398 ; converted to Christianity, v. 730; the poison for the English nobles concocted in his house, *ibid.*

121. PARIS, MATTHEW.—Historia Minor, edit. Sir F. Madden (R. S.), 1869. [Only items seemingly not in Ch. Majora.]

Decree concerning, at Lateran Council, i. 412.—Used magical arts at Ric. I.'s coronation, ii. 9.—Seven imprisoned for circumcising boy at Norwich, ii. 375, iii. 271.—New privileges from Pope, ii. 378.—Allowed to keep Christian servants, *ibid.*—Proclamation in England that no one should injure them, ii. 392.—Not to hold house after convicted of forgery, iii. 322.—Hen. III. orders shall not eat meat in Lent or on Fridays, iii. 320.

122. PALGRAVE, Sir F.—Rise of English Commonwealth.

ii., pp. xxv.-xxvii., Description of protracted litigation of Richard de Anesty in 1156-8, and of many loans contracted with Jews to carry on litigation.

123. —— Index to Printed Reports of.

Roll relating to, among Chancery Records in Rolls Chapel, VII., App. ii., 212.

Placita Judæorum, Hen. III. and Ed. I. removed from Carlton Ride to Stone Tower, IX. 19, App. i. 9, 26.

Jews' Rolls among Exchequer of Receipt Records, xviii. 15.

Documents relating to, among Miscellanea of Q. R., xx. 1, 31.

List showing place of deposit of Jews' Rolls in Record Repository on 21st Nov., 1858, xx. 159.

Bonds to, among Records removed from Chapter House to Repository in 1859, xxi. 20.

124. PARKER, J.—Early History of Oxford (Oxf. Hist.
Soc.), 1885.
Suggests fil' Manasse mentioned in Oxfordshire Domesday
was a Jew, as he is mentioned as being fined for holding
land without King's license, 224, 257. Passage given in
facsimile frontispiece.

125. PATENT ROLLS.—Ed. I.
[Analyses of these are being given in the successive Reports
of the Deputy Keeper from 1881, and contain many items
relating to Jews, but are unindexed.]

126. PECK, F.—Antiquarian Annals of Stamford.
iv. 17. Jossred, Abbot of Croyland, sent brother to
Cotenham to preach against Jews in Camb. Also to Stamford. Peter of Blesens, p. 115, 116.
v. 15. Permission to bury dead.
vi. 1. Massacre at Ric. I.'s coronation.
3-8. Suggests that Jews taught English hospitals. Massacres at Lynn, Stamford, York.
11. 1182. William de Burg pays Benedict of Burg to free
him from debt to Jews.
viii. 2. 1219. Jews to wear badges.
ix. 19. 1290. Their Synagogues at Huntingdon and
Stamford being profaned, Gregory de Huntingdon gets
their books and studies (v. Catalogue of Ramsay Library).
Leland Comment., p. 321.

127. PEARSON.—England in Early and Middle Ages.
Their condition and massacre, i. 548-9. Argue with
Christians, 420, 606.
Taxed by John, ii. 55; by Hen. III., 199-201, 211.
Massacred in London, 241.
Forbidden usury and to hold land, 303-306.
Expelled England, 347-349.

128. PIKE, L. O.—History of Crime in England (Smith,
Elder), 1873. [Frontispiece with early caricature of
Jews.]
Jewry pledged to the Caursins, 193, 264.—Statute of the,
194, 464.
Position of, in England, from Conquest to end of twelfth
century, 157-9, 451.
Admirable patience and tenacity, 159.
Massacre of, in London on Richard's coronation day,
164-171, 457.
At York, 161-2, 457-8; at Lynn, Stamford, and Lincoln,
162-3, 457-8.
Combination of clergy, barons, and traders against,
184-5.

Envy excited by their superior knowledge of commerce, 185.

Regulations for, under Ric. I., 186, 463.

Frauds and coin-clipping attributed to them, 186, 191, 463-4.

Their condition in reign of John : the Jew of Bristol and his teeth, 186-7, 463.

Hostility of clergy to, 187-8.

Are compelled to wear badges, if male, 188, 463.

Pandulf's wish to expel them, 188-9, 463.

Debts of the clergy to them, 189-90, 463.

Caricature of, in reign of Henry III., 190-1, 463-4, and frontispiece.

French usurers among them, 191.

Have rivals in the "Pope's money changers," 192, 464.

Bribe the Justices, 192-3, 464.—Their privileges restricted, 193, 464.

Forbidden to practise usury, 194.—Females as well compelled to wear badge, *ibid.* 464.

Accused of offences against Christian religion, 194-5, 465.

Cruelly expelled from England, 196-7, 465.—Divisions of their property, 197-8, 465.

"Jews' Rolls" referred to, 463-4.

129. PIPE ROLLS.—Magnum Rotulum Scaccarii, 31 Hen. I., edit. J. Hunter (R. C.), 1833.

Pp. 53, 146-9.

130. PIPE, GREAT ROLLS OF THE, 2, 3, 4 Hen. II., edit. J. Hunter (R. C.)

Pp. 8, 15, 36, 72, 96, 127, 133.

131. PIPE ROLL SOCIETY PUBLICATIONS, 1885, *seq.*

Introductory vol., pp. 8, 9, 64, 65.

5 Hen. II., 1, 3, 12, 17, 28, 35, 65.

6 Hen. II., 33, 50.

7 Hen. II., 43, 63.

8 Hen. II., 18, 24, 41, 61, 62, 69.

9 Hen II., 61.

10 Hen. II., 31.

11 Hen. II., 4, 6, 7, 11, 35, 61.

132. PIPE, GREAT ROLL OF.—1 Ric. I., edit. J. Hunter (R. C.).

Pp. 8, 59, 160, 219, 226, 229, 246.

133. PIPE, GREAT ROLL OF THE, 1189-90, edit. J. Hunter (R. C.), 1844.

Pp. 8, 20, 26, 39, 43, 44, 45, 50, 60, 73, 74, 75, 99, 109,

110, 144, 160, 165, 173, 208, 209, 216, 219, 226, 228, 229, 230, 242, 246, 251.

134. PIPE ROLL, 3 Jo., ROTULUS CANCELLARII, edit. J. Hunter (R. C.), 1833.

> Pp. 4, 14, 30, 36, 47, 59, 85, 88, 89, 96, 102, 122, 168, 169, 171, 188, 225, 244, 246, 271, 285, 286, 294, 326, 344. [Mostly debts of Aaron of Lincoln seized by King.]

134a. PLACITA DE QUO WARRANTO.—(R. C.), 1818.

> Pp. 572, 815.

135. PLACITORUM WESTMON. ABBREVIATIO.—(R. C.)

> Pp. 9, 36, 40, 58, 59, 62, 64, 97, 111, 114, 166, 168, 175, 223, 256.

136. PLOWDEN, F.—A Treatise on the Law of Usury, 1797.

> Chapters i.-iii. deal incidentally with Jews.

137. PROTHERO.—Simon de Montfort.

> Fined by Hen. III., 108, 125.
> Collision with police, 162.
> At London, 268 ; at Lincoln, 358.

138. PRYNNE, W.—A Short Demurrer to the Jews long discontinued Remitter into England, 1655-6.

> [In two parts. Part I. went into two editions. The fullest collection of records yet printed in connected series. The work was written with violent feeling against Jews, but from the author's official connection with the Record Office is full of information.]

139. PUGIN, E.—Specimens of Gothic Architecture.

> Plate 2 gives window and door of Jew's house at Lincoln (earliest in the chronological list), described pp. 4-5.
> N. p. 5. The chimney peculiar both in this and the other Jews' house.

140. RECORD OF CAERNARVON.—Record Com., 1838.

> Pp. 159, 163, 179, 181, 193, 196.

141. RECORDS OF THE BOROUGH OF NOTTINGHAM.— Vol. i., 1155-1399.

> Jew gallows in Lyngdalefield.
> Jew Lane = Venella Judæorum ; Dering = S. Nicholas Street, 116.
> Jews' synagogue and church house in street leading from St. Peter's to Friar Minn.

142. RECUEIL GENERAL DES ANCIENNES LOIS FRAN-
ÇAISES.—Paris.
> No. 291, p. 683. Ordonnance qui expulse les Juifs venus
> d'Angleterre et de Gascoyne.
> (Not given but reference made to C.L., I. 317, No. 86.)

143. REGISTRUM EPISTOLARUM J. PECKHAM, edit. C.
Trice Martin. (R.S.).
> Jews of London, i. 213, 239; ii. 407, 410. Preface, pp.
> lxxxvi.-c.

144. REGISTRUM MALMESBURIENSE.—Edit. Brewer and
Martin, 1880. (R.S.).
> Jewry, Statute of the, i. 233, 506.
> Jews, creditors of the abbey, ii. 81.

145. REGISTRUM ROFFENSE —Edit. John Thorpe.
> Acquietavit (Radulphus prior) domum de usuria versus
> Samson Judeum.

146. REVUE DES ETUDES JUIVES.—Paris, 1880, &c.
> i. 61. Several Jews mentioned with addition of "len-
> glais" or "lenglische," in Role de Juifs à Paris en 1294.
> By I. Loeb.
> iii. 4. Z. Cahn on R. Jomtob of Joigny.
> iii. 223. Catalogue des Actes dans la bibliotheque Na-
> tionale. No. 74 relates to expulsion of English Jews from
> Carcassone in 1291.
> iv. 14. Memorbuch de Mayence mentions massacre in
> London, 1264.
> v. 247. Un Schetar de 1258. By A. Neubauer (Col-
> chester deed, see Athen. 4 Nov. 1884. N. & Q., Sixth
> Series, vi. 138.)
> viii. 168. Moses "lenglische" mentioned at Vesoul about
> 1310.
> xi. 256. M. Schwab, Documents pour servir à l'histoire
> des Juifs en Angleterre.
> xii. 73. Moise le Naqdan. By W. Bacher.

147. RILEY, H. T.—Chronicles of London, 1863.
> Jewry of Winchester destroyed, 78 ; of London burnt, 234.
> Jews to plead before the citizens in certain cases, 17.
> Moiety of movables exacted by the King, 21.
> A Christian child slain by, 25 ; their punishment, *ibid.*
> Persecution of, 54 ; slaughtered in London, 61.
> Inquiry as to flesh sold by, and the buyers and sellers
> thereof, 177.
> Concerning advowsons of churches held by, 194 ; war-
> ships of Christians, 194, 196.
> 500 killed for extortion, 234.

Drawn and hanged for clipping coin, 239.
All in England imprisoned, 241.
Banished from England, 242.

148. RILEY, H. T.—Memorials of London, 1868.
Murder committed by, 15. [Abraham de Derkynge, Isaac of Canterbury, Cresse f. Isaac de l.ynton, 21st Sept., 1278.]
Jewry, Old, 15, 302, 479, 501, 503 (in the ward of Coleman Street).

149. RISHANGER, WILLIAM DE.--Chronicon St. Albani, edit. Riley (R. S.), 1865.
Shocking death of a Jew at Tewkesbury, 4.—At Cambridge are taken by the Disinherisoned, 44.—Grant made to Edw. I. for expulsion of, 118.—Banished beyond sea, 431.

150. RISHANGER, WILLIAM DE, Chronicle of, edit. Halliwell (Cam. Soc.).
Killed in London, 24, 126.

151. ROGERS, J. T.—History of Agriculture and Prices.
i. 285. It is said Jews never excluded from Oxford.
ii. 579, col. iii. A clerk hired at Farley, 1320, to translate Hebrew into Latin.
"Farley: In procuratia soluta cuidam clerico Oxon. exponenti Ebraicum in Latinum."
[J. T. R. suggests it might be for translating a "Starr."]

152. ROLL OF HOUSEHOLD EXPENSES OF BP. SWINFIELD (Cam. Soc.), 1855.
Money lenders, 127.—Cherished by Hen. III., xcix. n.—Account of them, their dress and wealth in Hereford, c.—Expelled the realm by Edw. I., ci.
[At marriage, in 1286, Aug., numbers invited and grand doings, but Bp. forbade and excommunicated all who attended ; there were displays of silk and cloth of gold, horsemanship, stage plays, sports, and games.]

153. ROSS, J.—Historia regum Angliæ, edit. T. Hearne.
Pp. 200-3. [Story of Oxford cross said to have influenced Edward I.]

154. ROTULI DE OBLATIS ET FINIBUS, 1199-1216, edit. Roberts (R. C.), 1844.
Pp. 41, 44, 56, 65, 66, 91, 92, 101, 121, 122, 130, 133, 188, 197, 198, 202, 208, 210, 218, 231, 236, 240, 246, 249, 256, 257, 258, 263, 264, 267, 271, 272, 280, 296, 297, 303, 314, 315, 322, 334, 345, 350, 358, 364, 365, 368, 370, 372, 373, 378, 388, 390, 391, 400, 402, 416, 418, 419, 420, 424, 425, 428, 430, 436, 440, 554, 560, 598, 6co.

155. ROTULI CHARTARUM, edit. Duffy (R. C.), 1837.
Pp. 6ᵇ, 7, 27, 29, 52, 55ᵇ, 59ᵇ, 61, 62ᵇ, 70, 75ᵇ, 96ᵇ, 98, 105ᵇ, 125ᵇ, 134, 150, 155ᵇ, 158, 165, 185ᵇ, 193, 198ᵇ, 200ᵇ, 201, 203, 204.

156. ROTULI CURIÆ REGIS, edit. F. C. Palgrave (R. C.), 1835. [1194-1199-1209.]
I. 9, 15, 16, 34, 79, 223, 289, 338. II. 62, 108.

157. ROTULI DE LIBERATE, temp. Johannis, edit. T. D. Hardy (R. C.), 1844.
24, 34, 35, 38, 39, 42, 44, 48, 49, 54, 71, 72, 73, 84, 86, 98.

158. ROTULI FINIUM, 1216-1272, edit. C. Roberts (R. C.).
I. 4, 6, 62, 76, 77, 78, 87, 104, 110, 170, 174, 179, 191, 194, 214, 226, 236, 264, 288, 294, 295, 297, 315, 322, 356, 360, 380, 390, 391, 399, 405, 408, 412, 415, 419, 422, 427, 438, 441, 442, 444, 445, 455, 461. [1216-1244.]
II. 14, 25, 47, 55, 58, 60, 65, 66, 67, 68, 73, 82, 84, 88, 93, 95, 110, 113, 124, 125, 148, 153, 155, 163, 165, 168, 232, 302, 309, 314, 335, 415. [1246-1272.]

159. ROTULI HUNDREDORUM (R. C.)
I. 119, 124, 126, 313, 318, 319, 321, 322, 355, 396.
II. 250, 282, 392, 789, 791, 792, 793, 794, 798, 808.

160. ROTULI LITERARUM CLAUSARUM (R. C.), edit. Hardy, 1844.
I. 1ᵇ, 11ᵇ, 20ᵇ, 23ᵇ, 25, 30ᵇ, 33ᵇ, 34ᵇ, 35, 44, 49, 49ᵇ, 73, 75, 80, 87, 88, 89ᵇ, 95, 107, 137ᵇ, 146, 152ᵇ, 166, 166ᵇ, 171, 172ᵇ, 181ᵇ, 186ᵇ, 189, 195, 196, 197, 198ᵇ, 203, 205, 220, 223ᵇ, 224ᵇ, 227ᵇ, 231, 242ᵇ, 243, 263ᵇ, 265ᵇ, 268, 272, 275ᵇ, 283, 286, 313, 321ᵇ, 323ᵇ, 328ᵇ, 330, 330ᵇ, 341, 354ᵇ, 357, 358, 366, 367ᵇ, 368, 386, 387, 399, 401, 407ᵇ, 409, 409ᵇ, 414, 426, 459, 513ᵇ, 521ᵇ, 530, 540, 548, 551ᵇ, 555, 567, 575, 598ᵇ, 628, 653ᵇ. [1204-1224.]
II. 9, 24, 29ᵇ, 40, 50ᵇ, 51ᵇ, 52ᵇ, 53, 53ᵇ, 63, 67ᵇ, 78, 87ᵇ, 88ᵇ, 89, 90, 92, 96, 108, 113ᵇ, 114ᵇ, 123, 123ᵇ, 129ᵇ, 135, 135ᵇ, 140ᵇ, 163ᵇ, 165ᵇ, 172, 176, 176ᵇ, 180, 194ᵇ, 198ᵇ, 200, 206. [1224-1227.]

161. ROTULI ORIGINALIUM (R. C.)
Pp. 2, 64, 73ᵇ-76ᵃ [List of Jews' houses at expulsion.]

162. ROLLS OF PARLIAMENT, INDEX TO THE.
Certain Jews complain that a Jew boy was baptised against their will, and pray justice : King will not revoke baptism, i. 46ᵃ.

Such as have charters to converted Jews to restore them :
a petition from the, 49ª.
Osbert de Long and others indicted for concealing chattels
of condemned Jews, 51ª.
R. le Clark bought house from Jew who had houses to
sell to plead thereon, 38ª.
Imperfect petition concerning, 61ª.
Arrears of rents to their lands since *in manu regis* to be
paid to landlords, 98ᵇ.
Prior of Bridlington accused of concealing money due to
King, property of Jew, 99ᵇ.
Archbishop of York impeached for purchasing a debt
due to an exiled Jew from Prior of Bridlington, *ibid.* 120ª.
R. Fitz Walter prays to have a chapel called the Jews'
Synagogue, 161ª.
R. de Stormeworth prays restitution of a messuage she
sold to a Jew, 303ª.
Ed. I. pardoned to Christians all usurious debts to Jews
if pay principal, 465ᵇ.
Pardon of debts to Jews by Ed. I. conferred by Act,
An. I, Ed. III., ii. 8ª, 11ᵇ.
Commons complain that many pretending to be Lombards
are Jews, 332ª
Church more injured by covetous Christians than by
them, 338ª.
J. Oldebury discharged of a debt to Jew in King's hand,
redress, 402ª.
Domus Conversorum conferred to Keeper of Rolls, iii.
31ª, v. 447ª.

163. ROTULI LITERARUM PATENTIUM, edit. Hardy,
1835.
13ᵇ, 14, 15ᵇ, 16, 16ᵇ, 22ᵇ, 24ᵇ, 30, 30ᵇ, 33, 37, 38ᵇ, 39ᵇ,
47, 47ᵇ, 54ᵇ, 75ᵇ, 81ᵇ, 83, 85ᵇ, 97, 102ᵇ, 112ᵇ, 116, 139ᵇ,
169ᵇ, 194. [1201-1216.]

164. —— SCACCARII NORMANNIÆ, edit. Stapleton
(E. H. S.), 1840-4.
I. cxli., cl.—II. l., li., liv., lxxxi., lxxxv., cxxvi., ccxliv.,
ccl., ccliii.

165. —— SELECTI, edit. Hunter (R. C.), 1834.
P. 210. [Plea about Jews of Northampton, 1265.]

166. RYE, W.—Pedes Finium. 1882.
Pp. 67, 140.

167. —— On the Circumcision of a Boy at Norwich in
1230 in *Norfolk Antiquarian Miscellany,* vol. i.,
pp. 312-344.
With twenty-three unpublished documents in Appendix,
some relating to Oxon and Lincoln; mostly to Norwich.

168. Rye, W.—Short History of Norfolk (Pop. County Hist.), 1886.

Persecution, 42.—St. William of Norwich, 46.—Lynn, 47.—At Norwich, 48.—Caricatures of, 51-2.—Jews' Ways by Burnham and Burgh Castle, 16.

169. Rymer's Fœdera (Syllabus in English, Hardy), 1885.

Jew of Lincoln, Aaron the, 18.—Benedict, son of Mossæus of London, a Jew, 56.—Cresse, a Jew, 59.—Edward Brussels, a Jew, 315.—Hagin, a Jew, 59.—Henry, a converted Jew, created a knight, 87.—Helias Sabot, a Jew of Bologne la Chase, doctor, 566.—John, the converted Jew, 56.—John de Chastel, a converted, 386.—Elizabeth, a converted Jewess, 547.—Jewesses throughout England, regulations to be observed by all, 94.—Jewry in England, 78.— Jews, 14, 24, 46, 50, 56, 59, 72, 78, 85, 89, 93.—Cemetery of, 46.—Coming to England, regulations concerning, 24.— Commanded to evacuate Northampton Castle, 72.—Converted Jews, 33, (56,) 87, 90, 154, 315, 386.—Chapel of the converted Jews, 182.—House of converted Jews in New Street in the suburbs of London, 33, 34, 94, 182, 315, 528.—Keeper of converted Jews, 147, 386, 495.—To be induced to attend the discourses of the provincial of the Friars Preachers, 90.— Regulations for the management of the houses of converted Jews in London, 91.—Elizabeth, daughter of Moyses, Bishop of the converted Jews, 547.—Hagin, son of Deulacres, appointed High Priest of Jews for life, 93.— Imprisoned by the King; excluded from a general pardon, 13.—Indicted for clipping coins, 89.—Inventory of all the debts due to the Jews to be made, 66.—Albertus Medici, judge of the Jews. 156.—Justices of the, 50.—Liberty to choose their high priest, 60.—Messuages of, 14.—Regulations concerning, 50.—Regulations to be observed by, 79, 94.—Privileges to the, in England and Normandy, 8.— Rabbi Moysis, bishop of the converted Jews, 547.—Tallages due by the, 82.—Tallages to be paid, 88.—Their help to Richard, brother of Hen. III., 59.—Ordered to leave the kingdom, 109.—To wear two white tablets on their breast, 24.—Under protection of Hen. III., 72.—Under protection of King John, 13.—Jews and Christians who clip the coin, 85.—In England, 8, 13, 79.—Assigned by Hen., III. to brother Richard in security for money advanced, 53.—Confirmation of privileges granted to Jewish priesthood of all the, 14.—Jews in Gascony, 83, 93.—Of Hereford, 24.—In Agen, seneschalcy of, 156.—Of London, 13, 46, (154).— Their coffins to be searched, 56.—Debts of the, 56.—Josce, a priest of, 14.—Masters of the law of, 46.—From Winchilsea, expulsion from, 80.—From Windsor, removal from ordered, 98.

170. SELDEN.—De Jure Naturali et Gentium, sec. Hebr.
On Jewish Medals and coins—one from Scheckard in
Persia, another in Surrey (fig.), 186-7.
Passage from " Shalsheleth Hakkebala " on persecution
of Jews in England, 1260, 186.
The Winchester inscription, 191.

171. —— Titles of Honour.
A Starr translated hence into Tovey, 644.

171A. SEYER, S.—Memorials of Bristol. 1821.
Pp. 527-9, Jews in Bristol [chiefly from Prynne].

172. SHIRLEY.—Royal Letters of Hen. III. (R. S.), 1866.
Of Ireland, i. 519 ; of Kent, 392 ; of Poitou and Gascoigne, i. 206 ; also ii. 23, 24, 46, 98, 110.

173. SKELTON, J.—Oxonia Antiqua, 1823.
Pl. 100. Domus Conversorum at Oxford. [Also in W. H.
Turner's *Records of Oxford*, p. 436.]

174. SOMNER, W.—Antiquities of Canterbury, 1640.
Jewry and Jewry Lane ; Synagogue where Saracen's Head
Inn, 124-5.

175. SPEED, J.—The Mighty Empire of Britain, 1676.
Jewry streets or lanes occur in maps of Hereford (6) ;
Warwick (B) ; Lichfield (? Jaye's Lane, 12) ; Winchester(4) ;
Canterbury (24), and Parish of Allhallows in Jewry in Cam-
bridge.

176. SPROTT, J.—Chronicon, edit. T. Hearne, 1719.
P. 75. Anno Domini MCCXC. quidam Judæus Parisiis
emit a muliere Christiana corpus Domini die Paschæ et
bullivit in patella et transfixit cultello et sanguis exivit et
die omnium Sanctorum ejecti sunt Judæi ab Anglia cum
omnibus facultatibus suis.

177. STATUTES OF THE REALM.
I. 100 [merchants] ; 202-3 [de Pistoribus] ; 221, 233, and
1 Edw. III., st. 2, c. 3.

178. STEINSCHNEIDER, M.—" Abraham ibn Ezra " in
Zeits. f. Math. und Phys. Hist. Lit. Abth., 1882,
pp. 59-128.
Joseph ben Jacob ממדויל, 61 ; Jesod Moreh, 99.

179. STEINSCHNEIDER, M.—Cat. Bodleian, 1860.
No. 7,068, col. 2475. Samuel b. Salomo (ex Dreux) de
Falaise. Sir Morel רבינו מורי״ל מאינגלטיר״א in הנהות
ממוני הלחות אישות, § 9. Tosaphoth to Aboda Sara.

180. STOW.—Survey of London, edit. Strype.
>Jewry a place in the liberties of Tower, Bk. ii., p. 32.
>First brought over by Will. I., Bk. iii., p. 54.
>Several hanged for circumcising a child, *ibid.*
>Seven hundred slain by Londoners, and why, *ibid.* 53.
>Treatment in several reigns, pp. 54, 55.
>Rolls' Chapel for converts, *ibid.* 262, 263.
>Their dwellings in London at expulsion, Bk. ii., 59.

181. STUBBS, W.—Constitutional History of England.
>i. 221, 223, Statute de la Juerie.
>ii. 197, Legislation respecting, 197.
>133, 300, 578-80, Banishment of.

182. —— Documents illustrating English History, 1870.
>Pp. 155, 262 [Capitula de Judæis], 294, 298 [Magna Charta], 382, 391 [Statutum de Judaismo], 435 [writ of expulsion], 476.

183. STUDDER, E.—Henry Vachel in "Dundee People's Friend," 4th Oct. 1871.
>[Account of expulsion of Jewish miners from Cornwall.]

184. TAYLOR, H.—Flint, 1883.
>P. 30. [Expulsion.]

185. THROSBY, J.—History of Leister.
>Jewry Wall, 2, 3, 17, 18, 40, 232, 392; also Plates I. and II.

186. TOVEY, D'BLOISSIERS.—Anglia Judaica, or the Histories and Antiquities of the Jews in England. Oxon., 1738.
>[The "standard" history of the pre-expulsion period. Illustrations: Seal of Jacob of London; the Bodleian ewer (without arms); and tomb of St. Hugh of Lincoln. Almost entirely derived from Prynne.]

187. TRIVET.—Annales, edit. Hog, 1845.
>Jew, Spanish legend of a, 239.
>Massacred at London, 116. Strict laws against them by Ric. I., 153.
>Expelled England by John, 182. Hung for clipping coin, 299.
>Expelled England by Ed. I., 316.
>Jews of Norwich crucify a boy, 18; another at Blois, 68; St. Hugh, Lincoln, 248. A fourth at Gloucester, *ibid.*

187a. TURNER, T. H.—Domestic Architecture in England, vol. i.   1851.

> P. 7, Jews' house, Lincoln.
> 36, Southampton houses earlier than Jews' house.
> 40, Lincoln house figured and described.
> 46, Moyses' Hall (Bury St. Edmund's) figured and described.

188. TWYFORD AND GRIFFITHS.—Records of York Castle, 1880.

> Frontispiece, Clifford's Tower.
> Plan of Castle, 9.
> The massacre described, 25-35.
> Mince Pye, or Clifford's Tower before the "blow up," 43.
> Gateway at Clifford's Tower,153.

189. TWYSDEN. — Historiæ Anglicanæ Scriptores X., London, 1652.

> Pp. 444, 609, 647, 651, 1005, 1043, 1050, 1081, 1159, 1160, 1171, 1258, 1403, 1450, 1458, 1728, 2394, 2401, 2402, 2435, 2437, 2444, 2454, 2462, 2466.

190. WALSINGHAM, THOMAS DE.—Ypodeigma Neustriæ (R. S.).

> Jewry at Lincoln, 162.   Jews, 147, 172, 178, 179, 252, 477.

192. [WEBB, P. C.]—The Question whether a Jew . . . was a Person capable by Law to purchase and hold Lands . . . Fairly stated and considered, London, 1753.

> [Valuable collection of records in Appendix.]

193. WENDOVER, ROGER DE.—Edit. Coxe (E. H. S.), 1842.

> English persecuted, iii. 7 *seq.* ; 19 *seq.*
> Plundered and tortured by King John, 231.
> Pay a tax of one-third to Hen. III., iv. 209.
> Outrage of at Norwich, iv. 324.
> Of Christendom obtain a protection from Pope against extortions, iv. 326.
> Quotes Holinshed, 1145; M. Paris, 1240; Tyrrell, ii. 972.

194. WOOD, ANTHONY À.—History of Oxford, edit. Gutch, vol. i.

> About middle of twelfth century gave money to Empress

Maud and King Stephen to save their houses from being
burnt, i. 148.
Obtained a burying place (1177), 165.
Forcibly take away a Jewish child that had been con-
verted and baptised, and are imprisoned, 220.
Not to receive from scholars more than 2d. in pound in a
sevennight, acc. to statute of Hen. III. (1248), 239.
One of them (1268) breaking cross in a procession, they
are obliged by the King to build a cross and present a port-
able one in silver for processions, 273, 274.
Chancellor had cognizance granted him by King Ed. I.
of causes between them and scholars, 325, 326.
Expelled Oxford and banished the kingdom (1289), 328.
Purchased tenements called Great and Little Jewries, 328.
Of their synagogue and burying place, *ibid.*
Of their enormities at Oxford about that time, 329.
Read Hebrew in their school, 397, v. ii. p. ii. 745, 746.
Settled in Oxford about 9 Will. I. (1075), i. 129.
Jews' school, iii. 651 [became London College=Burnett's
Inn].

195. WORCESTER, FLORENCE OF.—Chronicon ex Chro
nicis, edit. Thorpe (E. H. S.), 1849.

A boy murdered by them at Bury, ii. 155.
Many slain at coronation of Ric. I., 157; slain in various
places, 158.
Imprisoned, 169; executed at Norwich, 177.
Plundered and slain, 192.
Synagogue given up to Friars de Pœnitentiâ, 210.
Forbidden to practise usury, 214. Expelled from Cam-
bridge, 215.
Imprisoned, 220; hanged for clipping coin, 221.
Boy crucified by them at Northampton, 222; im-
prisoned, 238; expulsion, 243.

196. Year Books, edit. A. J. Horwood (R. S.).

30 Ed. I., "Defend" inserted in deeds to cover debts to
Jews, 190.
33 Ed. I., Annuity to a Jew (Simon), and a mortgage to
secure it.

197. ZUNZ.—Geographische Literatur der Juden, in *Ges.
Schr.*, I., p. 167.

§ 44. (3.) Joseph b. Baruch=the one who brought Je-
huda b. Kardinal's "Kusari" to England. Both Jewish
Crusaders (v. de Rossi cod. 625. S. D. L. in preface to
"Kusari," 1839, § 3. Orient., 1840, 588).
(4.) Meir b. Baruch, Joseph's brother=Meir of England,
R.A., on funeral customs.

D

198. Zunz.—Zur Gesch. und Literatur. 1845.

    Tosafists : (?) Sir Leon (35), Sir Muriel (37), Elias הק״פ of אובריון (? Eboracum), Jomtob of Joigny (52), Joseph b. Daniel (52, 89). Exegetes : Jacob of Orleans (75). Punctators : Moses der Nakdan = M. b. Joseph, Moses b. Isaac of England (112). Jurists : Meir of England (161), Jomtob of London, 1175 (193).

199. —— Die Ritus. 1865.

    20 Sivan, a fast for Jews of France, England, and Rhine for the martyrs of Blois, 1171, 127.
    Meir of Rothenburg (R. A. 4to., No. 117) treats France and England as one. A Machsor with notes from England mentioned in twelfth century.—Jacob of London translated " Hagada " for women and children, 62.

APPENDIX

TO PRE-EXPULSION PERIOD.

[Rough Notes (unverified), kindly communicated by Dr. C. Gross.

Allen, J., " Liskeard," p. 27.

Bemont, C., "Simon de Montfort," (Paris), 1884, pp. 62, 63, 124, 203, 210.

Brent," Canterbury,'' 116, 137.

Calendarium Rotulorum Patentium (R.C.), 1802, 2, 8[b], 11[b], 12, 13[b], 16, 18, 19[b], 21[b], 23, 27, 27[b], 28, 28[b], 29, 31, 32[b], 33, 35, 36[b], 37, 38[b], 39, 39[b], 42[b], 43, 43[b], 44, 44[b], 45[b], 46, 47, 47[b], 48[b], 49, 49[b], 50[b], 51, 53[b], 54[b], 55.

" A Chronicle of London," 1827, pp. 1, 20, 28, 34, etc.

" Chronicon Angliæ Petriburgense," ed. J. A. Giles (Cam. Soc.), pp. 107, 142, 145, 151, 155, etc.

" Chronicon Galfridi de Swinbroke" (Caxton Soc.), p. 36 [Expulsion].

Griffith, E., " Records of Huntingdon," 1827, p. 18.

Hedge, " Wallingford," i. 317.

" Historical Collection of a Citizen of London " (Cam. Soc.), pp. 68, 70, 72.

"Judæorum Memorabilia," Bristol, 1796.

Kent Archæological Society, "Archæologia Cantiana," vi. 306-17.

Leland, " Itinerary," iii. 71 (Winchester); iv. 165 (Warwick Jewry).

" Liber Custumarum " (R. S.), p. 255.

Liebermann, F., " Ungedruckte Anglo-Normannische Geschichtsquellen." Strassburg, 1879.

Mason, " History of Norfolk," i. 49.

Maynard, Sir J., " Reports," 1678, 1-19.

Morant, " Colchester," 1748, p. 8.

Morin, " Chronicle of Dunstaple."

" Palatine Note Book," 1881, p. 117.

Promptorium Parvulorum (Cam. Soc.), 1843; i. 267. IVRYE, where Ivys dwelle, *Judea, Judaismus.*

Pryce, " Bristol," pp. 22, 23.

Records of Gloucester Cathedral, 1884, ii. 125.

Report of Municipal Corporations Commission, 1835, pp. 2582. 2680, 2840.

Richards, W., " Lynn," i. 390.

Simpson, R., " Collection concerning Derby," pp. 36-37.

Sussex Archæological Society, " Collections," ii. 32; viii. 56, 63; ix. 161.

Waylen, " Devizes," p. 45.

II.—MIDDLE AGE.

1290—1656.

201. P. ABRAHAM.—Curiosities of Judaism, 1879.
>   1290. Proscribed Jews fled to Scotland, p. 45.

202. RYMER'S FŒDERA.
>   1308. Inquisition touching converts, Syl. 154.
>   1340. King allows Edward of Brussels, a converted Jew, to reside in House of Converts, Syl. 315.
>   1356. King allows John de Chastel a converted Jew, Syl. 386.
>   1410. Safe conduct for Helias Sabot, a Hebrew, Syl. 566.

203. ELLIS, Sir H.—Chronica Johannis de Oxoniæ, edited by H. E., 1859.
>   1310. Extract from Hargrave MS., relating to a mission of Jews to England, preface, p. iv.

203a. AYENBITE OF INWYT.—(Early English Text Society.)
>   1345. Jews employed by the great to lend money, p. 35.

203b. JOSEPH HA-COHEN. — Emek habacha, edited by Wiener.
>   1358. Jews attempt to return and are finally expelled, p. 54.

204. ROTULI PARLIAMENTARUM.
>   1376. Commons complain that many so-called Lombards in England are Jews, ii. 332a.

205. WILKS, T. E.—History of Hampshire, 1861.
>   1489. Masse Salaman, Jew Sheriff of Southampton, ii. 262.
>   [Note. Jews banished in 1287. More strictly expelled in 1610. In 1624 practically allowed.]

206. BARRY, JOHN S.—Town of Hanover, Mass., 8vo., 1853.
>   Jacob's family of Jewish extraction resident in England in 15th century.

207. AMADOR DE LOS RIOS.—Historià de los Judeos de Espana.

1492. Spanish Jewish fugitives in England, iii. 377.

207a. POCOCK, NICHOLAS.—Records of the Reformation, 2 vols. 1527-1533. Oxford. 8vo. 1870.

[Contains important documents bearing on the participation of Jews in the controversy on Henry VIII.'s divorce. Unfortunately the work is not provided with an index.]

208. NICOLAS, Sir HARRY.—Proceedings of Privy Council of England.

1421. Baptism of "Job, an apothecary from Italy," ii. 304.
1542. Arrest of Jews, vii. 304.

209. CALENDARS OF STATE PAPERS.—Domestic Series of the Reigns of Edward VI., Mary, Elizabeth, and James I. Edited by R. Lemon and M. A. E. Green.

Vol. i. (1547-1580). Ferdinando, Simon, a Portuguese, 541.
Jacob, Abraham, warrant addressed to, 700.
Lopez, Dr., petitions Burghley, 592.

Vol. ii. (1581-1590).
Gaunze, Joachim, 49.
—— a Jew, prosecution of, 617.
Loppez, Dr. Roger, to Walsyngham, 609.

Vol. iii. (1591-1594). Acosta, Josephus, History of the Indies, by, 67.
Jews, pp. 444, 446, 462.
Lopez, Jeronimo, Portuguese merchant, 379, 416, 418, 443.
Lopez, Dr. Roger or Ruy, Portuguese Jew, physician to the Queen, pp. 16, 82, 83, 92 (²), 93 (²), 94, 359, 413, 416, 418, 420, 422, 423, 425, 428, 430, 434 (²), 444, 450, 455, 458, 460, 482, 484, 485, 533, 538, 542, 553 (²), 558, 564.
—— Accusation of, pp. 434, 439 (²), 440, 445-449, 452, 455-457.
—— Indictment against, p. 445 (²).
—— Letter of, 443.
—— Letters to, 65, 69 (²), 434.
—— Present to, 416, 445, 447.
—— Reports on the treasons of, 453, 455, 456, 460-462, 564, 577.

Lopez, Dr. Roger, Trial of, 444, 448, 456.
—— Trial, abstract of evidence at, 445-448.
—— Death or execution of, 460.
—— Wife and children of, 434.
—— Daughter of, 413, 440.
—— Cousins of 16.
Vol. iv. (1595-1597). Hurtado [? Herrera], resident at Cadiz, 279.
Lopez, Dr. Roger, 76, 175, 466
—— Persons implicated in his conspiracy, 85, 141.
—— Present to, 15.
—— Sarah, widow of, grant to, 15.
Vol. vi. (1601-1603). Jacobs, Jacob, prisoner at Rye, 413.
Lopez, Dr., not yet hanged, 173.
Vol. viii (1603-1610). Jacob, Abraham, 329, 366.
Vol. ix. (1611-1618). Jacob, Abraham, 47, 535.
Jews at Melomocco, 188.
Jew pirate arrested, 260.
Vol. x. (1619-1623).—Jacob, Abraham, 27, 82, 91, 170, 175, 179, 232, 310.
Jews, book on conversion of, 248, 277.
Jews, cause of the, 320.
Vol. xi. (1623-1625).—Jacob, Mr. [Abraham], 190, 212, 234.
Jew, petition of a converted, 517.
Judaism, convert to, 435.
Vol. xii. (addenda 1580-1625). Jew of Barbary gives bill on London merchant, p. 587.
Judea, balm of, 71.
Lopez, Dr., 379.

CALENDARS OF STATE PAPERS, *cont.*—Domestic Series of the reign of Charles I., edited by J. Bruce and W. D. Hamilton.

Vol. i. (1625-1626). Danielson, Lieven, petition of, 271.
Jacob, Abraham, 40, 93, 245, 255, 379, 511, 571.
Jacobson, Jacob, petition of, 271.
Jew at Cambridge, 98.
Vol. ii. (1627-1628). Jacob, Abraham, 32, 299, 415, 421, 443, 582.
Vol. iii. (1628-1629). Maria Anthony de Verona, 26.
Vol. ix. (1635-1636). Judaism, prosecution of convert to, 132.
Vol. xvii. (1640-1641). Israelites, the, 164, 165.
Jews, certain M.P.'s so designated, 560.

CALENDARS OF STATE PAPERS, *cont.* — Domestic
Series during the Commonwealth, edited by M. A. E.
Green.

Vol. i. (1649-1650). Ferdinando, Bartholomew, 368.
Ferdinando, Don Antonio, 255.
Jews, 193, 194.
Vol. ii. (1650). Carvajal, Antonio Fernandez de, 373,
377, 380, 558.
Fernandez, Antonio or Anthony, 248, 347, 359-360,
380, 404.
—— son of, 143.
Jews, 189.
Rodrigues [? Robles], 360.
Vol. iii. (1651). Carvajal, Antonio Fernandez, 262, 418.
Casseras, Henrique de, 212.
—— Simon de, 212.
Vol. iv. (1651-1652). Carvajal, Antonio Fernandez, 213,
301, 361, 395.
Fernandez, Antonio, 296.
Jewish brokers, 49.
Jews, 49.
Mendes, Henriq. Jor., 408.
Moïse, David, 353.
Robles, Antonio Rodriques, 432.
Roduges [? Rodrigues], Leonora, 405.
Vol. v. (1652-1653). Caseres, Simon de, 98, 166, 194,
209, 211, 275, 618.
—— petition of, 378.
Mendez, Henrique Jor., 335.
Vol. vi. (1653-1654). Carvajal, Antonio Fernandez, 272.
Jacob, Israel, 537.
Mendez, Henriq. Jor., 330.
Vol. vii. (1654). Carvajal Antonio Fernandez, 28.
Carolus, Jacob, 91.
Chacon, Augustin Coronel, 443.
Mendez, Henriq. Jor., 389.
Vol. viii. (1655). Brito, Domingo Vaes de, 593.
Carvajal, Antonio Fernandez, 580.
Coronel, Augustin, 47.
Coste, Bento de la, 47.
Mendez, Henriq. Jor., 43, 44, 586.
Mercado, Abraham and Raphael, pass for, 583.
Solomons, Henricke, 578.
Vol. ix. (1655-1656). Carvajal, Antonio Fernandez, 60,
161.
Carcerts (? Casseres), Simon de, 128.
Robles, or Robelles, Antonio Rodriques Peremeun,
93, 227, 247, 260, 274 (^{2}), 295, 316, 325 (^{2}), 327.

Felix, an Augustine friar, formerly a Jew, 6445, 6581; App. 261.

Francis, Father, or Friar Francis George, 6149, 6156, 6159, 6165, p. 2756, 6173-4, 6192-4, 6197, 6207, 6209, 6229, 6232, 6235-7, 6239, 6242, 6250-1, 6266, 6280-2, 6287-1, 6300, 6310, 6316, 6326, 6339, 6352-4, 6372, p. 2863, 6388, 6403, 6406-7, 6413-14, 6416, 6423, 6425-6, 6428, 6434, 6445-6, 6463, 6465, 6470, 6472, 6491, 6500, 6543, 6567, 6581, 6613, 6620, 6624, 6633, 6637, 6669-71, 6694, 6696, 6702, 6713-14, 6785-6 ; App. 265 (19).

—— letters from, 6207, 6465, 6472.

—— letters to 6388, 6620.

Gabriel, *see* Raphael.

Helyas, Hebrew Dr. in Venice, 6266, p. 2863, 6445, 6786.

Jacob, the Jew, 6194, 6445, 6499.

Jews, the, 6105, 6140, 6149, 6161, 6170, 6463, 6479.

Mantineus [? Mantuanus], Jacob, 6165.

Raphael, Mark, a Jew, 6068, 6156, 6236, 6239, 6240, 6250, 6266, 6300, 6375, 6398, 6414, 6541, 6656, 6739, 6786.

Vol. v. (1531-1532). Francis George, 567.

Jew sent for by Henry VIII., 70, 120, 216, 1429.

Jews, 869.

Raphael, Mark, converted Jew, nephew of Francis George, 567 ; — 1065) (29).

Vol. vi. (1533). Raphaelle, Marke, 299 ii. ; ix. E., 1367.

Vol. vii. (1534). Raphael, Mark, 923 iv., xli.

Vol. ix. (1535). Jews, 84, 102.

CALENDARS OF STATE PAPERS, *cont.*—Foreign Series of the Reign of Elizabeth, edited by Rev. J. Stevenson, M.A., and A. J. Crosby, M.A.

Vol. iii. (1560 61). Tremellio, Immanuel, Canon of Carlisle, letter from, 1008.

—— letter to, 1022.

·—— letter to, 1008, 1020, 1030 (25).

Vol. iv. (1561-1562) —— 171, 189 (1), 190 (1), 197, 208 (5).

Vol. v. (1562). Jews, the, 158 (10), 190 (1), 197, 208 (5).

——Calendar of Letters, Despatches, and State Papers, relating to the Negotiations between England and Spain, edited by J. A. Bergenroth and P. de Gayanjos.

Vol. i. (1485-1509). Jews, conduct of certain, 51.

—— in England, 164.

Vol. iv. (1429-1533). Gabriello, Marco [? Raphael, Mark],
a converted Jew, 335.
—— invited to England, 761.
—— Imperial Ambassadors take measures for his
arrest, 825, 842, 844.
—— in London, 45.
Jews in Venice and Bologna consulted on divorce
case, 61, 552, 869.
—— one in Rome to be brought to England, 761 ;
ii. 535.
—— one in Rome compelled to marry his brother's
widow, 739.

209a. COOPER, W. H.—Athenæ Cantabrigienses.
1549. Emmanuel Tremellius, i. 423.
1596. Philip Ferdinand, ii. 209 and Supplement.

209b. BUTTERS, FRIEDRICH.—E. Tremellius, &c. Zwei-
brücken, 1859. 8vo.
Tremellius visited England in 1549 and 1567.

209c. WRIOTHESLEY, CHARLES.—A Chronicle of England (Cam. Soc.), 1875.
1550. Prosecution of Ferdinando Lopes, a Jewish
physician, ii. 36.

210. LEE, SYDNEY L.—The Original of Shylock.
[Rodrigo Lopez.]
Article in "Gentlemen's Magazine," Feb., 1880.

211. FORNERON, HENRI.—Histoire de Philippe II.,
Paris, 1882.
1560-94. Rodrigo Lopez, iv. 266 et seq.

212. TREMELLIUS, JOHN EMMANUEL.—Psalmi Davidis
ex Hebraico in Latinum conversi, 16mo., London,
1580.

213. GRAETZ, H.—Geschichte der Juden.
1590. Marranos in England, ix. 492-3.

214. HARVEY, GABRIEL.—A New Letter of Notable
Contents ; with a Strange Sonet, entitled, Gorgon ;
or the wonderful Jew. 1591.

215. BARRIOS, DAVID LEVY DE.—Historia Universal
Judaica.
1596. Abraham (Alonzo) de Herrera brought to England,
p. 20.

216. PIOT, LAZARUS.—The Orator: Handling a Hundred Severall Discourses. 1596.

[95th Declamation, "Of a Jew who would for his debt have a pound of the flesh of a Christian."]

217. HALEVI, ABRAHAM ABEN HASSAN.—Hæc sunt verba Dei, etc. Precepta 613. Collecta per A. fil. Kattani, translata in linguam Latinam per P. Ferdinandum. Cantabrig, 4to. 1597.

[Translation of מצות עשה ומצות לא תעשה by P. Ferdinand, teacher of Hebrew at Cambridge, and a converted Jew.]

218. ELLIS.—Letters Illustrative of English History, 1825.

1599. Letter from Esperanza Malchi to Queen Elizabeth, iii. 52.

218a. SYMONS, John.—Hull in ye Olden Times. 1886.

1599. David de Pomis, a Jew Rabbi, resident at Hull, p. 82.
[1618.] Israel Leoni, a Hull Merchant, p. 14.
[The documents referred to in this work belong to the series edited by Mr. Gunnell (see No. 223). David de Pomis is generally supposed to have died at Venice in 1588 (cf. Graetz, "Geschichte," ix. 483).]

219. NIXON, ANTH.—The Travels of Three English Brothers. 1607.

[Gives an account of the kindly treatment of Sir Thomas Shirley by a Jew in Constantinople. —This was turned into a bad account in Day, Rowley, and Wilkins' dramatisation of Shirley's travels in the same year].

219a. Jewes' Prophecy, or Newes from Rome. 1607. 4to.

219b. BULLEN, A. H.—"Old Plays," ("Everie Woman in her Humour," 1609).

"You may hire a good suit at a Jewes," (cf. *Academy*, May 14, 1887).

220. PATERSON, MARK.—Life of Isaac Casaubon, London, 1875.

1613. Jacob Barnett, a Jew, at Oxford, pp. 413-416.

220a. BACON'S APOPHTHEGMS.

1617. Anecdote of Gondemar.

220*b*. HARRISON, JOHN.—The Messiah already come;
or profes of Christianitie, both out of the Scriptures and aunctent Rabbins, to convince the Jewes
of their palpable and more than miserable blind-
nesse (if more may be), for their long, vaine, and
endlesse expectation of the Messiah (as they dream)
yet for to come. Written in Barberie in the year
1610, and for that cause directed to the dispersed
Jewes of that countrie, &c.   Amsterdam, 1619.
8vo., 68 pp.

220*c*. CASTRO, D. HENRIQUES DE.—Auswahl von Grabsteinen.   Leiden, 1883.   Part I.
> 1623. Burial of a child of an English proselyte, p. 28.
> „   Burial of a daughter of an English Jew, p. 28.
> 1625. Burial of a child of an English proselyte, p. 28.
> „   Burial of the wife of an English proselyte, p. 28.

221. The Wandering Jew telling Fortunes to Englishmen.   1625.
> [Reprinted in J. O. Halliwell's "Books of Character,"
> London, 1857.]

222. MARLOWE, C.—The Famous Tragedy of the Rich
Jew of Malta; as it was played before the King
and Queene in His Majestie's Theatre at Whitehall, by Her Majestie's servants at the Cock Pit.
1633.
> [Edited by W. Shone, with Notes, 1810.]

223. GUNNELL, W. A.—Sketches of Hull Celebrities.
Hull, 1876.
> 1600 (*circa*). A Jew goldsmith in Chepe, London, p. 183.
> 1618. Israel Leoni, Hull merchant, p. 9.
> 1649. Richard Ffranks, Chamberlain, and afterwards
> Mayor of Hull, pp. 118, 200.
> [The genuineness of the documents edited in this work
> has been strongly contested.]

223*a*. Reports of Historical MSS. Commission.
> 1641. Carvisall [Carvajal], iv. 73.
> „   Hawes v. Kilvart and Carvajall, iv. 274.
> 1644. Petition of Antonio Fernandez Cavajal, vi. 8a.
> 1645. Prosecution of Carvajal as a recusant, vi. 42b.
> „   Petition of Carvajal, vi. 51a.

1646. Carvajal advances money to the Parliament, vi. 102-3.
  1648. Petition of Carvajal, vii. 12.
224. A Parallel between the Israelites' desires of King Saul, &c. London, 1643. 4to.
225. The Gathering together of the Jews for the Conquering of the Holy Land. 1647. 4to.
226. CALVERT, THOMAS.—The Blessed Jew of Marocco. 1648. 8vo.
227. The Devilish Conspiracy executed by the Jews. 1648. 4to.
228. ISAAC, P. L.—Historical Notes on Shipping. 1879.
  1649. Michael ben Alexander petitions Parliament, p. 40.
229. WOOD, ANTHONY À, Diary of the Life of.
  [Prefixed to Athen. Oxon.]
  1650. Jacob, a Jew, sells coffee at Oxford, p. xix.
  1654. Cirques Jobson, a Jew and Jacobite, sells coffee at Oxford, p. xxiii.
230. VIOLET, THOMAS.—The Advancement of Merchandise. London, 1651.
  Advises Government to confer with Carvajal on question of transport of bullion, 13.
231. ——.—Petition against the Jews. 1661.
  Antonio Ferdinando [Carvajal] passed as a Christian before the Re-admission, 4.
231a. MARTIN, FREDERICK.—The History of Lloyds. 1655. Augustin Coronel, a Jew, p. 84.
232. THURLOE STATE PAPERS.
  1655. Indenization granted to Carvajal, iii. 688.
  ,, Simon de Casseres projects conquest of Chili, iv. 62.
  1656. "Jew named Da Costa, a great merchant in London," v. 572.
233. BURNETT.—History of his Own Times.
  Cromwell brought over Jews to serve as spies, i. 122.
234. "THE TIMES."
  S. L. Lee: "Jews in England," Nov. 1, 1883.
  F. E. Sawyer: "Jews in England," Nov. 1, 1883.
234a. "THE ATHENÆUM."
  J. E. Thorold Rogers: "Antonio de Verona," Sept. 3, 1887.
  Lucien Wolf: "Antonio de Verona," Sept. 10, 1887.

235. "THE ACADEMY."
S. L. Lee : "Jews in England," March 26, 1882.
―――― Baptisms of Jews in XIV. Century, Feb. 3, 1883.
W. E. A. Axon : Jews (?) in Lancashire in XIV Century,
Feb. 3, 1883.
1410. Sir James Ramsay : Jewish Physicians in England,
March 11, 1882.
1421. ―――― Jewish Apothecary in England, Jan. 27, 1883.
1643. S. R. Gardiner : Mention of Jews in Despatches of
Venetian Agent, March 4, 1882.

236. "THE JEWISH WORLD."
Queen Elizabeth's Jewish Physician, Jan. 1880.

237. "THE JEWISH CHRONICLE."
S. L. Lee : "The House of Converts," Jan. 26, Feb. 16,
April 27, and June 15, 1883.
1618. Jews probably began to settle in England, Dec. 5,
1884.

―――――――――

NATIONAL MOVEMENT FOR THE RETURN.

238. M. KAYSERLING. — Menasse ben Israel. Sein
Leben und Wirken. Zugleich ein Beitrag zur
Geschichte der Juden in England. Berlin. 8vo.
1861.
[Translated by Dr. de Sola Mendes in "Soc. Heb. Lit.,"
Misc. II.]

239. LUCIEN WOLF. — Re-settlement of the Jews in
England. With Notes and Appendix. 1888.
[Reprinted from *Jewish Chronicle* of Dec. 9, 16, 23, 1887,
and Jan. 13, 1888. German translation in *Oestereichische
Wochenschrift* of Dec. 16, 1887, *et seq.*]

240. P. T. [THOMAS POCOCK.]—De Termino Vitæ ; or,
the Term of Life, viz., whether it is fixed or
alterable ; with the sense of the Jewish Doctors,
both ancient and modern, touching Predestination
and Free Will. Written in Latin by the famous
Menasseh ben Israel the Jew, and now translated
into English. 1700.
[Contains a memoir of Menasseh based on information
supplied to the writer by Mr. Gomes Serra.]

241. MANASSE B. ISRAEL.—Gratulatio gentis suæ nomine, ad principem Fred. Henricum cum juxta reginam Henricam Mariam, Caroli Magnæ Britanniæ regis conjugem, synagogam lustraret. 4to., 12 pp. Amsterdam. 1642.

242. ROGER WILLIAMS.—The Bloody Tenent of Persecution for cause of conscience discussed in a Conference between Truth and Peace. 1644.
. [Reprinted by Hanserd Knollys Soc., 1848.]
P. 141, Jews, although heretics, may make good citizens.

243. LEONARD BUSHER.—Religious Peace ; or, A Plea for Liberty of Conscience. Presented to King James, and printed in the year 1614 ; reprinted 1646. 1646.
[Reprinted in collection of Hanserd Knollys Soc., 1846.]
Pp. 28, 47, 71, By not setting up liberty of conscience Jews are prevented from seeking to inhabit England, and their conversion is impeded.

244. A true and perfect relation of a . . . Conspiracy discovered by a Jew in Turkie. London. 4to. 1646.

245. THOMAS VALENTINE (Rector of Chalfont). — A Charge against the Jews and the Christian World for not coming to Christ . . . Delivered in a Sermon before the . . . House of Peers, . . . May 26, 1647, being the day of their Public Fast. 4to. 1647.

246. HUGH PETERS.—A Word for the Army, and Two Words to the Kingdom, to clear the one and cure the other. (Harleian Miscellany, v. 573.) 1647.
Art. 10 demands that "strangers, even Jews, [be] admitted to trade and live with us."

247. EDWARD NICHOLAS.—An Apology for the honourable Nation of Jews, and all the Sons of Israel. 8vo. 1648.

248. T. CALVERT. — A Large Diatribe of the Jews' Estate. York. 8vo. 1648.
[Added to a translation of R. Samuel's "Demonstration of the True Messiah."]

249. The Petition of the Jewes for the Repealing of the Act of Parliament for their Banishment out of

England, presented to his Excellency [Lord Fairfax]
and the Generall Councell of Officers, on Fryday,
Jan. 5, 1648, with their favourable acceptance
thereof. Also a Petition of Divers Commanders,
prisoners in the King's Bench, for the releasing of
all prisoners for Debt, according to the Custome of
other Countries. London. Printed for George
Roberts.   1649.

[Sm. 4to., 6 pp. The petitioners are "Johanna Carten-
wright, Widdow, and Ebenezer Cartwright, her Son,
freeborn of England, and now Inhabitants of the City of
Amsterdam." This is the first petition presented in connection with the National Movement for the Return]

250. MENASSEH BEN ISRAEL. — מקוה ישראל Esto es,
Esperanza de Israel (Relacion de Aharo Levi, alias
A. de Montezinos.)   Amsterdam.   1649.

[Dedicated to the English Parliament and Council of
State "in order to gain your favour and goodwill to our
Nation."]

251. JOHN SADLER.—Rights of the Kingdom.   1649.

P. 48 refers to Menasseh ben Israel, and pleads for justice
and mercy to Jews.

252. J. DURY.—An Epistolary Discourse to Mr. Thomas
Thorowgood, concerning his conjecture that the
Americans are descended from the Israelites. 1649.

253. E. S. [of] MIDDLESEX.—An Epistle to the learned
Manasse ben Israel in answer to his, dedicated to
the Parliament.   London.   8vo.   1650.

[Proposes twelve conditions for the re-admission of the
Jews. Among them are that Jews shall not circumcise; that
they shall attend a Conversion Sermon once a year on Good
Friday, and that they shall pay double customs.]

254. R. LEO JUDA.—History of the Modern Jews. Translated from the Italian of Juda, by E. Chilmead.
                                                  1650.

255. ANTONIO DE MONTEZINOS [=AARON LEVI].—The
Relation of . . . . Antony Montezinus of what befell
him as he travelled over the Mountains Cordillære.
                                                  1650.

[Another edition in 1651. 4to.]

256. T. Thorowgood, B.D.—Jews in America, or Pro-
babilities that the Americans are Jews.   1650.
      [Second Edition.]

257. Menasseh ben Israel. — The Hope of Israel.
Translated into English with the "Relation of . . . .
Antony Montezinos." 8vo. 2nd edit., 1851, with
Discourses upon the Point of the Conversions of
the Jewes, by Moses Wall.   1651.
      [The original, in Spanish, appeared at Amsterdam in
      1649 (No. 250), and a reprint in Madrid, 1881. It also ap-
      peared in Dutch, together with a translation of Nicholas'
      tract (see No. 247) at Amsterdam, in 1666.]

258. The Great Deliverance of the Whole House of
Israel : What it truely is, by whom it shall be performed, and in what year; in answer to the book
called "The Hope of Israel." London. 8vo.
                                            1652.

259. Sir Hamon L'Estrange.— Americans no Jews.
London. 4to.   1652.
      [Reply to No. 256.]

260. R[oger] W[illiams].—The Fourth Paper presented by Major Butler to the Honourable Committee of Parliament for the Propagating the Gospel
of Christ Jesus. London. 4to.   1652.
      [One of the questions propounded by Major Butler (p. 3)
      is, "Whether it be not the duty of the magistrate to permit
      the Jews, whose conversion we look for, to live freely and
      peaceably amongst us." On this R. W. comments at length
      in an affirmative sense (pp. 18-19).]

261. —— The Hireling Ministry none of Christ's, or
a Discourse touching the Propagating the Gospel
of Christ Jesus, humbly presented to such pious
and honourable hands whom the present debate
thereof concerns.   1652.
      P. 27.—"All consciences (yea, the very conscience of the
      Papists, Jews, &c.) ought freely and impartially to be per-
      mitted their severall respective worships, their ministers of wor-
      ships, and what way of maintaining them they freely choose."

262. The Wonderful and most Deplorable History of
the Latter Times of the Jews. London. 8vo. 1652.
                        E

263. ELEASAR BARGISHAI.—A Brief Compendium of the Vain Hopes of the Jews Messias, the Ignorant Fables of their Rabbies, and the Confuting of the Jewish Religion. Written by E. B., a born Jew, for the upholding of Christianity. 8vo., 21 pp. [A. N.]   1652.

> [Colophon : " This is the first part of this, my little Treatise, of the Jews superstitions and carnal hoping for their Messias, as they are taught from their babbling Talmuth and foolish blinde Rabbies and Teachers."]

264. HENRY JESSEY.—The Glory of Jehudah and Israel.   1653.

> [Referred to by Menasseh ben Israel in his " Humble Addresses " (see Nos. 275-6) as having been written in Dutch.]

265. Original Letters and Papers of State addressed to Oliver Cromwell concerning the affairs of Great Britain . . . found among the Political Collections of John Milton.   1743.

> P. 100.—Petition for the re-admission of the Jews addressed to the Short Parliament by Samuel Herring.

266. JOSEPH BEN ISRAEL.—The Converted Jew; or, the Substance of the Declaration and Confession which was made in the Publique Meeting House at Hexham, the 4th moneth, the 5th day, 1653, by J. ben I. Gateside. 8vo., 12 pp.   1653.

267. The Counterfeit Jew. Sm. 4to., 8 pp. [A. N.]
                                                        1653.

> [A person named " Josephus ben Israel," who came to Newcastle under name of Horseley. The tract wanders off into theological rhapsodies.]

268. THO. WELD, SAM. HAMMOND, CUTH. SIDENHAM, AND WIL. DURANT.—A False Jew; or, a Wonderful Discovery of a Scot, baptised at London for a Christian, circumcised at Rome to act a Jew, rebaptised at Hexham for a Believer, but found out at Newcastle to be a cheat. Newcastle. 4to., 14 pp.   1653.
Second Edition. London. 4to.   1654.

269. THOMAS TILLAM.—Banners of Love displaied over
the Church at Hexham; or, an Answer to a Narrative stuffed with Untruths by four Newcastle
Gentlemen. London. 4to. 1654.

270. ELIAZAR BAR-ISAJAH. — The Christian's Messiah
vindicated by One that was a Jew born. 8vo., 66 pp.
[Pp. 61-66, "Epistle to my former Brethren."]

271. ELIEZER BAR-ISAJAH.—The Messiah of the Christians and the Jew. 8vo. 1655.

272. MERCURIUS POLITICUS.
Distress of Jews in Poland, Nov. 1, 1655.
Hamburg full of fugitive Polish Jews, Dec. 17, 1655.
Polish Jews petition to be allowed to settle in Austria,
Dec. 20, 1655.
If Jews admitted to England, will be useful in war with
Spain, Jan. 24, 1656.

273. "PUBLIC INTELLIGENCER."
Distress of Jews in Poland, Nov. 12, 1655.
Polish Jews' petition to be allowed to settle in Austria,
Dec. 17, 1655.

274. SAMUEL BRETT.—A Narrative of the Proceedings of
a great Council of Jews, assembled in the Plains of
Ageda in Hungaria, about 30 leagues distant from
Buda to examine the Scriptures concerning Christ,
on the 12th of October, 1650. 1655.
[Reprinted in *Phœnix*.]

275. MENASSEH BEN ISRAEL.—To his Highnesse the
Lord Protector of the Commonwealth of England,
Scotland, and Ireland, the humble Addresses of
Menasseh ben Israel, a Divine and Doctor of Physic,
in behalfe of the Jewish Nation. 4to., 23 pp.
[1655.]
[No imprint or date. The British Museum copy is dated
in MS. "November 5th (London) 1655." Reprinted in
Soc. Heb. Lit., Misc. II. Also separately in facsimile
(Dwight), Melbourne, 1868.]

276. MENASSEH BEN ISRAEL.—To his Highnesse the Lord
Protector of the Commonwealth of England, Scot-
land, and Ireland, etc. 26 pp. 4to. [1655.]
[No imprint or date. Apparently a revised edition of
No. 275.]

277. JOHN DURY (in Hesse Cassel).—A Case of Conscience, whether it be lawful to admit Jews into a
Christian Commonwealth, resolved by Mr. J. D.,
written to Samuel Hartlib.   1655.
[Reprinted in *Harleian Miscellany*, vii., 240-244.]

278. W. PRYNNE.—Short Demurrer against the Jewes
continued remitter into England. Part I.   1655.
[A second part appeared in 1656, together with a second
edition of the first.]

279. A. R.—A View of the Jewish Religion, containing
Manner of Life, Rites, Ceremonies, and Customs of
the Jewish Nation throughout the World at this present time, with their Articles of Faith, as now
received.   1656.
[Announced in *Public Intelligencer*, Feb. 4, 1655-56.]

280. W. PHINEH.—The Law read June the 10, 1656,
unto the People Israel belonging to the returning
from Captivity at the Tent Judah. London. 4to.

281. J. COPLEY.—Case of the Jews is altered and their
Synagogues shut to all Evil-walkers, or a Vindication of the Jews. 4to., 6 pp.   1656.

282. ARISE EVANS.—Light for the Jews: or, the Means
to convert them, in answer to a Book of theirs,
called "The Hope of Israel." London.   1664.
[A note states that the pamphlet was written in March,
1656, but not published until 1664. The object of the work
was to prove to Menasseh ben Israel that "Charles Steward
is he whom you call your Messiah, Captain and Deliverer,
who will bring you to present happiness if you follow him."]

283. MENASSEH BEN ISRAEL.—Vindiciæ Judæorum, or
a Letter in answer to certain Questions propounded
by a Noble and Learned Gentleman, touching the
reproaches cast on the Nation of the Jewes;
wherein all objections are candidly and yet fully
closed. By Rabbi Menasseh Ben Israel, a Divine
and a Physicyan. Printed by R. D., in the year
1656. 8vo., 41 pp.   1656.
[A German translation by Mendelssohn was published at

Berlin, 1782, and reprinted at Bamberg, 1882, in connection
with the Anti-Semitic movement.   Translated into Polish in
1831.]

284. [HENRY JESSEY].—A Narrative of the late Proceedings at Whitehall concerning the Jews, who
had desired by Rabbi Manasse, an Agent of them,
that they might return into England, and worship
the God of their fathers here in the Synagogues.
Published for satisfaction to many in several parts of
England that are desirous and inquisitive to hear
the truth thereof.   16 pp.   1656.
   [Reprinted *Harl. Misc.* iii., pp. 578-83.   German in
Pantheon Anabaptist, p. 235 seq.]

285. Anglo-Judæus, or the history of the Jews whilst
here in England.   Relating their Manners, Car-
riages, and Usage from their admission by William
the Conqueror to their banishment, occasioned by
a Book written to his Highness the Lord Protector
(with a Declaration to the Commonwealth of England) for their re-admission by Rabbi Menasses
Ben Israel.   To which is also subjoyned a particular
answer by W. H.   1656.

286. THOMAS COLLIER.—A brief Answer to some of the
objections and demurs made against the coming in
and inhabiting of the Jews in this Commonwealth,
with a plea on their behalf or some Arguments to
prove it not only lawful, but the duty of those
whom it concerns to give them their Liberty and
Protection (they living peaceably) in this Nation.
                                                     1656.

287. The Case of the Jewes stated ; or, the Jewes Synagogue opened.   With their Preparations in the
Morning before they go thither, and their doings at
Night when they come home : their Practises in
their Synagogues and some select actings of theirs
in England upon Record.   R. Ibbitson.   Sm. 4to.,
6 pp.   [A.N.]   1656.

288. THOMAS BURTON, M.P.— Parliamentary Diary, edited by J. T. Butt. London. 8vo. 1828.

> Feb. 4, 1658. "The Jews, those able and general intelligencers, whose intercourse with the Continent Cromwell had before turned to a profitable account, he now conciliated by a seasonable benefaction to their principal agent resident in England."

289. The Great Trappaner of England Discovered; being a True Narrative of many dangerous and abominable Practices of one Thomas Violet, Goldsmith, to trappan the Jews and ruin many scores of Families in and about London. London. 4to., 6 pp. 1660.

290. TH. VIOLET.—Petition against the Jews, with several Reasons proving the East India, the Turkey, and the East Country Trade may be driven without transporting gold and silver out of England, 4to.
1661.

> References to the negotiations of the Jews with Cromwell, p. 7.

291. WOOD.—Athenæ Oxoniensis.

> Henry Martin proposed revocation of the Edict of Expulsion of Ed. I.

292. WILLIAM GODWIN. — History of the Commonwealth of England. 1828.

> Vol. iv., pp. 243-51. Chapter on Return of the Jews to England, in which reference is made to Dormido's Petition and the foundation of the first Jewish Burial Ground in London.

293. CALENDARS OF STATE PAPERS.—Domestic Series during the Commonwealth, edited by M. A. E. Green.

> Vol. iii. (1651). Menasseh ben Israel, 472.
> Vol. iv. (1651-1652). —— pass for, 577.
> Vol. v. (1652-1653). Jewish Rabbi, 38.
> Sanhedrin, 339.
> Jews, 120, 334.
> Menasseh ben Israel. pass for, 38.
> Mordecai, petition of Robert Rich, surnomer, on behalf of Jews in England, &c.

Vol. vi. (1653-54). Jews, 21, 42, 95, 167, 263, 289, 331.
  Menasseh ben Israel, pass for, 436.
Vol. vii. (1654). Abarbanel, David, 393, 407.
  Jews, 91.
Vol. viii. (1655). Dormido, Manuel, Petition of, 102.
  Jewish Rabbis, 7, 336.
  Jews or Hebrews, 62, 336, 402, 583.
  Menasseh ben Israel, 402.
  Samuel ben Israel, 585.
Vol. ix. (1655-1656). Jewish Hebrew, 866.
  Jewish nation, 15, 20, 51.
  Jews, 15, 23, 51-57, 58, 82, 128, 257, 294, 295, 316,
    473.
  —— in London, petition of, 237.
  Judaism, 16.
  Menasseh ben Israel, 15, 20, 23, 52, 366.
  —— petition of, 237.
  —— request of, 15.
Vol. x. (1656-1657). Menasseh ben Israel, petition of,
    284.
Vol. xi. (1657-1658). —— ——, 101.
  —— son of, 101.

294. CALENDARS OF THE CLARENDON STATE PAPERS.

Vol. ii. (1653). Consultations in Parliament for bringing
the Jews into England, p. 233.

295. THURLOE STATE PAPERS.

Vol. i. (1653). Debates in Parliament on readmission, 387.
Vol. iv. (1655.) Question of readmitting Jews, 308, 321.
    Menasseh ben Israel, 333.

296. "JEWISH CHRONICLE."

Israel Davis : "Resettlement of the Jews by Oliver Crom-
well," Nov. 26 and Dec. 3, 1880.
"The Return of the Jews to England," Dec. 10, 1880.
Philip Abraham : State Papers relating to the Return,
Aug. 8, 1884.

III.—MODERN PERIOD, 1657-1886.

(A.) HISTORIES.

280. S. OCKLEY.—The History of the present Jews
throughout the World : translated from the Italian
[of Jehuda de Modena], to which are subjoined
two supplements—one concerning the Samaritans,
the other of the sect of the Carraites, from the
French of R. Simon, with notes. 8vo.   1707.
[Another edition in 1711.]

281. T. TAYLOR, A.M.—The History of the Jews from
Jesus Christ to the present time ; translated from
the French of Basnagius.   1708.

282. HENRY HART MILMAN, D.D. (Dean of St. Paul's).—
The History of the Jews.

283. HANNAH ADAMS, of Boston, America.—A History
of the Jews from the Destruction of Jerusalem to
the Present Time. 8vo., pp. 576. [A.N.]   1818.

284. History of the Jews in All Ages. 8vo., pp. 528.
[A. N.]   1832.

285. JAMES A. HUIE.—The History of the Jews from
Titus to the Present Time.   104 pp.   [A. N.]
                                               1841.

286. JAMES FINN.—Sephardim, or History of the Jews
in Spain and Portugal. 8vo., 480 pp. [A. N.] 1841.

287. M. MARGOLIOUTH.—The Jews of Great Britain,
being a Series of Six Lectures. 8vo., 412 pp. 1846.

288. [G. AGUILAR].—History of the Jews in England.—
Chambers' Miscellany.   1847.

289. E. H. LINDO.—The History of the Jews of Spain
and Portugal from the Earliest Times to their final

Expulsion from those Kingdoms, and their subsequent Dispersion; with complete translations of
all the Laws made respecting them during their
long Establishment in the Iberian Peninsula.
8vo. London.   1848.

290. ISAAK DA COSTA.—Israel and the Gentiles: Contributions to the History of the Jews. Translated
by Kennedy.   1850.

291. HUIE.—The History of the Jews from the taking
of Jerusalem to the Present Time. 8vo., 304 pp.
[A. N.]   1851.
[? Second edition of No. 285.]

292. ADOLFO DE CASTRO.—The History of the Jews in
Spain, translated by the Rev. E. D. G. M. Kirwan.
Cambridge. 8vo., 276 pp.   1851.

293. Prize Essays on the Post Biblical History of the
Jews. London.   1852.
Written for prizes offered by the *Jewish Chronicle.*

294. MORRIS J. RAPHALL, M.A., PH. D.—Post Biblical
History of the Jews; from the close of the Old
Testament, about the year 420 B.C.E., till the Destruction of the Second Temple in the year 70 C.E.
2 vols., 8vo. London.   1856.

295. REV. MOSES MARGOLIOUTH.—The History of the
Jews in Great Britain. London. 3 vols.   1857.

296. JAMES BROWN.—An account of the Jews in the
City of Glasgow. London. 8vo.   1858.

297. W. J. RULE.—History of the Karaite Jews.   1862.

298. T. S. DUNSCOMBE.—The Jews of England: their
History and Wrongs.   1866.

299. DR. M. KAYSERLING.—Geschichte der Juden in
Portugal. 8vo., xi.-367 pp. Leipzig.   1867.
[The last chapter has some useful references to the early
history of the Portuguese Jewish community of London.]

300. REV. DR. HERMANN ADLER.—The Jews in England. A Lecture delivered to Jewish Working Men

at the Spanish and Portuguese Jews' School, on
Sunday, May 1st, 5630 — 1870. 8vo., 32 pp. Lond.
1870.

301. MARKS, REV. PROF. D. W.—The Jews of Modern
Times. London.

> Two Lectures delivered at the Philosophical Institution,
> Edinburgh, on Nov. 28 and Dec. 5, 1871.

302. ALEX. MURRAY.—History of the Jews.   1875.

303. JAMES PICCIOTTO. — Sketches of Anglo - Jewish
History. 8vo., xi.-420 pp. London.   1875.

> [Reprinted from the *Jewish Chronicle*, and dedicated to
> Sir Moses Montefiore. Gave the first authentic account
> from the Synagogue Records of the history of the Disraeli
> family and their secession from Judaism.]

304. FREDERICK DAVID MOCATTA.—The Jews of Spain
and Portugal and the Inquisition.   1877.

> [Translated into German, Italian, and Hebrew].

(B.) POLITICAL AND SOCIAL.

306. W. S.—An Epistle from the Spirit of Love and
Peace unto all upright Israelites. 4to.   1663.

307. DE CHEAUMONT, French Ambassador at Constantinople.—A New Letter concerning the Jews.   1664.

308. The Restauration of the Jews, or a True Relation
of their Progress and Proceedings . . . . being the
Substance of several Letters, viz. from Antwerp,
Legorn, Florence. 8vo., 31 pp. [A. N.]   1665.

309. JOHN EVELYN, F.R.S.—The History of the Three
Late Famous Impostors . . . . and Sabbatai Levi,
the Supposed Messiah of the Jews in the Year
1666 . . . . together with the Cause of the Final
Extirpation, Destruction, and Exile of the Jews
out of the Empire of Persia.   1668.

> [Another edition in 1669.]

310. JOSEPHUS PHILO - JUDÆUS GENT [pseud.].—News from the Jews, or a True Relation of a Great Prophet in the Southern Parts of Tartaria; pretending himself to be sent to gather together the Jews from all parts.   4to., 6 pp.   [A. N.]   1671.

[Addressed to R. Joshua ben Eleasar and the rest of our Brethren, the Jews in Amsterdam, "and signed by Gorion ben Syrach."]

311. HAZZARD'S REPORTS.   1673.

Vol. i.   Petition of Jews, 11 Feb., 1673.

312. E. BERNARD. — Translation into Latin of the Letters of the Samaritans, which Dr. R. Hemington procured them to write to their Brethren, the Jews in England, in 1673, while he was at Schem. Published in a Collection which the learned Job Ladolphius had written to himself and other learned, and who had received a Copy of the Translation from Dr. Smith.   1673.

313. L. ADDISON, D.D.—The Present State of the Jews, more particularly relating to those in Barbary, wherein is contained an exact Account of their Customs, Secular and Religious, to which is anexed a Discourse of the Misna, Talmud, and Gemara. 8vo.   1675.

[Also 1676, 12mo., and 1682, 12mo.]

314. JACOB JUDAH ARYEH (Templo).— A Relation of the Most Memorable Things in the Tabernacle of Moses and the Temple of Salomon, according to Text of Scripture.   Amsterdam.   4to.   1675.

[In English, preparatory, no doubt, to Templo's coming over to England to show his model of the Temple to Charles II.]

315. A Collection of the Names of the Merchants living in and about the City of London.   1677.

[The oldest printed list of the merchants and bankers of London.   Among the names are the following :—

Isaac Alvarez, *in St. Mary Ax.*
Jacob Jesrum (? Jessurum) Alvarez, *in St. Mary Ax, neer Bury Street.*

Mr. Andrado, *Leadenhall Street.*
Mr. Ashur, *Aldermanberry.*
Moses Berrew (? Baruch Lousada), *Duke's Place.*
Abra. Caris (? Caceres), *Mincin Lane.*
Mr. Cutteris (? Gutierrez), *Berry Street.*
Jacob David, *Little Tower Street.*
Alvaro Decosta, *Budge Row.*
Mr. Deco-tus, *Duke's Place.*
Sir (?) Ba. Degomaz, *Berry Street.*
Mr. Delieus (? De Leon), *Rood Lane.*
Jos. Delliviers ⎫
Lyon Delliviers ⎭ (?) d'Olivierrez, *Throgmorten Street.*
Mr. Demingo, *Mugwell Street.*
Solo. Demodina, *Great St. Hel.*
Mr. Depostus (?), *Duke's Place.*
Abrah. Deporta, *St. Mary Ax.*
Mr. Dermedo (? Dormido Abarbanel), *St. Mary Ax.*
John Elison (? Eliason), *Berry Street.*
Simon Francia, *Leadenhall Street.*
Dom. Francia,   *ditto.*
Mr. Gaseronne (? Jeshurun), *St. Mary Ax.*
Anto. Gounnesevares (? Gomes Suarez), *Creedchurch Lane.*
Anth. Gomeserd (? Gomes Serra), *Berry Street.*
Ja. Gonsalus, *Leadenhall Street.*
Peter ⎫
and ⎬ Henrique, *Walbrook.*
Pierce ⎭
Abraham Jacob, *Hatton Garden.*
Mr. Ibrook (?), *Duke's Place.*
John Israel, *Armitage.*
Sam. Lewin, *Barnaby Street.*
Jacob Luce, *Fan-Church Street.*
Michael Luce, *Duke's Place.*
Mose Lowman, *Fan-Church Street.*
Mr. Marandew (? Miranda), *Berry Street.*
Mr. Moria, *Great St. Hellens.*
Moses Mocate (Mocatta), *Camomile Street.*
Pet. Oleverez, *Duke's Place.*
David Persore, *Duke's Place.*
Movill ⎫
and ⎬ Perrera, *Duke's Place.*
Lopes ⎭
Henry Ricardus (? Ricardo), *at Ald.* Jeffery's, *Berry Street.*
Mr. Robulus (? Robles), *Berry Street.*
Gomez Rodrigues, *Berry Street.*
Mr. Samuel, *Duke's Place.*
Anth. Sexagomes (? Seixas Gomez), *Minories.*

5

Mr. Sigues (? Seixas), *Goodman's Fields.*

Isaac
and } Swares (? Soares), *Duke's Place.*
Jacob

Mr. Tares (? Teixeira), *Duke's Place.*

Isaac Tellis, *Berry Street.*

Among the " Goldsmiths that keep Running Cashes " is " Thomas Pardo, *at the Golden Anchor in Lombard Street.*

316. A Conference betwixt a Papist and a Jew, or a Letter from a Merchant in London to his Correspondent in Amsterdam. [A. N.], pp. 34, [signed, N. H.]. 1678.

317. A Conference between a Protestant and a Jew, or a Second Letter from a Merchant in London to his Correspondent in Amsterdam. 4to., 32 pp. 1678.

318. HAYNE.—Jews as Aliens. 1685.

319. London, Jews in.—*Begins:*—Whereas there is a clause in a Bill brought into the Hon. House of Commons, entitled : An Act for preventing Frauds and regulating Abuses in the Plantation Trade . . . those of the Hebrew Nation, residing at London, most humbly crave leave to offer to the consideration of the Hon. House. *Brit. Mus. Cat., Lond.,* vi.-49 pp. 1696.

320. Two Conferences; one between a Papist and a Jew, in Two Letters from a Merchant in London, to his Correspondent in Amsterdam. 12mo., 40 pp. [A. N.] 1699.

[Probably reprints of Nos. 316, 317.]

321. The Jews' Charter; or an Historical Account of the privileges granted them by the several Kings and Parliaments of England. . . . Extracted out of Baker's Chronicle, St. Ambrose's Letter to Theodosius the Emperor, &c. 8vo. 1702.

322. An Abstract of the Account of the Proceedings of

the Inquisition in Portugal. 8vo., 35 pp. Price, 6d. [A. N.]   1713.

[P. 32. Narrative of an escape from Lisbon to London, of a "New Christian," who reverted to his ancient faith.]

323. Reasons for Naturalising the Jews in Great Britain and Ireland, on the same foot with all other Nations. 8vo., 48 pp. [A. N.] (J. Roberts.)   1714.

324. A Confutation of the Reasons for Naturalising the Jews; containing their Crimes, Frauds, and Insolencies, &c. 8vo.   1715.

325. ELIZ. SHEMAJAH.—Letter to the Patriots of Change Alley, by Eliz. Shemajah, a converted Jew.   1720.

326. ANON.—A Historical and Law Treatise against the Jews and Judaism; showing that by the ancient established Laws of the Land, no Jew hath any Right to live in England, nor to appear without Yellow Badges upon his or her upper garment . . . together with a confutation of the two arguments us'd by some for the Re-Admission of the Jews. 8vo., 30 pp. Price, 4d. [A. N.] (J. Roberts.)
1725.

327. SOLOM. ABARBANEL [W. ARNALL].—Complaints of the Children of Israel concerning the Penal Laws; a Burlesque on the Dissenters petitioning for a Repeal of the Test Act.   1736.

328. Reasons offered for the consideration of Parliament for preventing the growth of Judaism.   1738.

329. The remarkable Life of Uriel Acosta, an eminent Freethinker, with his Reasons for rejecting all Revealed Religion, to which is added Mr. Lambert's Defence. . . . Price, 1s. [A. N.]   1740.

330. Consideration on the Bill for a General Naturalisation.   1748.

331. The Expediency of a General Naturalisation of Foreign Protestants and others.   1748.

[Reprinted, 1751].

THE "JEW BILL," 1753.

332. An Act to permit Persons professing the Jewish Religion to be naturalised by Parliament, and for other purposes therein mentioned. Anno vicesimo sexto Georgii II. Regis. Fol. 4, pp. 407-10. [A. N.]
1753.
[" Being the Sixth Session of the present Parliament."]

333. E. J. GENT.—Some Considerations on the Naturalisation of the Jews. 1753.

334. [J. HANWAY.]—Letters admonitory and argumentation from J. H——y, Merchant, to J. S——r, Merchant. 1753.

335. J. H. MERCHANT.—A Review of the Proposed Naturalisation of the Jews, being a Dispassionate Inquiry of the Present State of the Case. 8vo., 225 pp. 1753.

336. P. PECKARD.—The Popular Clamor against the Jews Indefensible. A Sermon preached at Huntingdon, Oct. 28th, 1753. 8vo., 28 pp. Cambridge. [A. N.] 1753.

337. JOSIAH TUCKER.—A Letter to a Friend concerning Naturalisations, showing (i.) What Naturalisation is; (ii.) What it is; (iii.) What are the Motives for the present Clamours against the Bill . . . . (v.) Proposing a scheme for the Prevention of all future Naturalisations. 8vo., 29 pp. Price 6d. [A. N.] 1753.

338. W. WARBURTON, Dean of Bristol.—Remarks on some Passages in a Dedication to the Jews. 1753.

339. [P. CARTERET WEBB, F.R.S.].—Question whether a Jew born within the British Dominions was, before the making of the last Act of Parliament, a Person capable by Law to hold Lands to him and to his Heirs, fairly stated and considered. 4to. 1753.
[See No. 385.]

340. Right Hon. E. WESTON.—A Pamphlet on the Memorable Jew Bill. 1753.

341. WINSTANLEY.—A Sermon preached at the Parish
Church of St. George, Hanover Square, Sunday,
Oct. 28, 1753, on Occasion of the Clamour against
the Act for Naturalising the Jews. 8vo., 28 pp.
[A. N.] (Dodsley.)   1753.

342. ARCHAICUS (Pseud.)—Admonitions from Scripture
and History, from Religion and common Prudence
relating to the Jews. 36 pp. (Baldwin) 8vo. 6d.

343. ARCHAICUS.—The rejection and restauration of the
Jews according to Scripture.   1753.

344. A. Z.—A Letter to the Publick on the Act for
Naturalising the Jews.   1753.

345. PHILO PATRIÆ [Pseud.].—An Answer to a Pamphlet entitled: Considerations on the Bill to permit
persons professing the Jewish Religion to be
naturalised. 8vo.   1753.
[In form of letters, all signed " P. P."]

346. Answer to a Pamphlet entitled "Consideration on
the Bill to permit Persons professing the Jewish
Religion to be Naturalised." 8vo., pp. 96. [A. N.]
[A Third edition also appeared.]

347. An Apology for the Naturalisation of the Jews,
containing an account of the Charters, Privileges,
and Immunities granted to the Jews by the Kings
of England five hundred years ago, &c. By a True
Believer. 8vo., pp. 30. London. (Cooper.) 8vo. cr.

348. An Appeal to the Throne against the Naturalisation of the Jewish Nation: in which are exposed
those Practices for which the Jews were expelled out
of England. 8vo., pp. 34. Price Sixpence. [A. N.]
(J. Bouquet.)   1753.

349. A Candid and Impartial Examination of the Act
passed last Session of Parliament for permitting the
Foreign Jews to be Naturalised without their re-
ceiving the Sacrament, &c. (Wright.) 8vo. 6d.

350. The Case of the Jews considered with regard to Trade, Commerce, Manufactures, and Religion, &c. By A Christian. pp. 33. (Reeve.) 8vo. 6d. 1753.

351. A Collection of the Best Pieces in Prose and in Verse concerning the Jews. 8vo., pp. 88. (M. Cooper.) 1753.

352. A Confutation of the Reasons for the Naturalisation of the Jews. 1753.

353. Considerations on the Bill to permit Persons professing the Jewish Religion to be Naturalised by Parliament in several Letters from a Merchant in Town to his Friend in the Country. 8vo, pp. 60. [A. N.] (R. Baldwin.) 1753.

354. An Earnest Persuasion and Exhortation to the Jews occasioned by the late Act of Parliament in their favour. 8vo., pp. 27. (Withers.) [A. N.].

355. An Epistle to the Freeholders on the Naturalisation of Foreign Jews. 1753.

356. Esther sent to King Ahasuerus on behalf of the Jews, in a Letter to a Member of Parliament. London. (Cooper.) 8vo. 6d. 1753.

357. A full Answer to a fallacious Apology artfully circulated through the Kingdom in favour of the Naturalisation of the Jews, inscribed to the Lord Mayor, Aldermen, and Common Council of the City of London. (Fox.) 8vo. 6d. 1753.
   [Went into second edition.]

358. Further Considerations on the Act to permit Persons professing the Jewish Religion, &c., in a second Letter from a Merchant in Town to his Friend in the Country. pp. 100. 1753.
   ["In this part the utility of the Jews in trade, their situation in other nations, and the expediency of continuing them on the present footing are fully considered and proved."]

359. The Humble Petition of several Merchants . . .

F

to the Honourable the Commons of Great Britain.
4 pp. fol.   1753.

> [In favour of the Bill. Attached to the petition, which
> only takes up first page, is an Affidavit serving to incri-
> minate Henry Symons, the Polish Jew. This must have
> been issued to counteract the Petition to which it was
> attached.]

360. An Historical Treatise concerning the Jews and
Judaism in England. London. (Baldwin.) 8vo. 6d.

361. Historical Remarks on the late Naturalisation Bill.
8vo., 72 pp. [A. N.]   1753.

362. The Jewish Gin; or, the Christians taken Napping;
and some Friendly Exhortations both to the Jews
and Christians. (Robinson.) 8vo. 6d.   1753.

363. The Jewish Naturalisation considered with respect
to the Voice of the People, its own Self-inconsis-
tency, and the Disingenuity of its Advocates. [By
George Coningesby, DD.] (Halkett and Laing.)

364. The Jew Naturalised, or the English Alienated ; a
Ballad ; to which is added the Parable of the
Chosen and the Unjust Servant. Lond. (Webb.)
fol. 6d.   1753.

365. The Jews' Advocate ; containing Mr. Locke's Sen
timents in respect to the Treatment of the Jews by
Christians. 8vo., 54 pp. London. (Cooper.) 1s.

366. The Jew's Triumph. A ballad. To be sung or
said to the children of Israel on all popular occasions by all Christian people. Fol.   1753.

367. The Kingdom of Israel . . . . the Doctrine of
Sacrifice examined . . . . in a Letter from a Gen-
tleman in the Country to his Friend in London,
occasioned by the Act for the Naturalisation of the
Jews, with Observations thereupon. 8vo., 32 pp.
(M. Cooper.) [A. N.]   1753.

368. A Letter to a Friend in the Country on the subject
of the Jew Bill. London. (Corbet.) 8vo. 6d.

369. A Letter to Sir John Barnard, Knt., &c., on the late Act for naturalising the Jews. 8vo., 19 pp London. (Bouquet.) 8vo., 6d.   1753.

370. A Letter to the Public on the Act for Naturalising the Jews. London. (Carpenter.) 8vo. 6d.   1753.

371. A Looking Glass for the Jews; or the Credulous Unbelievours, &c., with an Introduction by way of Answer to several late Pamphlets concerning the Jews. 8vo , 68 pp. London. (Dickenson.)   1s.

372. A Modest Apology for the Citizens and Merchants of London who petitioned the House of Commons against naturalising the Jews. (Webb.) 8vo., 4d.
    [Went into three editions.]

373. The Motives to a senseless Clamour against the Act concerning Jews exposed, and the Act set in a true Light. 8vo., 30 pp. London. (Cooper.) 6d.

374. A Narrative of the remarkable Affair between Mr. Simonds, the Polish Jew Merchant, and Mr. James Ashley, Merchant of Bread Street, London. 8vo. 50 pp.   Price One Shilling.   [A. N.]   1753.

375. Placard, "No Jews, no Wooden Shoes."
    [These were pasted up everywhere: no satisfactory explanation has been given for the second half of the inscriptions. Perhaps some reference to French peasants and their sabots was intended.]

376. The Other Side of the Question; being a collection of what hath yet appeared in Defence of the late Act in favour of the Jews; to which is prefixed a word or two by the Editor. 8vo. 56 pp. (Meanwell.) 8vo., 1s.   1753.

377. The Prancing Jew, or Solomon catch'd in a Bridle. fol. 1s.   1753.

378. Reasons offerred to the consideration of the Parliament for preventing the growth of Judaism, inscribed to the Right Hon. the Lord Mayor. (Brett.) 8vo. 6d.   1753.

379. A Review of the proposed Naturalisation of the Jews; being an Attempt at a Dispassionate Inquiry into the present State of the Case; with some Reflections on General Naturalisation. By a Merchant who subscribed the Petition against the naturalisation of the Jews. 8vo., 106 pp. (Waugh.) 8vo. 1s. [Went into second edition.]

380. Seasonable Remarks on the Act lately published in favour of the Jews; containing divers weighty reasons for a Review of the said Act. (Dodsley.) 8vo. 6d.   1753.

381. The Unprejudiced Christian's Apology for the Jews; humbly offered as a Reasonable Answer to the several Arguments lately set forth for a Repeal of the Jews Act; with some recommendatory Observations on the conduct of the Ministry. (Owen.) 8vo. 1s.   1753.

382. A True State of the Case concerning the good or evil which the Bill for the Naturalisation of the Jews may bring on Great Britain; with some Remarks on the Speeches of Sir J—— B—— and H——s F——y, Esq., upon the said Bill. By a Bystander. 32 pp. (Noon.) 8vo. 6d.   1753.

383. BRITON [Pseud.].—The Crisis; or, An Alarm to Britannia's true Protestant Sons by a Country Gentleman. Price Threepence. 18 pp.   1754.

384. Διασπορα.—Some Reflexions upon the Questions relating to the Naturalisation of the Jews considered as a point of Religion in a letter from a Gentleman in the Country to his Friend in Town. 8vo. 1754.

385. A Reply to the famous Jew Question. In which, ... is fully demonstrated, in opposition to that . . . . performance that the Jews born here before the late Act were never Intitled to Purchase and Hold Lands . . . . but were considered only as Aliens. . . . . In a letter to the Gentlemen of Lincoln's Inn. [P. C. Webb.] By a Freeholder of the County of Surrey. 4to.   1754.

386. The Jews impartially considered. (Millan.) 8vo.
6d. 1754.

387. The Impartial Observer; being a modest Reply to
what hath been lately published relating to the intended Naturalization of the Jews, considered in a
modest, serious, and religious view. Leven. 8vo.
6d. 1754.

388. An Act to Repeal an Act of the Twenty-sixth Year
of His Majesty's Reign, intituled "An Act to permit Persons professing the Jewish Religion to be
Naturalised by Parliament, and for other Purposes
therein mentioned." [A. N.] 1754.

389. A Letter to the Right Honourable Sir Thomas
Chitty, with an Appendix on the Naturalisation of
the Jews. 1760.

390. MARQUIS D'ARGENS.—The Jewish Spy, being a
philosophical, historical, and critical correspondence
by letters, which lately passed between certain Jews.
Translated from the original into French. Five
vols. 8vo. 1766.

391. R. SHYLOCK [Pseud.]—The Rabbi's Lamentation
on the Repeal of the Jews' Act, setting forth to the
respectable Brotherhood in Duke's Place how ill it
becomes any Dissenters from the See of Rome and
Britons more especially, to refuse them the Benefit
of a Naturalisation. 1768.

392. A Letter addressed to the Overseers of the Portuguese Jewish Synagogue in Bevismarks, London,
upon their extraordinary conduct in the Dispute
between Mr. Ximenes and Mr. Joshua Lara with a
full Explanation of the Affair, and an Inquiry into
the Propriety of their passing Sentence of Excom-
munication against Mr. and Mrs. Lara, Mr. and
Mrs. Furtado, and Mr. Cohen . . . . to which is
added a Postscript to Mr. Ximenes. 8vo., 55 pp.
Price 1s. [A. N.] 1772.

393. Religious Intolerance no part of the general plan.
1774.

394. ROBERT HILL.—The Character of a Jew.
Before 1777.

395. Letters from Perdita to a certain Israelite, and his Answers to them.   4to.   1781.

396. Copy of a Letter from the Right Honourable Lord George Gordon to E. Lindo, Esq., and the Portuguese, and [to] N. Salomon, Esq., and the German Jews.   1783.

397. COMTE DE MIRABEAU.—A Moses Mendelssohn sur la Reforme politique des Juifs et en particulier sur la Revolution tentée en leur Faveur en 1753 dans la Grande Brétagne.   London.   8vo., 130 pp.
1787.

398. ANGEL LYON.—A Letter from A. L. to the Right Hon. Lord George Gordon on Wearing Beards, with Lord George's Answer and a Reply from Angel Lyon.   8vo., 16 pp.   [A. N.]   1789.
[Lord George Gordon s letter is signed from Felon Side, Newgate, with the name " Israel bar Abraham G Gordon."]

399. A Collection of Testimonies in favour of Religious Liberty in the case of the Dissenters and Jews. 8vo.   1790.

400. ABBÉ GREGOIRE.—An Essay on the Physical, Moral, and Political Reformation of the Jews . . . to the Rights of Natural, Moral, and of Civil Society. 8vo.   4s.   1791.

401. An Appeal to Popular Prejudice in favour of the Jews, by a Letter addressed to a Member of Parliament.   8vo., 26 pp.   (Johnson.)   1796.

402. P. COLQUHUN, LL.D.—A Treatise on the Police of the Metropolis.   8vo., 444 pp.   1797.

403. P. COLQUHUN, LL.D.—The State of Indigence and the situation of the Casual Poor in the Metropolis explained.   1799.

404. JOSHUA VAN HOVEN.—Letters on the present state
of the Jewish Poor in the Metropolis, with Propo-
sitions for ameliorating their Condition. A Letter
to Abraham Goldsmid, Esq. 8vo. 1s. 1802.

405. L. ALEXANDER.—Answer to Mr. Joshua Vanoven's
Letters on the present state of the Jewish Poor in
in London, in which some of his hasty Mistakes
are rectified; with a word to P. Colquhoun, Esq.,
on the subject of the Jews as treated in his Police
of the Metropolis; with an Introductory Letter
setting in a conspicuous view some of the Jewish
By-laws as observed at present; and an exact copy
of the Bill now before Parliament for bettering the
state of the Indigent, Jews. 1802.

406. T. GILLILAND.—Jack in Office. Containing Remarks on Mr. Braham's Address. 1804.

407. T. WITHERBY.—An Attempt to remove Prejudices
concerning the Jewish Nation. 8vo. 1804.

408. L. COHEN.—Sacred Truth addressed to the Children
of Israel residing in the British Empire, containing
strictures on the Book entitled "The New Sanhedrin convened in Paris, &c." Exeter. 8vo.
1807?

409. DIOGENE TALMA.—Transactions of the Parisian
Sanhedrin, or Acts of the Assembly of Israelitish
Deputies of France and Italy, convoked at Paris by
an Imperial and Royal Decree, dated 20th May,
1806. 8vo., 334 pp. 1807.

410. סנהדרין and Causes and Consequences of the
French Emperor's conduct towards the Jews, includ-
ing Official Documents. 12mo., 190 pp. [A. N.]
(M. Jones.) 1807.
[By an Advocate for the House of Israel.]

411. T. WITHERBY.— A Vindication of the Jews by way
of Reply to the Letter addressed by Perseverans
to the Hebrew Israelite. 8vo., 287 pp. [A. N.]
1809.

412. An Essay on the Commercial Habits of the Jews.
8vo.   1809.

413. An Appeal to the Humanity of the English Nation
in behalf of the Jews. Dunstable. (J. Burkitt.)
8vo., 31 pp. [A. N.]   1812.

414. The Lamentations of the Children of Israel, respecting the hardships they suffer from the Penal
Laws, and praying that, if they are repealed, so as
to exempt the Catholics and Dissenters from their
influence, the Jews may also enjoy the benefit of
this indulgence.   By Abraham, Isaac, and Jacob,
Moses, Aaron, and Levi, David, Bethsheba, Solomon, 1,000 Wives and Concubines, Daniel Belte-
shazzar, Manasseh ben Israel, of the House of
David. [A. N.] 72 pp.   1813.

415. TH. WITHERBY.—An Attempt to remove Prejudices
against the Jews.   1814.

416. On the close conformity of Opinion between the
modern Jews and the Roman Catholics. Dublin.
8vo.   1815?

417. JOHN ALLEN.—Modern Judaism, or a brief Account of their Opinions, Traditions, Rites, and
Ceremonies. 8vo. 434 pp.   1816.

418. R. F. A. LEE, "Baroness Despenser."—A Translation of the Hebrew Epistle of Antonina Despenser,
entitled אגרת הכולל אל העברים or A Circular Epistle
to the Hebrews. Heb. and Eng. 4to.   1821.
    [Translated by H. V. Bolaffey. Preface to the Transla-
tion appeared in 1820 also by H. V. B.]

419. An Epistle from a High Priest of the Jews to the
Chief Priest of Canterbury on the extension of
Catholic Emancipation to the Jews. Second Edition.
26 pp. [A. N.]   1821.
    [Signed * * * "From the Place of my sojournment in
Synagogue Lane, the 25th day of the 3rd month, called
Nissan, Anno Mundi, 5825."]

420. VAN HERNERT.—State of the Jews at the beginning of the XIXth Century. Translated by L. Jackson. 1825.

421. M. J. MAYER.—Account of the Zoharite Jews. 1826.

422. The Religious Rites and Ceremonies of every Nation in the World, impartially described and beautifully illustrated with engravings on steel and wood from the celebrated and splendid work of Bernhard Picard by Colin Mackenzie. 1826.

423. R. MELDOLA.—Letter by R. Raphael Meldola to D. A. Lindo, Esq., of Leman Street, on the State of Jewish Education, June 19, 5587. 1827.

424. P. ANICHINI.—A few Remarks on the expediency and justice of Emancipating the Jews, addressed to his Grace the Duke of Wellington, K.G. By the author of "An Historical and Analytical view of the Catholic Religion." [A. N.] 82 pp. 1829.

425. JOSEPH CROOLL.—The Fifth Empire, delivered in a Discourse by thirty-six men : every one made a speech . . . . and it is decided among them that the Fifth Empire is to be the inheritance of the sons of Israel. 12mo. 1829.

426. JOSEPH CROOLL.—The Last Generation. Cambridge. 12mo. 1829.

428. M. E. LEVY.—Letters concerning the Present Condition of the Jews, being a correspondence between Mr. Forster and Mr. Levy. 1829.

429. M. E. LEVY. — Speech delivered at a Meeting of Christians and Jews in London in May, 1828. 1829.

[In T. Thrush's Letters to the Jews.]

430. APSLEY PELLATT.—Brief Memoir of the Jews in relation to their Civil and Municipal Disabilities. [A. N.] 8vo. 40 pp. London, 1829. 1829.

[With Appendix containing the Jews' Petition to Oliver

Cromwell; the Russian Ukaze ; and Ordinance of the King of Wurtemburg affecting the civil and religious liberty of the Hebrew Nation.]

431. TH. THRUSH (late Capt. R.N.).—Letters to the Jews, with a copy of a Speech said to have been delivered by Mr. Levy, of Florida. York. 8vo.
1829.

432. Correspondence between Mr. Forster and Mr. Levy on the Present Condition of the Jews.   1829.

434. Jewish Emancipation, a Poem by a Levite.   1829.

436. Two Letters in answer to the Objections urged against Mr. Grant's Bill for the Relief of the Jews, with an Appendix. 20 pp.   1830.

437. F. H. GOLDSMID. — Remarks on the Civil Disabilities of British Jews. 78 & 6 pp.   1830.
[On p. 69 an estimate of Jewish population of Metropolis as 17,986, based on an average number of deaths of 344 for the past three years.]

438. HYAM ISAACS.—Ceremonies, Customs, Rites, and Traditions of the Jews, interspersed with Gleanings from the Jerusalem and Babylonish Talmuds and the Targums, Mishna, Gemara, Maimonides, etc. Also a copious selection from some of their prayers.

439. BARNARD VAN OVEN.—Emancipation of the Jews. Copy of a Letter taken from the "Times" of February 3rd instant. Signed B. V. O.   8 pp.

440. Extracts from Journals on the Disabilities of the Jews.   1830.

442. Extracts from the Public Journals on the Disabilities of the Jews.   1830.

443. I. D'ISRAELI. — The Genius of Judaism. 8vo. 266 pp. (Second edition.)   1833.

444. FRANCIS HENRY GOLDSMID. — A few Words respecting the Enfranchisement of British Jews, addressed to the new Parliament. [A. N.]   London.

445. —— The Arguments advanced against the Enfran-

chisement of the Jews, considered in a series of
Letters. [A. N.] London. 1833.

446. HYMAN HURWITZ. — A Letter to Isaac Lyon
Goldsmid, Esq., F.R.S., Chairman of the Association for obtaining for British Jews Civil Rights
and Privileges, on certain recent Mis-statements respecting the Jewish Religion. [A. N.] London.

447. BASIL MONTAGU. — A Letter to Henry Warburton,
Esq., M.P., upon the Emancipation of the Jews.
Second edition. 40 pp. 1833.

[Refers to *Edinburgh Rev.*, Jan. 1831; *Mirror of Parliament*, April and May, 1830; *Westminster Rev.*, April,
1829, and July, 1830.]

448. RICHARD WHATELY, D.D. (Archbishop of Dublin).
—A Speech in the House of Lords, Aug. 1, 1833,
on a Bill for the Removal of certain Disabilities
from His Majesty's Subjects of the Jewish Persuasion, with additional remarks on some of the Objections urged against that Measure, also a Petition
to the House of Lords from the Clergy of the Diocese of Kildare, relative to Church Reform, with
Observations made on the occasion of presenting it,
Aug. 7, 1833. [A. N.] 8vo., 56 pp. London.

449. Remarks on the Disabilities of the Jews, with
Postscript. 1833.

450. Speeches of the Right Hon. Robert Grant, M.P.,
the Right Hon. T. B. Macaulay, M.P., Joseph
Hume, Esq., M.P., and D. O'Connell, Esq., M.P.,
in the House of Commons, on Wednesday, April
17, 1833, on Mr. Grant's moving a Resolution relative to the Civil Disabilities of the Jews. [A. N.]
8vo., 29 pp. London. 1833.

[Extracted from the *Mirror of Parliament*, part cciv.]

451. The British Jew to his Fellow Countrymen. 44 pp.
[A.N.] 1833.

452. J. COLES.—Observations on the Civil Disabilities
of the Jews. 1834.

453. JEAN CZYNSKI. — An Enquiry into the Political
Condition of the Polish Jews, considered in relation
to the general interests of Europe, in which are
delineated the Social State of Poland . . . . translated from the French of J. C. [A. N.] Price
One shilling. 35 pp.   1834.

454. B. MONTAGU.—A Letter to the Right Rev. the
Lord Bishop of Chichester, on the Emancipation of
the Jews.   1834.

455. BARNARD VAN OVEN. — Debates in the House
of Commons on a Resolution preparatory to the
introduction, and in the House of Lords on the
motion for the second reading of the Bill for removing the Civil Disabilities of the Jews; the pro-
tests of the Right Hon. Lords Holland and Clifford
against the rejection of the Bill, and a list of Petitions for and against the measure, presented during the session of [1833]. 8vo., 100 pp. London.
[A. N.]   1834.
  [Reprinted from the *Mirror of Parliament.* Has a pre-
  liminary address by Barnard van Oven, secretary to the
  committee of the Jewish Association for Obtaining Civil
  Rights and Privileges.]
  The date " 1833 " on the title page is written.

457. An Appeal to the Public on behalf of the Jews;
with considerations on the policy of removing their
Civil Disabilities; comprehending a brief historical
sketch of their residence in this country from their
first settlement. 8vo.   1834.

458. Correspondence between Chief Rabbi Herschell
and J. J. Lockhard.   1834.
  [On the Oath to be taken by Jews.]

460. DAVID SALOMONS.—A Short Statement on behalf
of His Majesty's subjects professing the Jewish
Religion, with an Appendix containing the Jews'
Relief Bill as passed by the House of Commons in
the two last sessions of the late Parliament, together

with the Oaths and Affirmations required from
persons of various Religious Denominations. [A. N.]
London, 1835.   1835.

462. [SIR] D. SALOMONS —Further Observations on
behalf of his Majesty's subjects professing the
Jewish Religion, with an Appendix.   1836.

463. BRITANNICUS.—The Case of Mr. Salomons, Alderman Elect of the Ward of Aldgate. Letters of
Britannicus reprinted from the *Morning Chronicle*.
20 pp. [A. N.]   1836.

464. ALEX. McCAUL, D.D.—Sketches of Judaism and
the Jews. 8vo., 171 pp. [A. N.]   1838.

465. M. SAMUELS.—Jerusalem : a Treatise on Ecclesiastical Authority and Judaism, by Moses Mendelssohn, translated by M. S. 2 vols. London.   1838.

466. A. A. LINDO.—A Word in Season from an Israelite
to his Brethren. No. 1.   1839.

467. A CHRISTIAN.—Jewish Admission into Parliament
considered in an Address to the English People.
12 pp. London, 1842. [A. N.]   1842.

468. A CONSERVATIVE.—Remarks on the Civil Disabilities of the Jews.   1842.

469. HENRY HAWKES, B.A., F.L.S.—The Position of
the Jews. A Sermon [on 2 Sam. iii. 38] addressed
to the High Street Congregation of Christians,
Portsmouth, in reference to the death of Rev.
Solomon Hirschel, D D., Chief Rabbi of the German and Polish Jews in the British Dominions.
London.   1843.

471. REV. SAM. ALEX. BRADSHAW.—A Tract for the
Times, being a Plea for the Jews. 47 pp. London.
                                             1844.

473. [SIR] D. SALOMONS.—The case of David Salomons,
being his Address to the Court of Aldermen on
applying for admission as Alderman of the Ward of
Portsoken. [A. N.]   1844.

78   BIBLIOTHECA ANGLO-JUDAICA.

474. MOSES SAMUEL.—An Address on the Position of
the Jews in Britain, with reference to their Literary,
Political, Civil and Religious Condition. 27 pp.

476. QUIZIMUS (Pseud.)—Cursory glances at the present
Social State of the Jewish people of Great Britain.
16 pp. Edinburgh.   1844.

477. A FRIEND OF TRUTH.—אמת אהבת A Few Words
addressed to the Committee for the Election of a
Chief Rabbi of England and to the Electors at
large. London.   1844.

478. A JEW.—Suggestions to the Jews for improvement
in reference to their Charities, Education, and
General Government. 8vo., 32 pp. London. 1844.
   The writer appeals to such of his readers as may desire
   to assist his suggestions to communicate with him. Letters
   to be addressed " F., at G. Galabin's, 91, Bartholomew
   Close."

480. REV. W. AYERST, A.M.—The Jews of the Nineteenth Century. 8vo. 431 pp.   1845.

481. LIEUT.-COL. GEORGE GAWLER.—Observations and
Practical Suggestions in furtherance of the Establishment of Jewish Colonies in Palestine, the
most Sober and Sensible Remedy for the Miseries
of Asiatic Turkey. 48 pp.   1845.

482. BENJAMIN GOMPERTZ.—Letter addressed to Mr.
Jacob Salomons, Secretary to the Hambro Syna-
gogue.
   On the necessity for a Society for relieving Deserving
   Mendicants.

483. E. MITFORD.—An Appeal in behalf of the Jewish
Nation in connection with British Policy in the
Levant. London.   1845.
   [" The purpose of the writer is threefold—first, to expose
   the injustice and cruelty which the Jewish nation still
   endure, especially at the hands of Mohammedans; secondly,
   to appeal to the British people in their behalf; and, thirdly,
   to point out how England may remedy the evils complained of,
   and at the same time very considerably promote the strength
   of her political position, and the prosperity of her colonial
   dependencies." Extract from Preface.]

484. AN ISRAELITE.—Jewish Emancipation. London.

485. The Jews in this and other Lands. 16mo. London.

486. Prospectus of a Jewish Society at Liverpool for the total suppression of Mendicancy. 1845.

487. The Jews, their present State and Prospects (forming No. 31 of *The Topic*). London. 1846.

488. REV. CLOTWORTHY GILMOR, M.A.—Jewish Legislators : A word in Season on the general subject of Jewish Disabilities. 8vo., 93 pp. London. 1847.

489. REV. MOSES MARGOLIOUTH.—The Jews in Great Britain : being a series of Six Lectures delivered at the Liverpool Collegiate Institution. London.

490. REV. W. L. POPE, B.A.—On the removal of Jewish Disabilities. A Letter to the Parishioners of Great Yarmouth. 8vo., 7 pp. London. 1847.

491. WILLIAM THORNBORROW.—Advocacy of Jewish Freedom. London. 1847.
[W. T. was chairman of the Liberal Committee in the Cornhill Ward ; Jews much indebted to his exertions.—J. C., July 23, 1847.]

492. BARNARD VAN OVEN, M.D.—Ought Baron De Rothschild to sit in Parliament ? An imaginary Conversation between Judæus and Amicus Nobilis. 8vo , 29 pp. London. 1847.

493. ANON.—A Clergyman's Apology for favouring the removal of Jewish Disabilities as bearing on the Position, Prospects, and Policy of the Church of England. 8vo., 28 pp. London. [A. N.] 1847.

494. BIGNON (late Member of the Chamber of Deps., for the Dept. de l'Eure).—On the Proscriptions and Persecutions of the Jews, with reflections on Religious Proscriptions. Translated from the French by a Lady. With an Introduction, Preface, and Explanatory Notes. London and Brighton. 1848.

495. REV. T. R. BIRKS, M.A. — A Letter to the Right Hon. Lord John Russell, M.P., on the admission of Jews to Parliament. 8vo., 60 pp. London.

496. REV. GEORGE CROLY, LL.D.—The Claims of the
Jews incompatible with the National Profession of
Christianity. 8vo., 40 pp. London.   1848.
[Replied to by the Rev. A. L. Green.]

497. CHARLES EGAN (Barrister-at-Law, late Fellow Com-
moner of Trinity Hall, Cambridge).—The Status
of the Jews in England, from the time of the
Normans to the reign of Her Majesty, Queen
Victoria, impartially considered. Including authentic
Notices, deduced from Historical and Legal Records
and Debates on the Jewish Disabilities Bill, with
Comments. 8vo. London.   1848.

498. HENRY FAUDEL.—A Few Words on the Jewish
Disabilities, addressed to Sir Robert Harry Inglis,
Bart., M.P., [in reply to his published speech on
the Jewish Disabilities Bill made Dec. 17th, 1847.]
London.   1848.

499. REV. OL. GILLMORE, M.A., (Vicar of Dartford,
Kent).—Jewish Legislators and Israel's Conversion.
A Word in Season. London.   1848.

500. FRANCIS HENRY GOLDSMID (of Lincoln's Inn,
Barrister).— Reply to the Arguments advanced
against the removal of the remaining Disabilities of
the Jews. London.   1848.

501. A. KEYZOR.—A Few Remarks on the Jewish Disabilities. (? Norwich.)   1848.

502. L. LEVASON.—Jewish Disabilities. To young Mr.
Pope. Great Yarmouth.   1848.

503. REV. JOHN TRAVERS ROBINSON, M.A.—Remarks
deprecating the proposed Admission of Her Majesty's
Jewish Subjects to Seats in the House of Commons.
8vo., 36 pp. London. [A. N.]   1848.

504. RT. HON. LORD JOHN RUSSELL. — Jewish Disabilities : a Speech delivered in the House of Commons, December 16th, 1847, on the Jewish Disabilities. London.   1848.

505. WILLIAM THORNBORROW.— Advocacy of Jewish Freedom. 2nd edit. 1848.
[Contains portrait of author "listening to the speech of Baron Lionel De Rothschild at the Hall of Commerce, on his appeal to the Livery of London for their votes"; also litho. of the testimonial presented to Sir David Salomons by the Jews (1836).]

507. ANON.—"Che Sara, Sara," or Lord John Russell and the Jews. 8vo., 16 pp. Lond. 1848.
[On the fly-leaf is an "Erratum. Page 10, for *Jew d'esprit* read *Jeu d'esprit.*"]

508. D. R.—A Christian's Appeal to the British People. An imaginary speech in Parliament against the Jewish Disabilities Bill. 8vo., 23 pp. Lond. 1848.

509. EUPHRON (Pseud.).—Remarks on the proposed Bill for Admitting Jews into Parliament. 8vo., 24 pp. London. 1848.

510. A GRADUATE OF THE UNIVERSITY OF CAMBRIDGE. —A few words on the proposed admission of Jews into Parliament. 8vo., 8 pp. London. [A. N.]

511. A LAYMAN.—Remarks on a letter to the Parishioners of Great Yarmouth by the Rev. Henry Mackenzie, M.A., on the subject of the removal of the Jewish disabilities. 8 pp. Yarmouth. [A. N.]

512. ONE OF THE PEOPLE.—A Word with the Earl of Winchelsea. London. 1848.

513. Progress of Jewish Emancipation since 1829. London. 1848.

514. HON. W. F. CAMPBELL (M.P. for Cambridge).— Substance of a Speech on the Jewish Question delivered in the House of Commons, May 4, 1848. 28 pp. London. [A. N.] 1849.

515. REV. HENRY HUGHES, M.A. — A few Plain Thoughts on the Christianity of excluding a Jew from Parliament, suggested by the recent Division in the House of Lords. London. [A. N.] 1849.

G

516. REV. HENRY STREET, M.A.—A Plea for the Removal of Jewish Disabilities. 8vo., 31 pp. London. [A. N.]   1849.

517. Don Adrian; or, The Harp of Judah. A Dramatic Poem, in ten acts, or two parts. Lond. 1849.

    " The author, in submitting the above work to the public,
regrets that Englishmen, ever foremost as the champions of
liberty, should still cherish vulgar prejudices against the
Israelite. . . . . Imbued with a real love of civil and religious liberty, he has produced the tragedy of Don Adrian,
&c." Advt., *J. C.*, Nov. 16th, 1849.

518. REV. AARON LEVY GREEN (Minister of the Jewish
Congregation, Bristol).—Dr. Croly, LL.D., *versus*
Civil and Religious Liberty. London and Bristol.
                                     1850.
    [*See* No. 496.]

519. REV. THOMAS PYNE, A.M., Incumbent of Hook,
Surrey.—Judæa Libera; or, The Eligibility of the
Jews to Parliament. London.   1850.

520. PHŒNIX (Pseud.).—Scripture Reasonings in support of the Jewish claims to sit in the Commons
House of Parliament, addressed to the conscience
of the Christian People of the British Empire.
London. [A. N.]   1850.

521. MacGILL, Rev. D. (Minister of the National Scotch
Church, Holloway).—The Claims of the Jews on a
Christian State; a Lecture. London.   1851.

522. Jewish Disabilities Bill. The Lord Chancellor's
Speech in moving the Second Reading. London.

    The profits of the sale to be applied to the fund for build-
ing the Shoreditch New Almshouses opposite Haggerstone
Church.

523. ELKALI, Rabbi JUDAH. — מבשר טוב The Har-
binger of Glad Tidings; an Address to the Jewish
Nation on the propriety of organising an Association to promote their regaining of their Fatherland.
8vo., 10 pp. English, 8 pp. Hebrew. London.
                                       1852.

524. ASSOCIATION FOR PROMOTING JEWISH SETTLE-
MENTS IN PALESTINE.—Address to the Public.
Fcp., 3 pp. 1852.

525. ALFRED BRANDON.—A Letter to the Right Hon.
Lord J. Russell on the Jewish measure. 12 pp.
London. [A. N.] 1853.

526. MILLS, Rev. JOHN.—The British Jews; being a
digest of the domestic habits, the religious cere-
monies, and the social condition of the Jews in
Great Britain. (Illustrated.) London. 1853.
Dedicated by permission to the Right Hon. Lord John
Russell.

527. The Lords and the Jews. 8vo. 1853.

529. ANON. [MRS. HORATIO MONTEFIORE.]—A Few
Words to the Jews, by One of Themselves. 8vo.
Lond. 1854.

530. ANON.—Jews' Disabilities Bill. Protest by a Believing Jew. 8 pp. London. [A. N.] 1854.
[The author explains that "love to the Jew and supreme
love to Christ" constrains me, a believing Jew, to protest
against the above measure.]

531. —— The Crisis and Way of Escape. An Appeal
for the Oldest of the Oppressed. Touching the
origin of the present War and conditions of durable
Peace. London. 1856.
[The object of the author is to induce the English Government "to prevail upon the Porte to allow the Jews facili-
ties of returning to their own land, to appoint Palestine, as a
place of refuge for them, from the anarchy and confusion
from which they suffer, but in which they have no share.]

532. The Stock Exchange Almanack for 1856. 4to.
7 pp. 1856.
[A *jeu d'ésprit* in verse? A "skit" on most of the prominent Jewish members of the Stock Exchange of the
period.]

533. A CLERGYMAN OF THE CHURCH OF ENGLAND.—
The Anglo-Hebrews; their past Wrongs and present Grievances. Two Epistles (with a Postscript)
written for all Classes of the British public. London.
[Advocates the removal of Jewish disabilities.]

534. ANON.—Exclusion no Intolerance. To the Right
Hon. S. H. Walpole, M.P. 8vo. 53 pp. London.
[A.N.]   1856.
[Protest against the Jews being admitted to Parliament.]

535. G. CRUIKSHANK.—A Slice of Bread and Butter cut
by G. C. Being the substance of a Speech delivered at a Public Meeting held for the benefit of
the Jews' and General Literary and Mechanics'
Institution. London.   1857.

536. REV. HAROLD H. SHERLOCK, M.A. (Rector of
Ashton-le-Willows.)—The Principles and Precedents
of Holy Scripture favour the complete Emancipation of the Jews. A Letter to his Grace the Archbishop of Canterbury. London.   1857.

537. The Author of the Phrase "Unchristianize the
Legislature."—The Admission of the Jews into
Parliament truthfully considered in connexion with
our National Christianity, Commerce, and the
British Constitution. 8vo. London.   1857.

538. JOHN SIEBBOLD EDISON. — The Impossibility of
admitting Jews into Parliament consistently with
the recognised principles of the Constitution,
demonstrated in a manner parallel to the demonstration of a theorem of Euclid. London. 8vo. 1858.

539. HORATIO MONTAGU.—The Jews in Parliament :
a National Evil not now to be escaped by us.
London. 8vo.   1858.

540. GEORGE S. YATES.—Is it desirable to admit Jews
into Parliament? An Essay. Liverpool.   1858.
[Originally read before the Liverpool Christian Society.]

541. REV. P. BEATON, M.A. — The Jews in the East.
From the German of Dr. Fränkl. 2 vols. 8vo.,
252 & 390 pp. London.   1859.
[Translation of *Nach Jerusalem.*]

542. J. S. EDISON.—The Question of the Admissibility
of the Jews to Parliament as yet undecided. 8vo.
London.   1859.

543. C. WRAY. — The Jews admitted to the Christian Parliament. A Sermon preached at Liverpool. 12mo. London. 1859.

544. THOS. CLARKE, M.D. — India and Palestine or the Restoration of the Jews, viewed in relation to the nearest Route to India. 1861.

545. JOHN SYMONS. — High Street, Hull, Some Years Since; and Biographical Sketches interspersed with historical accounts. Hull. 1862.
[Contains a few references to the Jews of Hull.]

546. F. G. G.—De Inglaterra a Marruecas. Algesiras (Spain). 1863.
[Gives account of Sir Moses Montefiore's mission to Morocco. It is apparently written by a Catholic Spaniard, who was interested from humanitarian motives in the mission.)

547. E. USLEY.—Trifles. 1865.
Pp. 44 to 60, "Jews."

548. Rabbis of Jerusalem. [A Letter stating the Calamity caused by the Cholera, and calling for assistance.] Hebr. and Engl. Fol. [1865].

549. THOMAS HODGKIN, M.D., F.R.G.D.—Narrative of a Journey to Morocco in 1863 and 1864, by the late T. H. (With portraits of the author and Sir Moses Montefiore, and other illustrations.) 1866.
[The author was medical attendant to Sir Moses Montefiore, and this work is an account of the mission of Sir Moses to Morocco in 1863.]

550. J. H. STALLARD, M.B., Lond.—London Pauperism amongst Jews and Christians. 8vo., xii.-327 pp. London. 1867.
[Dedicated by permission to the Baroness Lionel de Rothschild.]

551. BERNARD CRACROFT, M.A.—Essays, Political and Miscellaneous. 2 vols. 1868.
[Pp. 1-70 of vol. ii. on "The Jews of Western Europe," reprinted from the *Westminster Review*.]

552. W. C. (a Pole).—An Appeal to the Jews inhabiting the North Country. 16mo. 1868.

553. The Extraordinary Life and Trial of Madame Rachel [Sarah Rachel Levison] at the Central Criminal Court, September, 1868. The report copied verbatim from the *Times*. 1868.

554. ANNA MARIA GOLDSMID.—Persecution of the Jews
of Roumania. Translated from the French version
of the original Hebrew, by A. M. G.   1872.

555. Debate in the House of Commons, 10th April,
1872, on the Condition and Treatment of the Jews
of Roumania and Servia. 8vo., 16 pp. Lond. 1872.

556. ANONYMOUS.—The Jews in Roumania; Account
of the Proceedings at the Trial of the Jews at Busen.
Translated from the *Rumänische Post* for the Roumanian Committee. London. [A. N.]   1874.

557. An Open Letter, addressed to Sir Moses Montefiore, Bart., on his arrival in the Holy City of Jerusalem, together with a narrative of a Forty-days So-
journ in the Holy Land. With portrait. Hebr.
and Engl. 8vo., 188 pp.   1875.

559. LEOPOLD GLUCKSTEIN.—The Eastern Question and
the Jews. London. [A. N.]   1876.

560. Copy of an Address presented to W. Aronsberg,
Esq., of Manchester, by his Worship the Mayor, on
Friday, Oct. 27th, 1876, in the Mayor's Parlour,
Town Hall. 58 pp. Manchester.   [1876.]

561. PROF. DAVID KAUFMANN.— George Eliot and
Judaism. Translated by J. E. Ferrier.   1877.

562. HENRY SOLOMON.—Daniel Deronda, from a Jewish
point of view. 8vo., 11 pp.   [1875.]

563. [LORD STANLEY OF ALDERLEY.]—Speech of the
Right Honourable Lord S. of A. on moving for
a Paper respecting the Religious Persecutions in
Russia. Delivered in the House of Lords, Friday,
June 15, 1877. 8vo. 6 pp.   1877.
[Extracted from Hansard's Parliamentary Debate, vol.
ccxxxiv.]

564. ANON.—The Modern Jews on Capital Punishment.
1877. 8vo., 4 pp.   1877.
[An Editorial Article entitled "Death Punishment," and
a Letter on it by the Rt. Hon. John Bright, reprinted from
the *Jewish World* by the Howard Association.]

565. Principalities, No. 1, 1877. Correspondence respecting the . . . Jews in Servia and Roumania, ordered to be presented to the Houses of Parliament. Fol. 359 pp. 1877.

566. REV. D. MOSES MARGOLIOUTH.—The Destinies of Israel and the Claims of Hebrew Christians upon the Sitting Congress. 8vo., 82 pp. London. 1878.
[Inscribed to the Plenipotentiaries at the Berlin Congress.]

567. PHILIP ABRAHAM.—הנסתות והנגלת Curiosities of Ju'daism. Facts, Opinions, Anecdotes, and Remarks relative to the Hebrew Nation. 8vo., 300 pp. London. 1879.

568. DR. BLUNTSCHLI.—Roumania and the Legal Status of the Jews in Roumania. An Exposition of Public Law. 8vo., 31 pp. London. 1879.
[Translated from the German and published by the Anglo-Jewish Association.]

569. H. GUEDALLA.—Speech of his Excellency Don Antonio Canorus del Castillo, Spanish Minister of Foreign Affairs, on the Right of Protection by the European powers of the various Nationalities residing in the Empire of Morocco, translated from the Spanish by H. G., to which is added amongst other documents, Imperial Edict and Decree promulgated by Sultan of Morocco at the request of Sir Moses Montefiore, Bart., and the latter's Address to the Congregational Authorities of the Jews of Morocco, also copies of Correspondence between Mr. Guedalla and the late Marshal Prince, Señor Romersartiz and Marshal Serrano, relative to the re-admission of Jews into Spain. Fol., 22 pp. 1880.

570. —— Text of the Convention of the Morocco Conference as agreed to by the Eleven Powers, and their appeal to the Sultan for free exercise of all Worships and Religions in his Dominions. Fol. 4 pp.

570a. Russia, Nos. 3 and 4, 1881. Correspondence respecting the expulsion of Mr. L. Lewinsohn.

571. SYDNEY MONTAGU SAMUEL.—Jewish Life in the East. x.-199 pp. London. 1881.

[A Series of Travelling Sketches reprinted from the *Jewish Chronicle*.]

572. ANON. [ALFRED GEIGER.] —Die. Russischen Juden verfolgungen. Fünfzehn Briefe aus Süd-Russland. 8vo., 61 pp. Frankfort. 2nd edit. with "Nachschrift" same year. 1882.

[Translation of Letters sent to the *Jewish World* by the special Commissioner of that journal in South Russia.]

573. H. GUEDALLA.—Some account of the two journeys to Russia undertaken by Sir M. Montefiore, Bart., in 1846 and 1872 to further the interests of the Russian Jews. 8vo., 20 pp. 1882.

574. Russia, Nos. 1 and 2, 1882. Correspondence respecting the treatment of Jews in Russia.

575. [JOSEPH JACOBS.]—Persecution of the Jews in Russia, 1881. Reprinted from the *Times*, with Map and Appendix. 8vo., 31 pp. 1882.

576. CHARLES KENSINGTON SALAMAN.—Jews as they are. 8vo., pp. viii.—314. London. 1882.

[Went into a second edition.]

576a. J. M. SCHILLER-SZINESSY, M.A., Ph.D.—Persecution of the Jews in Russia. Speech . . . at the meeting in the Guildhall, Cambridge, Feb. 15, 1882.

[Printed by request.]

577. Russian Atrocities, 1881. Supplementary statement issued by the Russo-Jewish Committee in confirmation of the *Times* narrative. 8vo., 35 pp.

[Signed N. M. de Rothschild, Chairman.]

578. To the Chairman and Members of the Executive Committee for the Relief of the Russian Jews. 8vo., 12 pp. [1882.]

[Report on the International Russo-Jewish Conference (August, 1882) by Mr. B. L. Cohen, Delegate of the Mansion House Fund. The Conference met to devise means for the repatriation and dispersion of the refugees on the Austrian frontier.]

579. Persecution of the Jews in Russia. Mansion
House Relief Fund. Liverpool Commission. 8vo.,
14 pp. Liverpool.   1882.
[Report of the Commission.]

580. H. GUEDALLA.—A few words on the Jewish Question in Russia by Prince Demidoff San-Donato.
[Translated by H. G.] 4to., 9 pp. London.
                                               1883.

581. H. GUEDALLA.—כתר שם טוב The Crown of a
Good Name; a brief account of a few of the
doings, preachings, and compositions on Sir Moses
Montefiore's natal day, November 8th, 1883.
Hebrew and English. 8vo., 71 pp. [London.]
                                             [1883.]

582. [JOSEPH JACOBS.]—The "Blood Accusation," its
origin and occurrences in the Middle Ages. An historical commentary on the Tisza Eylor Trial. 8vo.,
12 pp.   1883.
[Reprinted from *Jewish Chronicle*, June 29, 1883.]

583. MARK SAMUEL (President of the Toronto Branch
of the Anglo-Jewish Association).—How to promote and develop agricultural pursuits among the
Jews. 8vo., 11 pp. Liverpool.   1883.

584. Address on the occasion of the presentation of the
portrait of Mr. Ernest Hart to his wife at Grosvenor
House, His Grace the Duke of Westminster, K.G.,
in the chair. 8vo., 29 pp.   1883.

585. Sir Moses Montefiore Commemoration; souvenir
containing line of route, order of procession, copy
of address, programme of fireworks, bonfire. 8th
November, 1883. Issued by order. Fcp., 4 pp.
[Ramsgate.]   [1883.]
[Programme of festivities in Ramsgate.]

586. J. MICHELL (H. M. Consul, St. Petersburg).—The
Jewish Question in Russia. By Prince Demidoff
San-Donato. 8vo., x.-105 pp. London.   1884.
[This work, dealing with a question which profoundly
agitated all the European Jewish communities at the time,
was translated at the cost of Mr. H. Guedalla, who also
supplied a Preface.]

587. [FLAMINIO SERI.]—Album Montefiore. 119 pp.
8vo.   Cassale Monferrato.   1884.
[Collection of Letters, Poems, Addresses, &c. written in
Italy on the occasion of Sir Moses Montefiore's 100th birthday. Mr. H. Guedalla contributes a Hebrew poem.]

588. I. STONE.—איין קורצע לעבענס בעשרייבונג פון איין
לאנדאנער שניידער An Historical (?) Sketch of a
London Tailor. London. 8vo., pp. 24.   1884.

589. ANON.—France and Tunis. London. 8vo. 51 pp.
[An account of the early stages of the dispute about the
Enfida estate in Tunis, which afterwards led to the occu-
pation of Tunis by France. It relates the case of an
English Jew, named Joseph Levy, who had sought to exercise his right of pre-emption with regard to the Enfida
property.]

590. Mansion House Fund for the Relief of the
Russian Jews. [Report of Messrs. B. L. Cohen,
S. Montagu, and A. Asher, M.D., on the Agri-
cultural Colonies in America.] 8vo.   1884.

591. ANON. [compiled by H. Guedalla].—The Montefiore Centenary. 44 pp. 8vo.   1885.
[Accounts of the festivities on the Montefiore Centenary
extracted from the *Jewish World*, *Jewish Chronicle*, *Life
and Shaare Zion*.]

591a. N. BERLIN.—דיא אמתע וועלט Reality in Fiction.
A satirical description of Life and Manners amongst
the Foreign Jews in Great Britain. Judeo-Germ.
London. 8vo., 40 pp.   1885.

592. JOSEPH JACOBS, B.A.—The Jewish Question, 1875-
1884; a Bibliographical Hand List. pp. xi.-96.
London.   1885.
[A Bibliography of the anti-Semitic agitation which arose
in Germany in 1875. Supplementary lists appeared in the
" Revue des Etudes Juives," 1885.]

593. DAVID F. SCHLOSS, M.A.—The Persecution of the
Jews in Roumania. A detailed account, compiled
from recent Official and other authentic informa-
tion. pp. 27. 8vo.   1885.
[Prepared at the request of the Council of the Anglo-
Jewish Association.]

594. מאררים ווינטשעװוסקי [Morris Wintshewsky].—
יהי אור איינע אונטערהאלטונג איבער דיא פעדקעהרטע
וועלט מיט זיין פריינד היימאן • Judeo-German.
London. 8vo., pp. 24.   1885.
[Described as ‑פאלקס ערסטעם העפט of a יידישע
ביבליאטהעק.]

595. The Jewish Roumanians and the Treaty of Berlin.
pp. 148. 8vo.   1885.
[No. 191 (vol. iv.) of "Diplomatic Fly Sheets." Reprint
of articles from *Vanity Fair*, August 22 and 29, 1885.]

(c.) ACTS OF PARLIAMENT.
[See also Part I., *sub voc.* Statutes.]

600. An Act to oblige the Jews to maintain and provide
for their Protestant Children. 1 Anne c. 30. 1702.
[Repealed in 1846.]

601. An Act for Naturalising such Foreign Protestants
and others therein mentioned (including Jews) as
are settled or shall settle in any of His Majesty's
colonies in America. 13 Geo. II. c. 7.   1740.

602. An Act to permit Persons professing the Jewish
Religion to be Naturalised by Parliament, &c. 26
Geo. II. c. 26.   1753.

603. An Act to Repeal an Act of the Twenty-sixth year
of His Majesty's Reign, intituled, An Act to permit Persons professing the Jewish Religion to be
Naturalised by Parliament, &c. 27 Geo. II. c. 1.

604. Barbados.—An Act concerning the Vestry of the
Hebrew Nation resident within the Island. S. sh.
                                            1820.
[For electing five representatives to settle taxation.]

605. Copy of a Bill which has recently passed the House
of Assembly in Jamaica.   1830.
[Repealing the clauses disabling Jews from being elected
members of the Corporation of Kingston.]

606. An Act for the Relief of Persons of the Jewish
Religion elected to Municipal Offices.   8 & 9 Vic.
cap. 52.   1845.

607. An Act to provide for the Relief of Her Majesty's
Subjects professing the Jewish Religion.   21 & 22
Vic. cap. 49.   1858.
> Sec. 1 empowers either House of Parliament to modify the
> form of oath, so as to enable a Jew to sit and vote. By sec. 3
> Jews are precluded from holding certain offices. By sec. 4 the
> right of presenting to any ecclesiastical benefice possessed by
> Jews is to devolve on the Archbishop of Canterbury.

608. An Act to Amend the Act of the Twenty-first and
Twenty-second years of Victoria, Chapter Forty-
nine, to Provide for the Relief of Her Majesty's
Subjects professing the Jewish Religion.   23 & 24
Vic. cap. 63.   1860.
> Repealed by 29 & 30 Vic., cap. 19, which removed the
> words "on the true faith of a Christian" from the oath.

609. An Act for Confirming a Scheme of the Charity
Commissioners for the Jewish United Synagogues.
33 & 34 Vic. cap. 116.

610. MISCELLANEOUS CLAUSES IN ACTS :—
(*a.*) 6 & 7 Wm. III., cap. 6, sec. 63.   1694.
> Jews cohabiting as man and wife to pay the duty
> imposed by this statute on marriages.

(*b.*) 26 Geo. II., cap. 33.   1753.
> Lord Hardwicke's Act for prevention of clandestine
> marriages. Sec. 18 exempts Jewish marriages.

(*c.*) 4 Geo. IV., cap. 76.   Repealing Lord Hard-
wicke's Act.   1823.
> Sec. 31 exempts Jews.

(*c*.*) 6 & 7 Wm. IV., cap. 85.   An Act for Marriages in England.   1836.
> Sec. 2. Jews may contract marriage according to
> Jewish usages, provided that both parties are of the
> Jewish religion, and that the Registrar's certificate has
> been obtained.

(*d.*) 6 & 7 Wm. IV., cap. 86.   An Act for registering Births, Deaths, and Marriages in England.
                                             1836.
> Sec. 30. The President of the London Committee of
> Deputies of the British Jews is to certify to the

Registrar-General the appointment of Secretaries of
Synagogues to act as marriage registrars.

(*e.*) 3 & 4 Vic., cap. 72.   An Act to provide for
the Solemnization of Marriages in the Districts
in or near which the Parties reside.   1840.
>Sec. 5. Jews exempted from operation of the Act.

(*f.*) 7 & 8 Vic., cap. 81.   An Act for Marriages in
Ireland.   1844.
>Sec. 12. Jews may contract marriages according to
their usages, provided they give notice to the Registrar
and obtain his certificate.
>Sec. 13. Jewish Registrars to be certified by the President of Jewish Board of Deputies.

(*g.*) 9 & 10 Vic., cap. 59.   An Act to relieve Her
Majesty's Subjects from certain Penalties and
Disabilities with regard to their Religious Opinions.   1846.
>Sec. 2. Jews are to be subject to the same laws as
Protestant Dissenters with regard to their schools, places
of religious worship, education, and charitable purposes, and the property held therewith.

(*h.*) 10 & 11 Vic., cap. 58.   An Act to remove
Doubts as to Quakers' and Jews' Marriages,
solemnized before certain periods.   1847.
>Declares all marriages amongst Jews solemnized in
England before the 1st April, 1837, or in Ireland before
the 1st April, 1845, according to their usages, are good
in law, if both parties were Jews.

(*i.*) 18 & 19 Vic., cap. 81.   An Act to amend the
Law concerning the certifying and registering of
Places of Religious Worship in England. 1855.
>Sec. 2. Synagogues may be certified as such to the
Registrar-General, and to be exempt from the provisions
of the Charitable Trusts Act, 1853, with certain exceptions.

(*j.*) 18 & 19 Vic., cap. 86.   An Act for securing
the Liberty of Religious Worship.   1855.
>Sec. 2 provides that 9 & 10 Vic., cap. 59 (*vide
supra*), is to be construed with reference to this Act.

(*k.*) 19 & 20 Vic., cap. 119.   An Act to amend the
provisions of the Marriage and Registration
Acts.   1856.
>Sec. 21. Marriages of Jews may be solemnised by
licence.
>Sec. 22. Twenty members of the West London Syna-

gogue of British Jews, or of any Synagogue in connection therewith, may certify a Secretary to the Registrar-
General, as a Registrar of Marriages.

(*l.*) 35 & 36 Vic., cap. 33.   The Ballot Act.   1872.
Schedule 1, sec. 26.   If a Parliamentary election
takes place on Saturday, the presiding officer may mark
a Jewish elector's ballot-paper for him.

(*m.*) 41 & 42 Vic., cap. 16.   An Act to consolidate
and amend the Law relating to Factories and
Workshops.   1878.
Sec. 50 provides means by which Jewish manufac-
turers closing on their sabbath may employ young persons and women in such a way as to make up the lost
time.
Sec. 51. Jewish employés in factories or workshops
are permitted to be employed on Sunday, subject to
certain restrictions.

(D.) TRIALS AND LEADING CASES.

611. Lilly's Practical Register, I., p. 3.   1673.
Religion of Jewish plaintiff was pleaded as a bar to an
action for debt.   Judgment for plaintiff.

612. BARKER *v.* WARREN.—2 Modern Reports, 271.
c. 1678.
Venue changed from London to Middlesex, to suit con-
venience of Jewish witness, who would not attend on Saturday.

613. ROBELE *v.* LANGSTON.—2 Keb., 314.   1680.
Jews sworn on Pentateuch : validity of evidence confirmed on appeal.

614. EAST INDIA COMPANY *v.* SANDYS.—2 Shower, 371 ;
State Trials, vii. 540, 563 (Cobbett's Edition, x.,
408, 444).
Jews regarded by English law as "alien friends," and
were in England by an implied license.

615. ANON.—The Information of Francis de Favia,
Delivered at the Bar of the House of Commons,

Thursday, the First day of November, 1680,
by Mr. William Williams, Speaker. Fol. 12 pp.,
[A. N.] T. Newcomb and Co.) 1680.

616. PARISH OF ST. ANDREW'S UNDERSHAFT, LONDON
v. JACOB MENDEZ DE BRETO.—1 Lord Raymond,
699. 1701.
Father ordered to pay to converted daughter an allow-
ance, under 43 Eliz., ii. 7 : order quashed, as no proof of
her needing asisstance.

617. The Case of Mr. Francis Francia, the reputed
Jew, who was accused of High Treason at the Sessions House in the Old Bailey, on Tuesday, Jan.
22, 1716. Fol., 12 pp. [A. N.] 1716.
[An adherent of the Old Pretender. He was acquitted.]

618. VINCENT *v.* FERNANDEZ.—1 Peere Williams, 524,
Vin. Abr. tit. Jew, sect. 12. 1718.
A Jewess turned Christian sued for maintenance from
her father's executor, as no legacy was left her : order that
the Master make inquiry if the charities given by the will
might not be under some secret trust for her if she turn
again.

619. The· Case of Mr. Anthony Da Costa with the
Russia Company. 1 sh. fol. 1727.
Claiming to be admitted. Claim refused as he was a
Jew. Attorney-General declared he ought to be admitted,
but the Company still refused, and petitioned Parliament to
modify their charter in that sense. The above broadsheet
was a protest against the charge.

620. The Proceedings at Large in the Arches Court of
Canterbury between Mr. Jacob Mendes Da Costa
and Mrs. Catharine da Costa Villa Real. 8vo.,
408 pp. [A. N.] 1734.
Breach of promise case. Portrait of Mrs. Villa Real.

621. The Famous Jew Case between J. M. da Costa and
Mrs. C. da Costa Villa Real. 8vo. 1735.

622. The Case of Mr. (Anthony) da Costa with Mr.
Monmartel relating to a Bill of Exchange. 1736.

623. ANDREAS *v.* ANDREAS.—1 Hagg. Cos.   1737.
     Restitution of marital rights : Jewess married *more
     Judaico* has marital rights.

624. VILLAREAL *v.* MELLISH.—2 Swanst. 538.   1737.
     A Jewish widow having turned Christian, recovers cus-
     tody of her children from her father, guardianship not being
     transferable.

625. DA COSTA *v.* DE PAS.—Ambler's "Report of Cases
     in Chancery," 228.   2 Swanst. 487.   1743.
     A bequest of £1,200 for founding a "Jesuba" declared
     invalid, as being for a superstitious purpose.

626. OMYCHUND *v.* BARKER.—1 Atkyns, 21.   1744.
     Jew's evidence legal, if sworn on Old Testament.

627. J. KATHER.—The Tryal of T. Kather and David
     Alexander for a Conspiracy against E. Walpole.
     4to.   1751.
     Also accused of a plot to kill Sir T. Hotham.

628. Memorial of Edward Wortley Montague, Esq.,
     written by himself in French, and published lately
     at Paris, against Abraham Payba, a Jew in Birth,
     who assumed the fictitious name of James Roberts.
     Translated into English from an authentic copy
     sent from Paris. 8vo., 78 pp. A. Mather. [A. N.]
                                                 1752.

629. The Sentence of the Lieutenant-Criminal at Paris in
     the Extraordinary Case between Abraham Payba
     alias James Roberts, Plaintiff, and Edward Wortley
     Montagu and Theobald Taaffe, Esq., Members of
     the Hon. House of Commons, Defendants. 8vo.,
     30 pp. J. Robinson. [A. N.]   Price Sixpence.

630. A Memorial or Humble Petition presented to the
     Judge in the High Court of Tournelle in Paris, by
     the Honourable Edward Wortley Montagu, Esq.,
     Member of Parliament for the County of Hunting-
     don, and Theobald Taaffe, Esq., against Abraham
     Payba *alias* James Roberts and Louis Pierre.
     [A. N.]   93 pp.   1752.

631. The Memorial presented to the High Court of La Tournelle at Paris, in favour of Abraham Payba, Jew, a native of London, against E——d W——y M——u, Esq., and T——d T——e, Esq. Translated from the French Original. 8vo., 76 pp. Price, 1s. 6d. [A. N.]   1752.

632. The Case of Henry Simons, a Polish Jew Merchant, and his Appeal to the public thereon, now published with the Tryal at Chelmsford for the benefit of him and his unhappy family. 115 pp.   1753.

633. The Case and Appeal of James Ashley of Bread Street, London, addressed to the Publick in general. In relation to the apprehending Henry Simons, the Polish Jew, on a warrant issued out against Perjury. Interspersed throughout with many very uncommon particulars. 8vo., 47 pp. Price 6d. [A. N.]   1753.
   [With print of Simons.]

634. NAPHTALI FRANKS.—Franks and Wife, Appellants; Martin Adolphus and Wife, Levy, widow, and others, Respondents. Case of the Respondents the Executors of M. Hart. Fol.   1760.
   The appellant's case was also printed and an appendix containing the Hebrew Contracts, &c.

635. ISAAC v. GOMPERTZ.—Ambler's Rep. 228. 7 Ves. 61.   1783.
   Will of Benjamin Isaac for support of Jewish charities at " Bromsall " and London held valid.

635a. GOWER v. LADY LANESBOROUGH.—Peake's Cases, 25.   1791.
   A Jewess may be permitted to give parol evidence of her own divorce in a foreign country, according to the custom of the Jews there.

636. LINDO v. BELISARIO.—1 Hag. Cons. Rep. 216.
                       1795.
   Jewish Marriage Law to be ascertained by testimony of its Professors.

H

637. VIGEVENA SILVERIA *v.* ALVAREZ.   1794.
    Question of legitimacy : marriage by Jewish rite held to
    be valid.

638. D'AGUILAR *v.* D'AGUILAR.—1 Hagg. Cors. Rep.
    776.   1794.
    First divorce suit between an English Jew and Jewess.

638*a.* REX *v.* GILHAM.—1 Espinasse's Reports, 1895.
                                                1795.
    A Jew, who had not formally abjured Judaism, sworn on
    the New Testament, held to be an admissible witness,
    though when sworn he had stated he considered himself a
    member of the established religion.

639. GOLDSMID *v.* BROMER.—1 Hagg. Cos. Rep., 324.
                                                1798.
    [Validity of a Jewish marriage decided by the Beth Din.]

639*a.* HORN *v.* NOEL.—1 Campbell's Reports, 61. 1807.
    Witnesses present at the marriage ceremony not sufficient
    to prove Jewish marriage ; written contract of marriage also
    necessary.

639*b.* JONES *v.* ROBINSON.—2 Phillimore's Reports, 285.
                                                1815.
    If Jews are married according to Christian rites, they must
    conform to the ordinary regulations of Marriage Acts.

640. ISRAEL AND OTHERS *v.* SIMMONS.—Starkie's Nisi
    Prius Reports, ii. 356.   1818.
    Synagogue declared to be a lawful establishment ; also
    that lessees could sue for rent from holders of seats.

641. *In re* TRUSTEES OF THE BEDFORD CHARITY.—2
    Swanston, 470.   1818.
    Jews not entitled to benefits of the Bedford Charity.

641*a.* EDENBOROUGH *v.* ARCHBISHOP OF CANTERBURY.—
    2 Russell's Reports, 119 (note).   1826.
    Jews were entitled to vote in the election of a vicar, but
    not Roman Catholics.

642. The Trial of John Kinnear, Lewis Levy, and
    Mozely Woolf, indicted, with John Meyer and
    others, for a Conspiracy on April 20 and 21, 1819,

with the Sentence. Taken in shorthand by Mr.
Fraser. 548 pp., and plan of St. Peter's Field,
Manchester. [A. N.]   1819.

643. STRAUS *v.* GOLDSMID.—8 Simon's Reports, 611.
1837.
A bequest to enable Jews to observe the rites of Passover
held to be good, notwithstanding the decision in Da Costa
v. De Pas.

644. BENNETT *v.* HAYTER.—2 Beavan's Reports, 1881.
1839.
Under "a bequest to the Jews' poor, Mile End," ordered
that fund be applied *cy pres* between Jews' Hospital and
Beth Holim.

645. DAVIS *v.* LLOYD AND OTHERS.—1 Carrington &
Kirwan's Reports, 275.   1844.
The entry by the Chief Rabbi in the Synagogue register
book of the circumcision of the plaintiff, a Jew, held not
admissible as proof of his age.

646. MILLER *v.* SALOMONS.—7 Exchequer Reports, 475.
1852.
Alderman Salomons, M.P., took his seat, after taking the
oath, intentionally omitting the words, "on the true faith of
a Christian"; was declared liable to penalties under 1
George I. statute 2, cap. 13, sec. 17.

647. GOODMAN *v.* GOODMAN.—33 Law Times Reports,
Chancery Appeals, 70.   1859.
A Jew and a Christian woman, who have cohabited as man
and wife for twenty-eight years, presumed to be married.

648. MICHEL'S TRUST.—28 Beavan's Reports, 39.
1860.
A bequest by a Jew in support of learning in the Beth
Hamedrash (or Divinity College), and to have the prayer
called "Kadish" repeated on the anniversary of his death,
held valid.

649. RE ESTHER LYONS.—22 Law Times, New Series,
770.   1869.
In the case of the abduction and baptism of a young
Jewess for proselytising purposes, £50 damages recovered
by father.

650. LINDO *v.* ROSENBERG. — Annual Report Jewish
Board of Deputies for 1883.   1882.

A Jewish girl having been abducted by Roman Catholics
for proselytising purposes, the Roman Catholic bishop and
lady superior ordered by Court to attend there to be examined. The domicile of the girl's father being foreign, no
order as to her custody could be made, but lady superior's
costs disallowed,

(E.) POLEMICS—EXTERNAL.

651. D. NIETO.—Respuesta al Sermon predicado por el
Arçobispo de Craganor, etc. Por el author de las
Noticias Recónditas obra posthuma impresso en
Villa Franca [London]. Por Carlos Vero. A la
insigna de la verdad.   1729.

[In answer to Diogo da Annunziazam, Arcebispo de
Cranganor, *Sermam do Auto da Fè que se celebran em 6
de Sept.* 1705. Translated into English by M. Mocatta.
1845 (see No. 709).]

652. STEHELIN.—The Traditions of the Jews with the
Expositions and Doctrines of the Rabbins, contained in the Talmud and other Rabbinical writings,
translated from the High Dutch. 2 vols. Sm. 8vo.
                                              1732-4.
[English adaptation of Eisenmenger.]

653. J. H.—The Covenant of the Cherubim, showing
the Hebrew writing perfect and the alterations by
the Rabbis forged. 8vo., 476 pp. [A. N.]   1734.
[Plates by Gravelot.]

654. DAVID ABOAB.—Remarks upon Dr. Sharp's two
Dissertations concerning the Etymology and Scrip-
ture-Meaning of the Hebrew words Elohim and
Berith. [A. N.]   1751.

655. S. SALTEL, D.D.—Some Queries relative to the
Jews, occasioned by a late Sermon, with some other
Papers occasioned by the Queries. Lond. (Payne).
8vo. 6d.   1751.

656. RAPHAEL BARUH.—Critica Sacra examined, or an Attempt to show that a new Method may be found to reconcile the seemingly glaring variations in parallel passages of Scripture. 8vo., 254 pp. [A.N.]
1775.

657. H. OWEN, D.D.—Supplement to Critica Sacra, in which the principles of that treatise are fully confirmed and the objections of Mr. R. Baruh clearly answered.   1775.

658. REV. R. BEERE.—An Epistle to the Chief Priests and Elders of the Jews, containing an answer to Mr. D. Levi's challenge to Christians, respecting the accomplishment of the prophecy predictive of the time of the First Coming and Crucifixion of the Messiah.   1787.

660. DUNCAN SHAW, D.D. — The History and Philosophy of Judaism, or a Critical and Philosophical Analysis of the Jewish Religion. 8vo., 388 pp. [A. N.]   Edinburgh.   1787.

661. JOHN H. SWAIN.—The Objections of David Levi to the Mission, Conduct, and Doctrine of our Lord Jesus Christ examined. 76 pp. See No. 667. 1787.

662. ANTISOCINUS. — Remarks on David Levi's Letters to Dr. Priestley. (See No. 667.)   1787.

663. The Reply of the Jews to the Letters addressed to them by Dr. Priestley and Solomon de A. R. Rivingtons. 8vo. 1s.   1787.

664. PHILIP DAVID KRAUTER, D.D.—A new succinct and candid Examination of Mr. David Levi's Objections against Christianity and the Gospel History in his Letters to Dr. Priestley. Bath. 72 pp. 1788.

665. JACOB BARNET. — Remarks upon Dr. Priestley's Letters to the Jews, upon his Discourse on the Resurrection of Jesus, and upon his Letters to the Members of the New Jerusalem, introductory to an Address to the Jews.   1792.

666. An Appeal to the Elders of the Spanish and Portuguese Jews. 8vo., 26 pp. (Minerva Press.)
[A. N.]   1796.

667. JOSEPH PRIESTLEY.—Letters to the Jews inviting
them to an amicable Discussion of the Evidences
of Christianity. 8vo., 54 pp.   Parts I. and II.
                                                 1797.

668. D. LEVI.—Letters to Dr. Priestley, in answer to
those he addressed to the Jews, inviting them to an
amicable discussion on the Evidences of Christianity.
8vo., 99 pp.   1797.

669. DAVID LEVI.—Series of [7] Letters addressed to
Tom Paine.   208 pp.   1797.

670. —— Letters to Dr. Priestley in answer to his
Letters to the Jews, Part II., occasioned by Mr.
David Levi's Reply to the former part; also Letters,
1, to Dr. Cooper in answer to his "One Great Ar-
gument in favour of Christianity from a single
Prophecy;" 2, to Mr. Bicheno; 3, to Dr. Krauter;
4, to Mr. Swain; 5, to Anti-Socinus *alias* Anselm
Bayley.   48 pp.   1799.

671. JOSEPH PRIESTLEY.—An Inquiry into the Knowledge of the Ancient Hebrews concerning a Future
State.   8vo., 67 pp.   [A. N.]   1801.

672. DR. S. HERSCHELL.—Against Missionary Schools,
Sermon.   1807.

673. SOLOMON BENNETT. — נצח ישראל.   The Constancy of Israel.   An unprejudiced Illustration of
some of the most important Texts of the Bible, or
a Reply to a Public Letter by Lord Crauford, addressed to the Hebrew Nation.   1809.
   [Translated into German by F. L. W. Wagner. Darm-
stadt, 1835.]

674. T. GOODMAN.—An Address to the Committee of
the London Society for Promoting Christianity

among the Jews; in which the conduct of the Committee is investigated. 8vo., 27 pp. 1809.

675. Talib.—Remarks upon David Levi's Dissertations on the Prophecies relative to the Messiah. 1810.

676. Investigator (Pseud.).—Strictures on "Lectures to the Jews at Artillery Street Chapel." 1810.

677. Chas. Leslie.—A Short and Easy Method with the Jews, wherein the certainty of the Christian Religion is demonstrated. New edition, published under direction of the London Society. 8vo., 147 pp. [A. N.] 1812.

678. P. P. Pasquin (Pseud.).—Jewish Conversion, a Poetical Farce, got up with great effect under the direction of a Society for making bad Jews worse Christians. Dedicated to His Royal Highness the Duke of Kent, with whose approbation it has been recently played, and will be repeated this Friday, May 6th, 1814. 8 pp. [A. N.] 1814.
[A poem in heroic couplets.]

679. J. Nikelsburger. — קול יעקב Koul Jacob in Defence of the Jewish Religion; containing the arguments of the Rev. C. F. Frey, one of the Committee of the London Society for the Conversion of the Jews, and the answers thereto. 8vo., 79 pp. Liverpool. [A. N.] 1814.
[Reprinted New York, 1816.]

680. A Letter to the London Society for Promoting Christianity among the Jews; containing Strictures on the Letter of a Jewish Correspondent, by the author of Remarks on David Levi's Dissertations on the Prophecies respecting the Messiah. (Gale and Co.). 8vo. 1814.

681. Copy of Correspondence between the Chief Rabbi, Dr. Solomon Herschell, and J. J. Lockhart, of Oxford, on the validity of oaths taken by Jews. Copied from the *Morning Chronicle*, June 26th, 1817.

682. M. Samuel.—Address to Missionary Preachers at
Liverpool.   1819.

683. A Letter from a Jew to a Christian, occasioned by
the recent Attacks on the Bible. Original. [A. N.]
                                                              1820.
[Pamphlets, Vol. XVI., No. xxxii.]

684. M. Sailman.—Mystery Unfolded; against the
London Society for the Promotion of Christianity
among the Jews.   1822.

685. M. Samuel.—Address to the Patrons of the Institute for the Promotion of Christianity among the
Jews.   1822.

686. Zailick [Selig] Solomon. — An Exposure of
Hypocrisy and Bigotry and a strenuous Vindication
of the Israelites, in an Address to the Members of
a Society formed for promoting Christianity among
the Jews.   1822.

687. H. Simmonds.—Letter to G. V. le Grice concerning some words used in his Sermon about the
Jews. Penzance.   1824.

688. M. Samuel.—An Address from an Israelite to the
Missionary Preachers assembled at Liverpool, Aug.
28, 1827. With Remarks upon the Conversion of
Rebecca Lyon. 8vo., 16 pp. [A. N.] Liverpool.
(W. Wales.)   1827.

689. Joseph Mitchell.—A Lecture on the Origin,
Progress, and Proceedings at Home and Abroad of
the London Society for promoting Christianity
among the Jews delivered by Mr. J. M. at Providence Hall, Finsbury Square. 8vo., 16 pp. 1836.

690. Rev. Alexander McCaul, D.D.—נתיבות עולם.
The Old Paths; or, a comparison of the principles
and doctrines of Modern Judaism, with the religion
of Moses and the Prophets. 8vo., viii.-240 pp.
London.   1837.
[Issued in sixty weekly parts, price 1d. each part, the

publication extending from January 15, 1836, to March 3,
1837.   Translated into German and Hebrew.]

691. REV. DR. McCAUL.—Reasons for believing that
the charge lately revived against the Jewish people
is a Baseless Falsehood.   London.   [A. N.]
1840.
On the Damascus Blood Accusation.   Dedicated by permission to Her Most Gracious Majesty the Queen.

692. [SIR] D. SALOMONS.—An Account of the recent
Persecution of the Jews at Damascus ; with reflections thereon ; and an Appendix.   [A. N.]   1840.

693. C. E. JENKINS, K.M.—A Speech delivered at the
Public Vestry of St. Mary, Whitechapel, on Thursday, July 16, 1840, on the subject of the Persecution of the Jews at Damascus.   8vo., 10 pp.
London.   1840.

694. J. LEVINSOHN. — Efes Dammim.   A Series of
Conversations at Jerusalem, between a Patriarch
of the Greek Church and a Chief Rabbi of the
Jews concerning the Malicious Charge against the
Jews of using Christian blood.   Translated from
the Hebrew as a tribute to the memory of the
Martyrs of Damascus, by Dr. L. Loewe, Member
of the Royal Asiatic Society of Great Britain and
Ireland, &c.   London.   1841.

696. THOMAS O'BRIEN, M.A., T.C.D.—Two Lectures
upon Jewish Claims delivered at the " Crown and
Anchor " Tavern, on March 17th and April 19th,
1841.   8vo., 43 pp.   London.   [A. N.]   1841.

697. The Destiny of the Jews and their Conversion with
the Gentile Nations, viewed practically, in a Course
of Lectures delivered at St. Bride's Church, Liverpool, by several Clergymen of the Church of
England.   12mo.   London.   1841.

698. M. J. RAPHALL.—Judaism defended against T.J.C.
1842.

699. REV. H. HIGHTON (Assistant Master of Rugby
School).—A Letter to Sir Moses Montefiore ; con-

taining Observations on the subject of an Address lately presented to him, signed by nearly 1,500 Continental Jews.   London.   1843.

700. MOSES MARGOLIOUTH.—The Fundamental Principles of Modern Judaism investigated, together with a Memoir of the Author.   Illustrated.   8vo. pp. xx., xvi. (Memoir), 259.   London.   1843.
[Dedicated to the Rev. Alexander McCaul.]

701. J. OXLEE (Rector of Molesworth, Hunts.).—Three Letters humbly addressed to the Lord Archbishop of Canterbury, on the inexpediency and futility of any Attempt to Convert the Jews to the Christian Faith in the way and manner hitherto practised. London.   1843.

702. RIDLEY H. HIRSCHELL.—Brief Sketch of the present State and future Expectations of the Jews. 18mo.   1844.

704. Ten Lectures on the Conversion of the Jews, delivered at the National Scotch Church, Regent Square, in the Spring of 1843, by Ministers of different Denominations.   12mo.   London.   1844.

705. Narrative of a Mission of Enquiry to the Jews. 12mo.   London.   1844.

706. STANISLAUS HAGA.—The Controversy of Zion: a Meditation on Judaism and Christianity.   2nd ed. 84 pp.   1845.

707. H. LEVEAUX.—A Letter to the Rev. Dr. McCaul by H. L., in refutation of a work entitled the "Old Paths," and the Rev. Doctor's answer to the same. London.   1845.

708. H. LEVEAUX.—A Casual Dialogue between a Christian and an Israelite.   London.   1845.

709. M. MOCATTA.—The Inquisition and Judaism: a Sermon addressed to Jewish Martyrs, by the Arch-

bishop of Cranganor, 1705; also a reply to the Sermon by Castos Vero. Translated by M. M. 8vo.,
191 pp. 1845.

710. REV. JOHN OXLEE (Rector of Molesworth, Hunts.)
—Three more Letters to his Grace the Lord Arch-
bishop of Canterbury, on the culpability and un-
authorised presumption of the Gentile Christian
Church, in requiring the Jew to forsake the Law of
Moses, &c., containing also Metaphysical Disqui-
sitions on the Godhead and a Confutation of the
Diabolarchy. London. 1845.

713. JUDAH MIDDLEMAN.—ספר נתיבות אמת חלק ראשון|
העומר למגן בעד חכמי התלמוד. Paths of Truth;
being a Defence of the Talmudical Traditions
against the attacks in the "Old Paths," by Dr.
McCaul. . . . Translated into English by M. H.
Breslau. Part I., 8vo. London. 1847.
[No more published.]

715. DR. MORRIS RAPHALL and C. N. NEWDIGATE, M.P.
—Jewish Dogmas; a Correspondence between R.
and N. 8vo., 49 pp. London. [A. N.] 1849.
The correspondence arose out of some remarks regarding
Jewish Dogmas made by Mr. Newdigate in the course of
the Debate on the third reading of the Parliamentary Oaths
Bill.

716. MOSES MOCATTA.—חזוק אמונה, or Faith Strength-
ened. 1851.
[Translation from Hebrew.]

717. M. H. BRESLAU.—The Re-opening of the Great
Synagogue, being a few Observations in reply to
the *Times* report of Friday, Sept. 3, 1852. 8vo.,
5 pp. 1852.

718. SELIG NEWMAN.—The Challenge Accepted. A
Dialogue between a Jew and a Christian, the former
answering a challenge thrown out by the latter

respecting the accomplishment of the Prophecies
predicative of the Advent of Jesus.   New York.

719. ANON.—The Turk and the Hebrew; or the Rule
of the Crescent.   A Story of Real Events and
Living Persons.   1854.
[Refers to Damascus Blood Accusation of 1840, and states
that Father Thomas is still alive.]

720. DR. A. BENISCH.—The Question at issue between
Judaism and Christianity and Israel's Mission as
exhibited in the Controversy between the *Eclectic
Review* and the *Jewish Chronicle*.   London.   1858.

721. DR. A. BENISCH.—The Principal Charges of Dr.
McCaul's "Old Paths" against Judaism, as stated by
Mr. Newdigate in the House of Commons, con-
sidered and answered.   London.   1858.

722. REV. MORTLOCK DANIELL (of Ramsgate).—Can
Jews, as Jews, be Saved?   A Tract most respect-
fully dedicated to Sir Moses Montefiore, Bart.,
F.R.S.   London.   1859.

723. M. N. NATHAN (Kingston, Jamaica).—A Defence
of Ancient Rabbinical Interpretation of the Pro-
hibitory Law of Deuteronomy xxiii. 3, being an
Answer by M. N. N. to a Polemic Essay on that
Subject by the Rev. J. M. de Sola.   (Montego
Bay.)   London.   1859.

724. REV. JOHN OXLEE.—The Mysterious Stranger; or
Dialogues on Doctrine.   1859.
[Dialogue the first is between "The Jew Rabbi and the
Stranger."]

725. M. N. NATHAN.—A Defence of Ancient Rabbinical
Interpretation of the Prohibitory Law of Deut. xxiii.
3, being an Answer by M. N. Nathan, Kingston,
Jamaica, to a Polemic Essay on that Subject by the
Rev. J. M. de Sola, Montego Bay.   Kingston,
Jamaica.   40 pp.   (See No. 723.)   1861.

726. A. SCHNEIDER (of Edinburgh.) — The Mosaic Miracles, with reference to the Treatises on Divine or Special Providence contained in Nos. 344-350 of the *Jewish Chronicle*. London.   1862.

[An Attack on the Treatises in question, which are described as "destructive of the Jewish Religion."]

727. DR. A. BENISCH.—Bishop Colenso's Objections to the Historical Character of the Pentateuch and the Book of Joshua (contained in Part I.) critically examined.   1863

[Reprinted from the *Jewish Chronicle*.]

729. ANON. (Jewish Assoc. for Diffusion of Religious Knowledge.)—A Jewish reply to Dr. Colenso's Criticism on the Pentateuch.   1865.

730. DR. A. BENISCH.—The Sabbath of the Jew in its relation to the Sunday Question. London.   1868.

[Reprint of a Series of Articles from the *Jewish Chronicle*.]

731. H. GUEDALLA. — Vice-Chancellor Sir Matthew Page Wood's able Defence of Scripture against Rationalists contrasted with Dr. Kalisch's "High Criticism on the Old Testament," and fallacious cavilling against its contents by specious arguments as contained in his "Historical and Critical Commentary on Leviticus," and a decision asked after perusal from those of all religious denominations. [Not published.] London.   1868.

Another edition was issued in 1881, under the title "In Memoriam William Page, Lord Hatherley."

732. HERSCHELL FILIPOWSKI.—Biblical Prophecies, including those relating to the expected Advent of the Messiah as interpreted by the Hebrew Nation agreeably with the view of Ancient Hebrew commentators thoroughly investigated and considerably augmented. London. [A. N.]   1869.

733. CLEMENTINE DE ROTHSCHILD.— Letters to a Chris-

tian Friend on the Fundamental Truths of Judaism.
8vo., 93 pp.   1869.

734. THOS. GRIBBLE.—The Semi-Barbarous Hebrew
and the Extinguished Theologian. 8vo., 72 pp.
[A. N.]   1871.

735. ANNA MARIA GOLDSMID.—The Deicides. Analysis
of the Life of Jesus, and of the several phases of
the Christian Church in their relation to Judaism.
Translated from the French of Joseph Cohen by
A. M. G. 8vo. London.   1872.

736. ISRAELITE [CHARLES KENSINGTON SALAMAN].—A
Letter to the Bishop of Manchester.
> [Reply to a conversionist sermon preached by the
> Bishop.]

737. "GEORGE ELIOT."—Impressions of Theophrastus
Such.   1879.
> [The modern "Hep! Hep! Hep!" pp. 313-357.
> Translated into German by E. Lehmann, 1880.]

738. OSWALD JOHN SIMON.—Extempore Speech on
Monday evening, 15th November, 1880, by Mr.
O. J. S. 8vo., 7 pp. [London.]   [1880.]
> [Delivered in the course of a debate at Cambridge, and in
> reply to some disparaging remarks anent the Hebrew race.]

739. HON. GEORGE SOLOMON (of Jamaica).—The Jesus
of History and the Jesus of Tradition. London.

740. M. C.—עד כי יבא שילה   Until he (Judah) cometh
to Shiloh. A Letter addressed to the Editor of the
Jewish World. 8vo., 15 pp.   1882.

741. REV. GEORGE MARGOLIOUTH.—What is Judaism?
A Question of To-day. 8vo., 25 pp. London.
                                                [1884.]
> [Reply, "For private circulation only," to an article
> bearing the same title in the *Fortnightly Review* for August,
> 1884.]

742. MRS. BOOLE.—Jews and Gentiles. 7 pp.
> [Reprint from *Jewish Chronicle*, 14 Nov., 5 Dec. 1884.]

(F.) POLEMICS—INTERNAL.

744. Decision del Doctissimo, y Excellentissimo Señor H. H. Hassalem, M.A.A.B.D.R.M.R. Zevi Asquenasi, con su Betdin, sobre el problema si Naturaleza, y Dios, y Dios, y Naturaleza es todo uno? Segun lo predico el Señor H.H.R. David Nieto en el K. K. de Londres, en 23 de Kisleu, 5464. En Londres. Por Tho. Hine en Aldersgate Street. 18 pp.   1704.
[Another edition in 1712.]

745. De la Divina Providencia o sea Naturaleza Universal o Natura Naturante, Tratado Theologico. Dividido en dos Dialogos.   89 pp.   1704.
Imprint : En Londres. Por James Dover en Tower Hill. En el Mes de Elul, Ano 5464.

747. JOHANAN BEN ISAAC.—משה רב פה ק״ק לונדון [against U. P. Hamburger's decision on a divorce]. Amsterdam. 4to.   1707.
[In תשובות הגאונים ff. 6 seq. : containing responses of Jehuda Loeb Charif (Amsterd.), Zebi Ashkenazi (Hamburg), Jehuda Loeb Ascher (Rotterdam), on the decree of divorce declared by Uri Phöbus Hamburger.]

748. URI PHÖBUS HAMBURGER.—אורים ותומים · · · על גט אחד שסדרתי פה. 4to.   1707.
[Answering Johanan b. Isaac.]

749. JOSEPH IRGUS.—תוכחת מגולה והצד נחש.   1714.
[Edited by M. ben J. Chagiz. The second title is a play upon the name of Nehemiah Chajon, against whom the work is directed.]

750. MOSES BEN JACOB CHAGIZ.—שבר פושעים. Amsterdam.   1714.
[Polemic against Nehemiah Chajon, Abraham Michael Cordoso, and Samuel b. Jacob Ailion, whose names by Gematria = פושעים.]

751. SHALOM BEN MOSES BUZAGLIO.—תוכחה לשובבים ותקנה לשבים.
[Two Letters to Israel Meshullam Solomon concerning B's. disputed opinion in a lawsuit.]

753. SHALOM BEN MOSES BUZAGLIO.—כך שהיה מעשה
היה בדקרוק רב. Report of the proceedings of a
lawsuit.   1774.

754. M. GOMPERT LEVISON.—תוכחה מגולה. [Against
Wardens of Duke's Place Synagogue.]   1775.

755. JUDAH IN LONDON.—תשובת הפרושים. Refutation
of G. Levison's תוכחת מגולה.   1775.

756. J. MOCATTA.—An Address to the Congregation of
Portuguese Jews, delivered at a meeting of their
Elders on the examination of the report presented
by the Committee on the Ecclesiastical state, A. M.
5563. London.   1803.

757. LEVY ALEXANDER.—The Axe laid to the Root; or
Ignorance and Superstition evident in the character of the Rev. S. Hirschell, High Priest of the
Jews in England, in several Letters to him, on occasion of his having ordered the trees to be felled
in the old burial ground at Mile End Road. 8vo.
London.   1808.

758. Z. SOLOMON.—גלוי מזמות Exposure of hypocrisy
and bigotry of the Society for the Promotion of
Christianity among the Jews.   1822.

759. ANONYMOUS.—תורה שבעל פה. Is there an Oral
Law of Divine Origin, and therefore binding upon
the Jews? By One of Themselves. London. 1841.
      A defence of the orthodox standpoint, issued during the
Reform agitation.

760. DAVID NIETO. — The Rod of Judgment, which
proves to demonstration, by natural inferences, the
truth of the Oral Law, transmitted to us by the
Sages of Israel, the authors of the Mishna and the
Talmud, written by the Rev. David Nieto (of blessed
memory), Chief Rabbi of the Spanish and Portuguese Congregation of London in the year 5474.
Translated from the Hebrew by Dr. L. Loewe,
London.   1842.
      Issued during the Reform Agitation. Vol. ii. publ. in
1845.

761. DE SOLA, REV. D. A. and RAPHALL, REV. M. J.— י״ח מסכתות מששה סדרי משנה־משניות. Eighteen Treatises from the Mishna. London. 8vo., 368 pp. 1842.

Second edition (issued in weekly and monthly parts) 1845. Fragmentary translation of treatises Berachoth, Kilaim, Sabbath, Erubin, Pesachim, Yomah, Succah, Bezo, Rosh Hoshanah, Taanith, Meguillah, Moed Katan, Yebamoth, Ketuboth, Gittin, Kedushin, Cholin, and Yadaim, with brief indications of the scope of the remaining treatises. The work was projected by Messrs. Moses Mocatta and Horatio Montefiore during the discussions which preceded the Reform movement, and was executed for those gentlemen by Messrs. De Sola and Raphall, in 1839 (cf. " Biography of D. A. de Sola, by A. de Sola, Philadelphia, 5624). Subsequently, after the schism had taken place, it was put to press by Mr. Benjamin Elkin, a prominent member of the Reform Congregation, without the revision or consent of the authors. The preface, which was unsigned, and referred in equivocal terms to the Oral Law, was written by Mr. Elkin. Messrs. De Sola and Raphall by advertisement in the *Times* of Dec. 23rd, 1842, formally repudiated responsibility for the work ; and the *Voice of Jacob* of Jan. 6th, 1843, was authorised to deny that the Reform Congregation had authorised its publication. An angry controversy ensued. Mr. Elkin issued a pamphlet (No. 765), in which he explained that no discourtesy was intended to the translators, and that their names had been placed on the title-page by accident. In the second edition, however, the names were retained, although the preface remained unsigned, and its obnoxious references to the " Divinity of the Oral Law," were neither expunged nor modified.

762. ANONYMOUS.—Is the Oral Law of Divine Origin, and therefore binding on the Jews? The Advocacy of this Question contested,—by a Member of that Community. London. 1842.
Answer to "One of themselves." No. 759.

763. The Oral Law and its Defenders, a Review by a Scripturalist. 8vo., 51 pp. [A. N.] 1842.

764. B[ENJAMIN] E[LKIN]. — Rejected Letters. 8vo. 24 pp. London. 1842.
Contains letters and documents vindicating the Reform Movement which the Editor of the *Voice of Jacob* had declined to insert in his Journal.

I

765. ANON. [Benjamin Elkin].—Letters addressed to
the Editor of the "Voice of Jacob," being replies
to the observations contained in Nos. xxxvii. and
xxxix. of that publication. By the writer of the
preface to the lately published Mishna. 8vo., 29 pp.
London. [A. N.]   1843.

766. RABBI MOSHE ISRAEL HAZAN (Dayan of Jerusalem). דברי שלום ואמת, Words of Peace and Truth.
London.   1845.
    In Hebrew and English, On the Reform Secession.
Written and published during the author's temporary stay
in London "on a Mission from the Holy City." Reply
to an "Address to the Israelites of Great Britain," by a
Levite, published in No. 110 of the V. of J.

767. מקראי קדש, Holy Convocations. 41 pp., 8vo. (To
be had of M. H. Simonson, Manchester.) 1846 (?).
    "Illustrates astro-geographically the reasons the ancient
Rabbins must have had in ordering the celebration of the
חוץ לארץ, (Second Day's Festivals) י"ט שני של גליות
founded on the varied expressions of Scripture."

768. The Appeal of the Congregation of the West London Synagogue of British Jews to their Brother-
Israelites throughout the United Kingdom. 8vo.,
27 pp.   1846.

769. ALBU, ISRAEL (from Berlin).—דבר בעתו. A Word
in due season relating to the Divine Service. 8vo.,
218 pp. London.   1853.

770. T. THEODORES. — The Rabbinical Law of Ex-
communication, considered in its bearing on the
case of the Margaret Street Congregation of British
Jews. Manchester. 8vo., 27 pp.   1854.
    [A lecture delivered at the Jews' School House, Man-
chester, on Jan. 29, 1854.]

771. JUSTITIA.—A Year at the Jews' Orphan Asylum,
being the Narrative or Statement read by the late
Headmaster to the Committee of Investigation,
Jan. 1857. Edited, with notes and an introduction
by Justitia. London.   1857.

772. "A Victim of Jewish Congregational Disunion" [Michael Henry].—A few Words on Jewish Congregational Union. 8vo., 20 pp. 1868.

773. Two Orthodox Members of the Jewish Community [B. Kisch and Numa Hartog.]—The Second Days of the Festivals. A Reply to a Sermon delivered by the Rev. the Chief Rabbi. London. [A.N.] 1868.

773a. WALTER JOSEPHS. 1874.

[Circular without title, dated November, 1874, advocating "the desirability, nay, the necessity of a modification in the Liturgy and Ritual of the Synagogue . . . on Talmudical principles." The circular, which is signed "Walter Josephs," asks "those who share these sentiments . . . to communicate with the undersigned." Privately circulated. Single 4to sheet printed on one side.]

774. DAVID NUÑEZ MARTIN. — The Desirability of Reforms in the Sephardi Congregation at Kingston, Jamaica. Kingston. 8vo. 1875.

775. ANON. [Assur H. Moses.] — Another Battle of Talking. 1875.

[Squib on the Debates on the Bayswater Enlargement Scheme.]

776. ANON.—The Jewish Prayer Book as it is and as it ought to be. With an introduction by "A Layman." 8vo. vii.-77 pp. Melbourne. 1876.

[Reprinted from the *Jewish World* with the object of inducing the Australian Jewish communities to revise the Prayer Book.]

777. A RESIDENT IN CANONBURY. — Is the Dalston Synagogue worthy of Support? 8 pp. London. 8vo. 1876.

[Attacks the scheme of the proposed Dalston Synagogue on the ground that it will not be situated in Dalston, and that it is calculated to injure the North London Synagogue.]

778. H. GUEDALLA.—Refutation of an anonymous article in the *Jewish World*, entitled "Secret History of Sir M. Montefiore's Mission to Morocco in 1863-4." 40 pp. 8vo. London. 1880.

779. H. GUEDALLA.—Observations on the Jewish Ritual of the Present Time. 15 pp. 8vo. London. 1885.

780. [ALFRED A. NEWMAN.]—A Chapter of Anglo-Jewish History. 47 pp. 8vo. London. 1886.
[Account of the proceedings of the Bevis Marks Synagogue Anti-Demolition League, of which the author was Chairman.]

780a. F. M. SEE.—An Advocacy for the change of the Hebrew as now used to the English Language, as a means of Prayer in the West London Synagogue. 8 pp. London.   1886.
[Privately printed.]

(G.) CONVERSIONISM.

[Up to 1840: chiefly biographies.]

785. Lettra scritta all' Hebrei da Rabbi Moisè Scialitti, Hebreo di Firenze, batizzato alli 14 di Giug. 1663, demostrando le raggione della sua Conversione esortandoli ad' Abracciate la Fede Christiana. A Letter written to the Jews by Rabbi Moses Scialitti, a Jew of Florence, baptised June 14, 1663, declaring the Reasons of his Conversion and exhorting them to embrace the Christian Faith. Italian and English. 39 pp., 4to.   1663.

786. PAUL TARCZALI.—Brevis Dissertatio de Vocatione Gentium et Conversione Judæorum . . . . Oxon. [A. N.]   1672.

787. JOHN JACOB [Convert].—The Jew turned Christian; or the Corner-stone, asserting Christ to be the Messiah. London. 4to.   1678-9.
[Translated into Dutch in 1682. Wolf iv. 815c.]

788. COMPEIGNE DE VEIL, M.A.—Catechismus Judæorum in disputatione et Dialogo Magister ac discipuli scriptus a Rabbi Abrahmo Jagel. 12mo., 58 pp. Hebrew and English. [A.N.]   1679.

789. EVE COHAN.—The Conversion and Persecutions of Eve Cohan now called Elizabeth Verboom, a person of Quality of the Jewish Religion, baptised Oct. 10, 1680, at St. Martin's in the Fields. 1680.

790. ISRAEL ISAAC.—Christ Jesus, the true Messiah, delineated in three Œconomics agreed on all sides. By I. I., formerly a Jew, but now a Christian. 8vo., 25 pp. [A. N.] 1682.

791. ALEXANDERSON.—A Declaration of the Christian Faith, with a Letter to those of his own nation from the Syriac. 1688.
[Republished in 1703.]

792. ASSEMBLY OF DIVINES, ENGLAND.—חנוך דת המשיח. היותר קצר לכנסת דרשני האי בריטניא הנכבדים. Catechesis religionis Christianæ brevior . . . in linguam sanctam Hebræam fideliter versa, operâ G. Geaman. 1689.

793. SHALOME BEN SHALOMOH.—A true Narrative of God's gracious dealings with the soul of Shalome b. Shalomoh, of the Circumcision after the flesh; as delivered to the Church of Christ assembled at their Meeting House, Rosemary Lane, Sept. 29th, 1699. 1699.
[A second edition in 1700.]

794. A Declaration of the Conversion of Solomon de Almanza, a Spanish Gentleman, with his Two Children and Nephew, from Judaism to the Protestant Religion. Drawn up by himself in Spanish, and by his order translated into English. 8vo., 16 pp. Price 2d. [A. N.] 1703.

795. JOHN XERES.—An Address to the Jews, containing His Reasons for leaving the Jewish, and embracing the Christian Religion. 8vo., 115 pp. [A. N.] 1710.

796. GEORGE HICKES, D.D.—Peculium Dei. A Discourse about the Jews as the Peculiar People of

God, in a Sermon preached before the Aldermen
and Citizens of London, on the sixth of February,
1681.   1713.

797. MOSES MARCUS.—The Principal Motives and Circumstances that induced M. M. to leave the Jewish,
and embrace the Christian Faith; with a short
account of his Sufferings thereupon. 8vo., 126 pp.
Price 2s. [A. N.]   1724.
[With recommendation from D. Wilkins, Chaplain to
Archbishop of Canterbury.]

798. JOSEPH OTTOLENGHI.—An Answer to Two Papers
lately published by Gabriel Treves, a Jew of the
City of Exeter. The one enittled A Vindication
of the Proceedings of Gabriel Treves against Joseph
Solomon Ottolenghi, now a Prisoner in Southgate,
Exon.: the other is intituled An Advertisement,
wherein is contained the said Joseph Ottolenghi's
Vindication of himself, against the Aspersions cast
on him in the said Papers. 8vo. iv. and 32 pp.
[A.N.]   1735.

799. L. STEPHENS.—Discourse Preach'd before the Inhabitants of the Parish of St. Patrick, in Exeter, on
Sunday, the 6th of July, 1735: Occasioned by their
delivering Joseph Ottolenghi, a Poor Convert Jew,
out of South-gate Prison; into which he was cast
by a Jew, after his Conversion to Christianity.
4to., 42 pp. Price One Shilling. [A.N.] Exeter.

800. D. ABOAB.—ספר חסד ואמת. The Mercy and Truth;
or a brief account of the dealings of God with
D. A., a native of Venice, converted from . . . .
Judaism to the Gospel.   1748.

801. DAVID ABOAB.—A Short, Plain, and Well-grounded
Introduction to Christianity. . . . . Published first
at Venice in Arabic and Italian, in order to be dispersed among the Neighbouring Mahometans and
Jews. Translated into English by D. A. 8vo., 30
pp. [A. N.]
[Pp. 25-30 Religious poems.]

802. E. GOLDNEY.—A Friendly Epistle to the Jews
. . . . humbly dedicated to the Archbishop of Canterbury. 8vo., 176 pp. [A. N.] 1761.

803. DANIEL TRINGHAM ALEXANDER.—A Call to the
Jews; setting forth in what surprising manner he
was converted to Christianity. 4to. 1770.

804. B. BEN MORDECAI.—The Apology of, to his
Friends for embracing Christianity in seven Letters
to Elisha Levi, Merchant, of Amsterdam. 4to.,
205 and 187 pp. [A. N.] 1771.

805. The Conversion of Jonathan the Jew as related by
himself; designed as a Familiar Illustration of the
Nature of Christianity. [A. N.] 1779.

806. The New Testament in Hebrew, corrected by
Richard Caddick. 1798.

808. L. MAYER.—Restoration of the Jews, containing
an Explanation of the Prophecies. . . . Addressed
to the Jews. The Third Edition, with Additions.
8vo., 24 pp. [A. N.] Price Sixpence. 1806.

809. JOHN EVANS.—An Address . . . . upon the Baptism, by Immersion of Mr. Isaac Littleton, one of
the Israelitish Nation, on his Profession of Christianity, to which is added an Account of his Conversion. 8vo., 34 pp. Price One Shilling. [A. N.]
1808.

810. J. S. C. F. FREY.—His Narrative, with an Address
to Christians of all Denominations in behalf of the
Descendants of Abraham. 1813.
[" His Narrative " alone first appeared in 1809.]

811. HYAM ISAACS.—A Solemn and Affectionate Address to the Jews, clearly demonstrating . . . . that
Jesus . . . . is the only and true Messiah. Exeter.
1820.
[Went into three other editions, 1825, 1835, 1835. An
eighteenth edition in 1840.]

812. The Claims of the Children of Aaron on the immediate attention of the whole Christian World. Dublin. 4to. 1822.

813. JOHN HATCHARD.—A Sermon preached on Wednesday, June 22nd, 1825, on the Baptism of Mr. Michael Solomon Alexander, late Reader in the Jewish Synagogue, with an Appendix. 8vo., 40 pp. Price 1s. 6d. [A. N.] 1825.

814. H. H. NORRIS.—The Origin, Progress, and Existing Circumstances of the London Society for Promoting Christianity among the Jews. 8vo. 1825.

815. ABRAHAM ELIAS CAISSON.—An Affectionate Appeal to the Sons of Israel, the chosen Nation, by one of their Brethren, addressed to Mr. Joseph Wolff and other lost sheep of the House of Israel, who believe Jesus to be the Messiah. 8vo., 12 pp. [A. N.] 1827.

816. The History and Conversion of the Jewish Boy, by the author of the "Twin Sisters," &c. 8vo., 127 pp. [A. N.] 1829.

817. REV. A. McCAUL.—Israel Avenged by Don Isaac Orobio; translated and answered by Rev. A. McC., T.C.D. Part First. 198 pp. [A. N.] 1839.

(H.) BIOGRAPHIES.

821. L. ALEXANDER.—Memoirs of the Life and Commercial Connections of the late B. Goldsmid, of Roehampton; containing a Cursory View of the Jewish Society and Manners. 1808.

822. D. MENDOZA. — Memoirs of the Life of Daniel Mendoza . . . to which are added Observations on the Art of Pugilism. 8vo., xxiii.-320 pp. [A. N.] 1810.

[A second edition in 1816.]

823. R. HUMPHREYS (Edited by).—The Memoirs of J. de Castro, Comedian. Portrait. London. 8vo., 279 pp. 1824.

824. Memoirs of the Life and Writings of David Ricardo, Esq., M.P. 8vo., 32 pp. [A. N.] 1825.

825. M. LISSACK (of Bedford).—Jewish Perseverance; or, the Jew at Home and Abroad. Bedford and London. 1850.
[An Autobiography.]

826. GODFREY ZIMMERMAN.—Autobiography of Godfrey Zimmerman, formerly in the Commissariat Department of the Army under Napoleon. 8vo., 126 pp. London. 1852.

827. HIRSCH EDELMANN.—כולל קורות · · · גדולת שאול
הרב מ' שאול וואהל · · · עם תוספות. Biography of . . . S. Wahl . . . containing also a genealogical and chronological sketch, &c. [Partly translated by M. H. Bresslau.] 8vo. 1854.

828. J. G.—Sir Moses Montefiore, Bart., F.R.S., and his many efforts for the relief of suffering humanity. 8vo. 1864.

829. REV. DR. ABRAHAM DE SOLA.—Biography of David Aaron de Sola, late Senior Minister of the Portuguese Jewish community in London. 61 pp. Philadelphia. 1864.

829a. M. N. ADLER, M.A.—Memoir of the late Benjamin Gompertz, F.R.S., F.R.A.S. [1865.]
[Extracted from *Assurance Magazine*.]

830. [SAMUEL VALLENTINE.]—Memoir of Isaac Vallentine. 1868.
[In P. Vallentine's Hebrew and English Almanack for 5629-30.]

831. Memoir of Maurice Alexander Alexander, Sydney. 1874.

832. DR. L. LOEWE.—תולדות הרב החכם הגדול מו' אליעזר הלוי. Lyck. 12mo., 41 pp. 1878.

833. REV. PROF. MARKS and REV. A. LÖWY.—Memoir
of Sir Francis Henry Goldsmid, Bart., Q.C., M.P.
8vo.; second edition, xiv.-273 pp. Portrait. Lond.
1879.

[The work is divided into two parts, the first, by Prof.
Marks, being a general biography, and the second, by the
Rev. A. Löwy, dealing with Sir Francis' career in connec-
tion with the Anglo-Jewish Association. Among the
Appendices to the first edition is a letter from David
Ricardo, M.P., in which it is claimed that the principle of
toleration should be extended as much to the Atheist as the
Jew. This is omitted from the second edition, presumably
because of the Bradlaugh controversy which was then
raging.]

834. JOSEPH ELLIS.—Mr. Cohen. 8vo., 41 pp. 1881.

[Extract from the *Brighton Guardian*, Nov. 28th, 1860.
Biography of Emanuel Hyman Cohen, founder of the
Brighton Guardian.]

835. J. KOHN ZEDEK.—נוה תהלה. Lemberg. .8vo., 18
+ 23 + 69 + 80 + 55. Portrait.

836. SOLOMON HART.—Memoirs. 1882.
[Privately printed.]

837. ISRAEL DAVIS.—Sir Moses Montefiore, a Biographical Sketch. 8vo., 35 pp. Portrait. 1883.
[Reprinted from the *Times* with additions.]

838. LEONE RACAH.—Sir Moses Montefiore, Biografia
di un Centenario. 16mo., 101 pp. Leghorn.
1883.

839. LUCIEN WOLF.—Sir Moses Montefiore. A Centennial Biography, with Extracts from Letters and
Journals. 8vo., xv.-290 pp. Portrait. 1884.

Published on the occasion of the Centenary. American
editions: 4to., 63 pp. With portrait. (New York, 1884.)
8vo. (illustrated), xiv.-254 pp. (New York, 1884).

840. ANON.—A Sketch of the Life and Work of Sir
Moses Montefiore, compiled from various authentic
sources. Illustrated. 8vo., 27 pp. Ramsgate. 1884.

841. JAMES WESTON.—Sir Moses Montefiore; the Story
of his Life. 8vo., 96 pp. 1885.

[See *Athenæum*, March 14, 21, and 28; and April 11, 1885.]

MISCELLANEA BIOGRAPHICA.

Cat.—ANGLO-JEWISH HISTORICAL EXHIBITION CATALOGUE.
J. C.—JEWISH CHRONICLE.
J. R.—JEWISH RECORD.
J. W.—JEWISH WORLD.

843. AARON, BARNEY, Pugilist. 1800-1859.
Egan, "Boxiana" (Portrait : Rogers, sculp.) : "Pugilistica": Cat., p. 62.
AARON, RABBI. *See* LEVY.

844. ABENDANA, ISAAC, Teacher and Author. D. circa 1710.
Wolf, "Bibliotheca Hebræa," i. 627 ; iii. 539 : Carmoly, "Médicins Juifs" : *J. W.*, Dec. 5, 12, and 26, 1879

845. ABENDANA, JACOB, Chacham, 1630-1686.
Wolf, "Bibliotheca Hebræa," i. 579 : Kayserling, "Analekten," &c. (Frankel's "Monatschrift," ix. p. 29): Schröder, "Hamburger Schriftsteller": *J. W.*, Dec. 5, 12, and 26, 1879: Chalmers, "Biog. Dict.," i. 54 : Didot, "Nouv. Biog. Gen.," i. 114 : Rose, "Biog. Dict.," i. 49.
ABOLAFIAH. *See* BOLOFFEY.

846. ABRAHAM, ABRAHAM, Sheriff of Southampton. 1798-1887.
Southampton Times, April 6, 1887.
Hampshire Independent, April 6, 1887.

847. ABRAHAM, ABRAHAM, Author and Communal Worker. D. 1863. *J. C.*, Apr. 10, 1863.

848. ABRAHAM, HENRY, Mayor of Southampton, 1824-1881.
Southern Reformer (Portrait), Aug. 21, 1886.

849. ABRAHAM, J., Mayor of Bristol. D. 1867.
J. C., Feb. 3, 1867.

850. ABRAHAM, SAMUEL, Merchant at Mottancheree (India). Circa 1772.
Forbes, "Oriental Memoirs."

851. ABRAHAMS, ABRAHAM, Writer on Schechita. 1801-1880.
J. C. and *J. W.*, Feb. 13, 1880. Autobiography in זכור לאברהם.

852. ABRAHAMS, BARNETT, Dayan. 1831-1863.
J. C., Nov. 20, 1863.

853. ABRAMS, HARRIET, Musician. B. 1760.
Brown, "Dictionary of Musicians."
ABUDIENTE. *See* GIDEON.

855. AELYON, SOLOMON, Chacham. 1667-1728.
Wolf, "Bibliotheca Hebræa," iii. 1016 : Graetz, "Geschichte der Juden," x., note 6 : Cat., p. 48 (Portrait : J. Houbraken, sc.)

856. AGA, ISMAEL, Noted Beggar and Character. Circa 1812.
Evans, Catalogue of Prints (Portrait : pub., R. Wilkins, 1812.)

857. AGUILAR, EPHRAIM LOPEZ PEREIRA, BARON D', Eccentric and Miser. 1739-1802.
Wilson, "Wonderful Characters," ii. 92-97 (Portrait : Page, sc.) : Cat., p. 51.

859. AGUILAR, GRACE, Novelist. 1816 1847.
Mrs. S. C. Hall, *Art Journal*, May, 1851 : "Dictionary of National Biography": Kayserling, "Judischen Frauen," pp. 278-284 : Memoir by Sarah Aguilar, prefixed to "Home Influence," 1849.

860. AGUILAR, MOSES (DIEGO) LOPEZ PEREIRA, BARON D', Financier and Ex-treasurer to Maria Theresa of Austria. 1700-1759.
L. A. Frankl, *Zeitung des Judenthums*, 1854, p. 657 : Graetz, "Geschichte der Juden," x. pp. 392, 393, 394.

862. ALEX, EPHRAIM, Founder of Board of Guardians. 1800-1882.
J. C. and *J. W.*, Nov. 17, 1882.

863. ALEXANDER, A., Hebraist and Printer. Circa 1770.
Steinschneider, "Biblio. Bodl."

864. ALEXANDER, LEVY, Author and Printer. 1754-1853.
Steinschneider, "Biblio. Bodl."

865. ALEXANDER, MAURICE ALEXANDER, Australian Politician. 1820-1874.
Memoir (*see* No. 831) : *Town and Country Journal*: Heaton, "Australian Dict. of Dates."

866. ALEXANDER, MICHAEL SOLOMON, Bishop of Jerusalem ; 1799-1845.
"Dict. Nat. Biog."

867. ALEXANDER, WILLIAM W., Alderman at Bristol. D. 1874.
J. C., Aug. 28, 1874.

868. ALMEIDA, JOSEPH D', Stockbroker. 1716-1788.
(Portrait : Lauranson pinx., Jones sc., 1783).

869. ALMEIDA, MANUELA NUÑEZ D', Poetess. Circa 1720.
Kayserling, "Jüdischen Frauen," p. 174.

870. ALMOSNINO, HASDAI, Ab Beth Din. D. 1802.
Carmoly, "La Famille Almosnino," p. 27.

871. ALMOSNINO, ISAAC, Chief Rabbi of Gibraltar. D. 1785.
Carmoly, "La Famille Almosnino," pp. 26-27 ; Picciotto, "Anglo-Jewish History," pp. 191 and 193.

872. ALMOSNINO, ISAAC, Chazan. D. 1843.
Carmoly, "La Famille Almosnino," p. 27.

873. ALMOSNINO, SOLOMON, Secretary to Bevis Marks Synagogue, 1792-1878.
    J. C. and *J. W.*, January 18, 1878.

878. ARTOM, BENJAMIN, Chacham. 1835-1879.
    J. C. and *J. W.*, Jan. 10, 1879; *Times*, Jan. 7, 1879.
    Portraits and Memoirs in *Graphic* and *Pictorial World*, Jan. 18, 1879.

    ARYEH, JACOB JEHUDAH. *See* TEMPLO.

879. ASCHER, JOSEPH, Musical Composer. 1830-1869.
    J. R., June 25, 1869 : Brown, " Dict. of Musicians."

880. ASCHER, SIMON, Chazan. 1789-1872.
    J. C., Dec. 6 and 13, 1872.

881. ASHENHEIM, LOUIS, Physician and Surgeon. 1817-1858.
    J. C., Dec. 3 and 10, 1858 : *Falmouth (Jamaica) Advertiser*, Oct. 1858 : *Falmouth Post*, Oct. 1858.

882. ASHENHEIM, MICHAEL, Journalist and Musician. 1824-1851.
    J. C., Nov. 31, 1851.

883. ASHER, EDWARD L., Engineer. 1838-1874.
    Allen's Indian Mail : J. C., June 12, 1874.

884. AZEVEDO, MOSES COHEN D', Chacham. D. 1785.
    Cat., p. 50.

885. AZULAY, ISAAC LEONINI, M.A., Tutor of Princess Royal of Prussia. D. 1840.
    J. W. ("Among the Tombs"), Nov. 5, 1880.

886. BAPUGEE, EZEKIEL, Major in Indian Native Army. D. 1878.
    Cat., p. 46.

887. BARLIN, FREDERICK BENJAMIN, Portrait Painter. D. circa 1803.
    Cat., p. 55.

888. BARNETT, A. L., Dayan. 1797-1878.
    J. C. and *J. W.*, Feb. 15, 1878.

890. BARNETT, JACOB, Hebrew Teacher. Circa 1613.
    Pattison, "Life of Isaac Casaubon," pp. 413-416.

891. BARNETT, MORRIS, Dramatist and Actor. 1800-1850.
    "Dict. Nat. Biog.," iv. 260.

892. BARUH, RAPHAEL, Author. D. 1800.
    Lysons, "Environs of London," iii. Supp. pp. 303 and 441.

893. BASEVI, JOSHUA (GEORGE), Architect. 1794-1845.
    "Dict. Nat. Biog."

895. BEDDINGTON, EDWARD H., Communal Worker. 1819-1872.
    J. C., Nov. 1, 8, and 15, 1872.

126   BIBLIOTHECA ANGLO-JUDAICA.

896. BELAIS, ABRAHAM, Hebrew Author. D. 1853.
    J. C., Sept. 2, 1853.
897. BELASCO, ABY, Pugilist. B. 1797.
    "Boxiana" : "Pugilistica" (Portrait: Sharpello, pinx. ;
    Cooper, sculp.)
898. BELINFANTE, SIMON, Australian Physician and Lawyer. D.
    1874.
    Heaton, "Australian Dict. of Dates."
899. BELISARIO, ISAAC MENDES, Preacher. D. 1791.
    Lysons, " Environs of London," iii. p. 479.
900. BELMONTE, BIENVENIDA COHEN, Poetess. Circa 1720.
    Kayserling, "Jüdischen Frauen," p. 174.
901. BELMONTE, JACOB ABRAHAM DE. *See* SCHONENBERG.
902. BENEDICT, SIR JULIUS, Composer and Musician. 1804-
    1883.
    "Dict. Nat. Biog."
903. BENISCH, ABRAHAM, Theologian and Journalist. 1811-1878.
    " Dict. Nat. Biog."
904. BENJAMIN, JOSEPH ISRAEL, Traveller. D. 1864.
    J. C., May 13, 1864.
905. BENJAMIN, JUDAH PETER, Statesman and Lawyer. 1812-
    1884.
    "Dict. Nat. Biog. ": Appleton, "Cycl. Amer. Biog." :
    Drake, "Dict. Nat. Biog." : Cat., p. 66 (Portrait :
    Piercy, pinx., —— sc.) : *J. C.* and *J. W.*, May 9, 1884,
    and *J. W.*, May 16.
906. BENJAMIN, MICHAEL HENRY, Cape Politician. 1822-1879.
    Cape Argus, July 10, 1879 : *J. C.*, June 13, 1879, and
    Aug. 15, 1879 : *J. W.*, June 13, 1879.
907. BENMOHEL, NATHAN LAZARUS, first conforming Jew who
    obtained degree in an English University. 1800-1869.
    Cat., pp. 22, 33, and 62.
908. BENNETT, SOLOMON, Hebraist. Circa 1815.
    (Portrait ; Engraved by himself after Frazer, frontispiece
    to " Temple of Ezekiel," by S. B.)
909. BENOLIEL, JUDAH, Banker and Moorish Consul at Gibral-
    tar. D. 1839.
    Anglo-Jewish Association Report, 1877-78, pp. 113-114.
910. BERLIN, SAUL, Hebrew Author. D. 1794.
    Orient (Literaturblatt), 1844, p. 714 : Landeshut, " Ber-
    liner Rabbinen " : Carmoly, *Revue*, p. 249.
911. BERNAL, RALPH, Politician and Art Collector. D. 1854.
    Bagenal, "Life of R. Bernal Osborne," *Gentleman's
    Magazine*, 1823, Part ii., 92 ; 1854, Part iii., 628 : "Re-
    turn of Members of Parliament" : Piccioto, "Anglo-

Jewish History," 157-8 : Cole, "Biography" (1885),
i. 289-91 : "Dict. Nat. Biog.," ix. 373 (Portrait:
Wivell, pinx. ; Thomson, sc., 1822).

912. BETH-HILLEL, DAVID D', Beni Israel Traveller and Author.
Circa 1832.
Cat., p. 47.

913. BLAND, MARIA THERESA, Actress. 1769-1810.
"Thespian Dictionary " : "British Theatrical Gallery "
Cat., p. 56. (Portrait : Conde, sculp.).

914. BLUMENFELD, J. C., Poet. Circa 1839.
Graetz, "Geschichte," xi., pp. 468-470.

BLUMENTHAL. See SCOTT.

915. BOLAFFEY, HANANIAH, Hebraist and Author. B. 1779.
" Biography of D. A. de Sola," (see No. 829), p. 16.

916. BORTHWICK, FRANCIS, Convert to Judaism. Circa 1681.
Cobbett, " State Trials," xiii., p. 939.

917. BOYNO, [? EPHRAIM BUENO], Physician. Circa 1660.
De Castro, " Auswahl von Grabsteinen," Part I. (Portrait : Lyryrus, sculp.).

918. BRAHAM, JOHN, Composer and Singer. 1774-1856.
"Dict. Nat. Biog." : London Chronicle, July 7, 1787 :
Cat., p. 57 (Portrait : Wood, pinx., Cardon, sculp.).

919. BRESLAU, MARCUS HEYMANN, Author and Journalist.
D. 1864.
J. C., May 20, 1864.

BRIL. See LEEP-BRIL.

920. BUZAGLO, ABRAHAM, Inventor. D. 1788.
Lyson's " Environs of London," iii., p. 479.

922. CARDOSO, AARON, Diplomatist. Circa 1805.
" Anglo-Jewish Association Report," 1877-78, p. 113.

923. CARVAJAL, ANTONIO FERNANDES DE, Financier. D. 1659.
Wolf : Re-settlement of the Jews in England (see
No. 239).

924. CASTELLO, DANIEL, Communal worker. 1831-1833.
J. C. and J. W., August 10, 1883.

925. CASTRO, HANANEL DE, Communal worker. 1796-1849.
J. C., March 30, 1849. Reprinted in "The Voice of
Lament," London, 1849 : Cat., p. 58.

926. CASTRO, JACOB DE, Comedian. B. 1758.
Memoirs, edited by R. Humphreys (see No. 823.) (Portrait : Stanfield, pinx. ; Sherwood, pub.)

927. CHAMBERLAIN, COMMODORE. Circa 1700.
Picciotto, "Anglo-Jewish History," p. 54.

928. CHARLEMONT, COUNTESS, Proselyte. D. 1882.
J. C., June 9, 1882.

929. COHEN, ANDREW.
     (Portrait "Coffee's the Thing! Go it, ye Tigers," drawn,
     etched, and published by R. Deighton, 1823.)

930. COHEN, EDWARD, Australian Statesman.   1822-1877.
     Heaton, "Australian Dict. of Dates" : *J. C.*, Jan. 14,
     1870, and April 27, 1877 : *J.R.*, Jan. 13, 1871.
     COHEN, FRANCIS. *See* PALGRAVE.

932. COHEN, ISAAC, Communal Worker.   D. 1845.
     J. C., Jan. 23, 1846.

933. COHEN, LEVY BARENT, Communal Worker.   B. 1740.
     Cat., p. 51 (Portrait : Drawn, etched, and published by
     R. Deighton, 1817, reissued 1824).

934. COHEN, LEVY EMANUEL, Journalist.   1796-1860.
     Memoir by J. Ellis (*see* No. 834) : *J. C.*, Nov. 17, 1860
     (Portrait : Leahy, pinx. ; Vernon, sc., 1863.)

935. COHEN, LIONEL LOUIS, Communal Worker, Financier, and
     Politician.   1832-1837.
     J. C. and *J. W.*, July 1, 1887 : *Times*, June 29, 1887 :
     The Craftsman, Oct. 1885 (Portrait).

936. COHEN, LOUIS LOUIS, Communal Worker.   1799-1882.
     J. C. and *J. W.*, March 17, 1882 : Cat., p. 61.

937. COHEN, NATHAN, Journalist.   D. 1873.
     Brighton Guardian, 1873.

938. COHEN DE LISSA, J., Journalist.   D. 1879.
     J. C., July 25, 1879.

939. CORONEL, SIR AUGUSTINE, Merchant and Portuguese Agent.
     Circa 1660.
     Wolf : Re-settlement of the Jews in England (*see*
     No. 239.)

940. CORREA, A. A., Philanthropist.   D. 1846.
     J. C., Dec. 11, 1846.

941. CORTISSOS, JOSEPH, Army Contractor.   1656-1742.
     "Statement of the case of C. J. Cortissos," &c. : Cat.,
     p. 48.

942. COSTA, BENJAMIN MENDEZ DA, Philanthropist.   1704-1764.
     Picciotto, "Anglo-Jewish History," pp. 89, 95, 155.

943. COSTA, EMANUEL MENDEZ DA, F.R.S., Scientific Writer.
     1717-1791.
     Nichols, "Literary Anecdotes."

944. COSTA, SOLOMON DA, Donor of Hebrew Library to British
     Museum.   Circa 1760.
     Zedner, "Catalogue of the Hebrew Books in the British
     Museum" (preface), *J. C.*, Dec. 2, 1859.

945. CRASTO, ISRAEL DAVID DE, Dayan. D. 1785.
Picciotto, " Anglo-Jewish History," p. 193.

946. CROOL, JOSEPH, Teacher and Controversialist. Circa 1838.
J. C., June 30, 1848. (Quotation from *Cambridge Independent Press*, June 11, 1848.)

947. DAINOW, HIRSCH, Magid. 1832-1877.
J. C. and *J. W.*, March 9, 1877.

948. DAVID, AARON HART, Canadian Physician and Professor.
1812-1882.
J. W., Nov. 24, 1882.

949. DAVIDS, ARTHUR LUMLEY, Orientalist. 1811-1832.
Hebrew Review, i. pp. 145-152 : *Der Jude*, Jan. 11 and
22, 1833 : *Asiatic Journal*, Dec., 1832 : *Literary Gazette*,
July 16, 1832.

950. DAVIDSON, ELLIS A., Author and Technologist. 1828-
1878.
J. C. and *J. W.*, March 15, 1878.

951. DAVIS, ALFRED, Philanthropist. D. 1870.
J. C. and *J. R.*, Jan. 14, 1870.

953. DEUTSCH, EMANUEL OSCAR, Orientalist. 1829-1873.
Memoir in " Literary Remains " (London, 1874), by Lady
Strangford : *Times*, May 14, 1873 : *Athenæum*, May
17, 1873, by R. S. Poole : *Contemporary Review* (1873),
by H. R. Haweis.

DIAS. *See* FERNANDEZ.

954. D'ISRAELI, BENJAMIN, Merchant and Financier. 1730-1816.
Introduction to I. D'Israeli's Collected Works, 1858.

955. DISRAELI, BENJAMIN, EARL OF BEACONSFIELD, Statesman,
1805-1881.
Biogs. by G. Brandes, Cornelius Brown, J. McGilchrist,
P. W. Clayden, W. Crosbie, T. Macknight, A. Cuche-
val Clarigny, E. Drew, A. C. Ewald, T. J. Finkelhaus,
G. H. Francis, T. T. Hayes, F. Hitchman, F. A. Hynd-
man, P. Leclerc, Janetta Manners, J. Mill, T. P.
O'Connor, P. Valmont, &c.

956. D'ISRAELI, ISAAC, Author. 1766-1848.
Memoir prefixed to Collected Works, 1858.

958. DORMIDO, DAVID ABARBANEL, Pioneer of Anglo-Jewish
Community. D. 1667.
Wolf : " Re-settlement of the Jews in England " (see
No. 239).

959. DRACH, S. M., Orientalist, 1816-1879.
J. W., Feb. 14, 1879.

K

960. DYTE, D. M., Saved life of George III.   Circa 1800.
  Howell, "State Trials."

962. ELIAS, SAMUEL (Dutch Sam), Pugilist.   1775-1816.
  Egan, "Boxiana" (Portrait) : "Pugilistica": Cat., p. 57
  (Portrait: Fores, pub. 1819).

963. ELKIN, BENJAMIN, Prominent Reformer.   D. 1848.
  J. C., Jan. 1 and 14, 1848.

964. ELLIS, SIR BARROW HELBERT, Indian Statesman.   1823-
  1887.
  Times, J. C. and *J. W.*, June 24, 1887 : *J. W.*, July 1,
  1887 : *Voice of Jacob*, July 21, 1843.

965. ELLIS, EDMUND HELBERT, Ensign, Bombay Native Infantry,
  1829-1851.
  J. C., March 7 and April 4, 1851 : *Bengal Telegraph*,
  Jan. 22, 1851.

965. ELMALEH, JOSEPH DE A., Morocco merchant and Rabbi.
  D. 1886.
  J. C. and *J. W.*, Jan. 15, 1886.

966. ELZAS, ABRAHAM, Minister and Author.   D. 1880.
  Hull and Lincolnshire Times, August, 1880: *J. W.*,
  Aug. 6, 1880.

967. EMANUEL, EDWARD JANVERIN, Communal Worker, 1852-
  1885.
  J. C. and *J. W.*, Jan. 16, 1885.

969 EVANS, SAMUEL, "Young Dutch Sam," Pugilist, 1801-1843.
  Egan, "Boxiana" (Portrait : Rogers, sc.): Pugilistica."

970. EZEKIEL, EZEKIEL ABRAHAM, Engraver.   1757-1806.
  Trewman's Flying Post, Dec. 18, 1806 ; *Devonshire Freeholder*, July 12, 1822 ; Cat. p. 53.

971. EZEKIEL, SOLOMON, Author.   1781-1867.
  J. C., March 23, 1867.

972. FALK, HAIM SAMUEL DE, Baal Shem.   1710-1782.
  Alexander, "Memoirs of B. Goldsmid" (see No. 821) :
  Wolf: *Leisure Hour* (Portrait) July, 1886, p. 451: Archen-
  holz, "England und Italien," I. p. 249 : Von Gleichen,
  "Denkwürdigkeiten" : Scharffenstein, "Das Entlarvte
  Judenthum" : *J. C.*, Dec. 19, 1884: *J. W.*, Nov. 7,
  1873.

973. FAUDEL, HENRY, Emancipation worker.   D. 1863.
  J. C., Sept. 25, 1863; Oct. 2, 1863 ; Dec. 18, 1863.

974. FERDINAND, PHILIP, Hebraist.   1555-1589.
  Athenæ Cantab., ii. 209, and supplement.

975. FERNANDEZ, BENJAMIN DIAS, Author.   Circa 1720.
  Dias's Letters, Introduction: *Voice of Israel*, March 2,
  1846.

976. FILIPOWSKI, HERSCHELL, Hebraist and Mathematician. 1817-1872.
   Morais, "Eminent Israelites," pp. 71-74.

977. FRANKE, RICHARD, Mayor of Hull. 1610-1684.
   "Hull Celebrities" (see No. 223), pp. 118, 200-204.

978. FRANKL, ——, Artist. 1846-1876.
   J. C., Aug. 11, 1876.

979. FRANKLIN, ISAAC A., Surgeon. 1812-1880.
   J. C. and *J. W.*, Dec. 31, 1880.

980. FRANKLIN, JACOB ABRAHAM, Journalist and Philanthropist. 1809-1877.
   J. C., Aug. 10 and 17, 1877: *J. W.*, Aug. 10, 1877.

981. FRANKS, ISAAC, Colonel in the American Revolutionary Army and Aide-de-Camp to Washington. 1759-1822.
   Cat., p. 54.

982. FREUND, JONAS, Physician and Founder of the German Hospital. D. circa 1880.
   J. W., Dec. 3, 1886.

983. FREY, JOSEPH SAMUEL CHRISTIAN FREDERICK, Christian Missionary. 1773-1850.
   "Cyc. Amer. Biog."

984. FRIEDBERG, Physician.
   Carmoly, "Medicins Juifs."

985. FURTADO, JOHN, Musician. Circa 1798.
   Brown, "Dict. Mus."

986. GAMA, GASPAR DA, Traveller. Circa 1500.
   Jahrbuch für die Geschichte der Juden, &c., iii. 309: Kayserling, "Juden in Portugal," pp. 161-163 : Sternberg, "Juden in Polen," pp. 103-105.

988. GELDERN, SIMON VON, Traveller and Author.
   Memoirs of Heinrich Heine (English edit.), pp. 167-172.

989. GEMALIEL BEN PEDAZZUR, Hebraist. Circa 1738.
   Allg. Zeit. d. Jud., 1839 ; Lit. Beibl., n. 13, p. 50.

990. GIDEON, SAMPSON, Financier. 1699-1762.
   Francis, "Chronicles of the Stock Exchange," pp. 88-90: Picciotto, "Anglo-Jewish History," pp. 60-64, 84, 113 : Nichols's "Lit. Anec."

991. GOLDSMID, ABRAHAM, Financier and Philanthropist. 1756-1810.
   Gentleman's Mag., lxxx., pp. 382 *et seq.*: *European Mag.*, lviii., pp. 244-247 : *Morning Post*, Oct. 9, 1810 (Portrait : Medley, pinx. ; F. Bartolozzi, sculpt; View of Seat (Morden, Surrey), Gylford, delin. ; Hawkins, sculp.)

992. GOLDSMID, BENJAMIN, Financier and Philanthropist. 1755-1808.
   " Memoirs " by L. Alexander (*see* No. 821) : *Gentleman's Magazine*, lxxviii., pp. 373-457.

993. GOLDSMID, SIR FRANCIS. Philanthropist and Politician. 1808-1878.
   Life by Marks and Löwy (*see* No. 833) : *J. C.* and *J. W.*, May 10, 1878 : *Times*, May 4, 1878.

994. GOLDSMID, FREDERICK, Politician. 1811-1866.
   J. C., March 23, 1866.

995. GOLDSMID, SIR ISAAC LYON, Financier and Philanthropist. 1778-1859.
   Bankers' Magazine, xix., pp. 375, 449 ; xx., p. 220 : *J. C.*, May 6 and June 17, 1859 : *J. W.*, March 5, 1878.

996. GOLDSMITH, LEWIS, Journalist and Author. 1763-1846.
   Didot, " Biog. Gen.": Rose, " Biog. Dict." : Quérard, "La France Littéraire."

997. GOMPERTZ, BENJAMIN, Actuary and Mathematician. 1779-1865.
   "Memoir " by M. N. Adler (*see* No. 829 a).

998. GOODMAN, TOBIAS, Preacher and Author. Circa 1819.
   J. W., Oct. 31, 1879.

999. GORDON, LORD GEORGE, Convert to Judaism. 1750-1793.
   Life by Robert Watson, 1795.

1000. GREEN, AARON LEVY, Minister and Preacher. 1821-1883.
   J. C. and *J. W.*, March 16, 1883.

1001. GUEDALLA, JUDAH, Eminent Morocco merchant. 1760-1858.
   J. C., June 18, 1858.

1002. HALIVA, REV. ABRAHAM, Dayan. D. 1853.
   J. C., Aug. 5, 1853.

1003. HARRIS, HERBERT WORMSER. 1858-1880.
   J. C. and *J. W.*, May 7, 1880.

1004. HART, AARON, Chief Rabbi. 1670-1756.
   Wolf, " Bibliotheca Hebræa," iii. 921 : Cat., p. 49 (Portrait : Dandridge, pinx. ; McArdell, sculp.)

1005. HART, EZEKIEL, Canadian Politician. 1771-1844.
   Voice of Jacob, Feb. 2, 1844.

1006. HART, HENRY JOHN, Australian Magistrate. 1820-1884.
   J. W., June 20, 1884.

1007. HART, MOSES, Founder of Duke's Place Synagogue. D. 1756.
   Picciotti, "Anglo-Jewish History," p. 133 : Cat., p. 49.

1008. HART, SOLOMON ALEXANDER, R.A., Artist. 1806-1881.
    J. C. and *J. W.*, June, 1881 : *Times,* June 13, 1881.
    Memoirs (privately printed). (*See* No. 836).
1009. HARTOG, NUMA, Senior Wrangler. 1846-1871.
    J. R., Feb. 5, 1869 : *J. C.* and *J. R.,* June 23, 1871 :
    Morais, "Eminent Israelites," pp. 119-122.
1010. HENRIQUES, AMOS, Physician. 1812-1880.
    J. C., June 18, 1880.
1012. HENRIQUES, JACOB, Financier. B. 1683.
    J. C., Oct. 11, 1867 : *British Magazine,* 1764.
1013. HENRY, EMMA, Poetess. 1788-1870.
    J. C., Jan. 6. 1871.
1014. HENRY, HENRY A., Minister and Hebraist. 1800-1879.
    J. W., Sept. 26, 1879 : *J. C.,* Oct. 3, 1879.
1015. HENRY, MICHAEL, Journalist and Mechanician. 1830-1875.
    J. C., June 25, 1875 : Memoir prefixed to "Life
    Thoughts," *Jews' College Journal,* June, 1875 : Morais,
    "Eminent Israelites," 139-132.
1016. HERRERA, ALONZO DE, Cabalistic Writer. 1570-1631.
    De Barrios, "Historia Universal Judayca," p. 20 :
    Graetz, "Geschichte der Juden," ix. 494
1018. HERSCHELL, SOLOMON, Chief Rabbi. 1762-1842.
    European Magazine (by Van Oven), reprinted in *J. C.,*
    Feb. 10, 1860 : *Voice of Jacob,* Nov. 11, 1842 : Morais,
    ' Eminent Israelites," pp. 142-144 : Landschudt,
    "Berliner Rabbinen "; *J. W..* (pedigree), Jan. 16, 1885.
    (Portrait : Barlin, pinx.; Holl, sc.)
1019. HIRSCH, ZEVI. *See* LYON, HART.
1020. HURWITZ, HYMAN, Professor of Hebrew and Author. 1770-
    1844.
    Voice of Jacob, Aug. 2, 1844.
1021. ISAAC, ——, Dancing Master. Circa 1730.
    Grainger's "Biog. Hist." (cont. by Noble), iii. 426.
    (Portrait : Goupy, pinx.; White, sc.)
1022. ISAAC, SAMUEL, "The Mersey Lesseps." 1812-1886.
    Times, Nov. 23, 1886. *J. C.* and *J. W.,* Nov. 26, 1886.
1024. ISAACS, DAVID MYER, Minister and Professor of Hebrew.
    1810-1879.
    J. C. and *J. W.,* May 9, 1879.
1025. ISAACS, NATHANIEL, African Traveller.
    Isaac, "Travels in Eastern Africa," 1836.
1026. ISAACS, REBECCA, Singer. 1828-1877.
    J. C., March 2, 1849 ; and Aug. 24, 1849.
1027. ISAACS, SAMUEL MYER, Minister and Journalist. 1804-1878.
    Morais, "Eminent Israelites," pp. 153-157 : *Jewish Mes-
    senger* (New York) : *J. C.,* June 7, 1878.

1028. ISAACSON, JOSEPH J., Naturalist. 1803-1879.
    J. C. and *J. W.*, May 23, 1879.

1029. ISRAEL, ELLAJEE DAWOODJEE, Major in Indian Native
    Army. Circa 1829.
    Cat., p. 45.

1030. ISRAEL, EZEKIEL BABUJEE, Major in Indian Native Army.
    Circa 1862.
    Cat., p. 44.
    ISRAEL, MENASSEH B. *See* MENASSEH.

    ISRAEL, SAMUEL B. *See* SOEIRO.

1031. JACKSON, HARRY, Actor. D. 1885.
    Era, Aug. 22, 1885 : *J. C.* and *J. W.*, Aug. 21, 1885.

1032. JACOBS THE WIZARD, Prestidigitateur. D. 1870.
    J. R., Nov. 18, 1870.

1033. JACOBS, BETHEL, Communal worker at Hull. D. 1869.
    J. C., Jan. 7, 1870.

1034. JACOBS, JOSEPH LYON, Communal worker at Hull. 1836-
    1883.
    J. C. and *J. W.*, Dec. 21, 1883 : *Eastern Morning
    News*, Dec., 1883.

1034*a*. JACOBS, Miss, Actress, and pupil of Mr. Crouch. Circa
    1792.
    " Thespian Dict."

1035. JACOBS, SIMEON, C.M.G., Judge in Supreme Court at Cape
    of Good Hope. 1832-1883.
    Zingari, March 14, 1873 : *Cape Argus*, July, 1883 : *J. C.*
    and *J. W.*, June 22, 1883.

1036. JAFFÉ, DANIEL JOSEPH, Manufacturer. D. 1874.
    Belfast newspapers, Jan. 21, 1874.

1037. JEREMIE, —, Physician.
    Carmoly, " Medicins Juifs," pp. 229-230.

1038. JESSEL, RIGHT HON. SIR GEORGE, Master of the Rolls.
    1824-1883.
    Times, March 22, 1883 (and other newspapers of the
    same date) : *J. C.* and *J. W.*, March 23, 1883, and
    J. W., March 30, 1883 : Peter, " Decisions of Sir G. J."

1039. JOHNSON, JOHN MORRIS, Printer. 1803-1880.
    J. C., April 16, 1880.

1040. JOSEPH, ELIJAH, Chazan at Bombay. D. 1871.
    Cat., p. 46.

1041. JOSEPHS, MICHAEL, Hebraist. 1763-1849.
    J. C., Feb. 16, 1849 : Morais, " Eminent Israelites," pp.
    165-167.

1042. KALISCH, MARCUS, Hebraist and Bible Commentator. 1828-1885.
Times, Aug. 31, 1885 : Athenæum, Sept. 5, 1885 : J. C. and J. W., Aug. 28, 1885 : Jewish Herald (Melbourne), Oct. 16, 1885 : Morais " Eminent Israelites," pp. 170-173.

1043. KEELING, HENRY L., Philanthropist. 1805-1180.
J. C., May 14 and June 4, 1880 : Grocer, Feb. 22 and March 1, 1862.

1044. KHARCELKHAR, SAMUEL EZEKIEL, Soldier in Indian Native Army, and distinguished at siege of Seringapatam. Circa 1799.
Cat., p. 45.

1045. KIMHI, JACOB, Hebraist and Pedler. 1739-1820.
Azulai שהג s. v. מהר״י שמואל קמחי: Cat., p. 54 : Leisure Hour, Aug., 1886 (Portrait: Humphreys, pinx.; Singleton, sculp., 1799 ; Butterworth, sculp., 1886).

1046. KING, JOHN, Author. D. 1824.
Picciotto, " Anglo-Jewish History," pp. 302-3.

1047. LAGUNA, DANIEL ISRAEL, Hebraist and Poet. 1660-1720.
Kayserling, " Sephardim," p. 297 et seq. : De los Rios, " Estudios," p. 626 : Graetz, " Geschichte," x. 329.

1048. LAMEGO, MOSES, Philanthropist. D. 1768.
Ascamot of Portuguese Congregation, p. 95.

1049. LANDESHUT, SAMUEL, Secretary Board of Guardians. 1825-1877.
J. C., Nov. 30, 1877.

1050. LARA, MOSES NUÑES, Philanthropist. Circa 1827.
" Ascamot of Portuguese Congregation," p. 100.

1051. LARA, Mrs., Philanthropist, 1780-1859.
J. C., Dec. 9, 1859.

1052. LAWRENCE, J. ZACHARIAH, Surgeon. 1828-1870.
J. C., July 22, 1870.

1053. LAWSON, LIONEL, Newspaper Proprietor. 1823-1879.
Daily Telegraph, Sept. 22, 1879.

1054. LEEP-BRIL, JUDAH ZEKIAH, Hebrew Journalist and Traveller. 1835-1886.
Times, November 18, 1886: J. C. and J. W., November 19, 1886.

1055. LEO, LEWIS, Musician. 1809-1876.
J. C., Nov. 24, 1876.

1056. LEON, HANANEL DE, Physician. Circa 1821.
Munk, " Roll of Coll. Phys.," iii.
LEON, JACOB JEHUDA. See TEMPLO.

1057. LEON, SOLOMON DE, Physician. Circa 1791.
Munk, " Roll of Coll. Phys.," ii. 361.

LEONI. *See* LYON, MYER.

1059. LEVI, DAVID, Hebraist and Author. 1742-1801.
European Magazine, May, 1799 (Portrait): "Memoirs of B. Goldsmid " (*see* No. 821), Lysons, "Environs of London," Supp., pp. 430-31.

LEVIN, HIRSCHEL. *See* LYON.

1060. LEVISOHN GEORGE (GOMPERTZ), Surgeon. D. 1797.
Schroeder, "Hamburgischen Schriftstellern," Carmoly, "Medicins Juifs," pp. 217, 219.

1061. LEVISON, J. L., Physician. 1800-1874.
J. C., July 17, 1874.

1062. LEVY, —, Mayor of Rochester. 1807-1871.
J. R., Feb. 10, 1871.

1063. LEVY, AARON, Dayan. 1794-1886.
J. C., Aug. 25, 1876.

1064. LEVY, BENJAMIN, Financier. Circa 1750.
Picciotto, "Anglo-Jewish Hist.," p. 134.

1065. LEVY, JOSEPH, Landowner at Tunis. D. 1882.
J. W., Feb. 4, 1881.

1067. LEVY, JUDITH, Philanthropist. 1706-1803.
"Notes and Queries," vol. xii. (1885): Cat., p. 51: Lysons, "Environs of London," Supp., p. 68.

1068. LEVY, MYER, Chazan at New Synagogue. Circa 1750.
Cat., p. 54: Portrait, Polok, sc.

1069. LEVY, SOLOMON HYAM, Crier, Noted Character. D. 1858.
J. C., Jan. 22, 1858.

1070. LEWIS, DAVID, Merchant. 1823-1885.
Liverpool Leader, 1875 (Portrait and Biog.) : *J. C.* and *J. W.*, Dec. 11, 1885.

1071. LEWIS, JAMES GRAHAM, Eminent Solicitor. D. 1873.
J. C., Jan. 24 and Feb. 21, 1873.

1072. LINDENTHAL, ISRAEL L., Clergyman and Author. 1796-1863.
J. C., Jan. 1, 1864 : Cat., p. 60.

1073. LINDO, DAVID ABARBANEL, Communal Worker. 1765-1851.
Cat., p. 56 (Portrait : Hanhart, pinx.; Lynch, sc.).

1074. LINDO, ELIAS HAIM, Jewish Historian. 1783-1865.
J. C., June 23, 1865.

LISSA. *See* COHEN DE LISSA.

1076. LOPES, SIR RALPH, Bart., Politician. 1788-1854.
Burke, "Baronetage."

1078. LOPEZ, SIR MENASSEH, Bart., Politician. D. 1831.
Picciotto, "Anglo-Jewish History," p. 59.

1079. LOPEZ, RODRIGO, Physician. Circa 1525-1594.
Munk, "Roll of Coll. of Phys.," i. 64: *J. W.*, Jan. 23,
1880: *Gentlemen's Mag.* (S. L. Lee), Feb., 1880:
Portrait in "A Thankfulle Remembrance of God's
mercy, in an Historicall Collection," &c., by George
Carleton, p. 177.

1080. LOUSADA, EMANUEL DE, Duke de Losada y Lousada.
1809-1875.
Burke, "Peerage" (1887), p. 1538.

1081. LOUSADA, FRANCIS DE, Marchese di San Miniato. 1813-
1870.
Burke, "Peerage," &c. (1887), p. 1538.

1082 LOUSADA, ISAAC DE, Duke de Losada y Lousada. D.
1857.
Burke, "Peerage" (1887), p. 1538.

1083. LÖWENTHAL, J. J., Chess Player. 1810-1876.
Times, July 21, 1876 ; Cat., p. 64 ; (Portrait : Anon.)

1084. LUCAS, HORATIO JOSEPH, Artist. 1839-1873.
J. C., Dec. 26, 1873.

1085. LUCAS, LOUIS A., African Explorer. 1851-1876.
Times, Dec. 26, 1876 : *Athenæum* : *J. C.*, Dec. 15, 1876.

1086. LUCAS, SAMPSON, Communal Worker. 1821-1879.
J. C. and *J. W.*, Aug. 8, 1879.

1087. LUMLEY, BENJAMIN, Director of H. M. Theatre. D. 1875.
Times, March 19, 1875.

1088. LUZZATTO, EPHRAIM, Hebrew Poet. Circa 1768.
Orient (Memoir by D. A. de Sola).

LYON, EMMA. *See* HENRY.

1089. LYON, HART, Chief Rabbi. 1721-1800.
Landschudt, "Berliner Rabbinen": Graetz, "Ge-
schichte der Juden," xi. 45 *et seq.* : Carmoly, *Revue
Orientale*, iii. 219 ; Auerbach, "Geschichte der
Israelit. Gemeinde von Halberstadt," p. 89, *et seq.*:
Cat., p. 50 (Portrait : Turner, pinx. ; Fisher, sc.).

1090. LYON, MYER, Operatic Singer and Chazan. Circa 1800.
"Thespian Dict.": "Memoirs of J. de Castro" (See
No. 823), pp. 9-10: *J. C.*, Dec. 26, 1873.

1091. LYON, ROBERT, Journalist. 1810-1858.
Morais, "Eminent Jews," pp. 221-223.

1092. LYON, SOLOMON, Hebrew Teacher. D. 1821.
J. C., Nov. 24, 1871 ; June 6, 1879.

1093. LYONS, ISRAEL, Hebrew Teacher and Author. D. 1770.
Nichols, "Lit. Anec."

138   BIBLIOTHECA ANGLO-JUDAICA.

1094. LYONS, ISRAEL, Astronomer, Botanist, and Mathematician. 1739-1775.
   Maunders, "Treasury of Biography": Carmoly, "Medicins Juifs": *J. C.*, Nov. 27, 1863.
1095. LYONS, JAQUES J., Clergyman and Author. 1812-1877.
   J. C. and *J. W.*, Aug. 31, 1877.
1096. MAAS, JOSEPH, Musician and Singer. 1847-1886.
   Times, Jan. 18 and 23, 1886.
1097. MAGNUS, SIMON, Founder of Chatham Synagogue. 1800-1875.
   J. C., Dec. 10, 1875.
   MARCHENA, ANTONIO NUNEZ. *See* MOCATO.
1098. MARGOLIOUTH, MOSES, M.A., LL.D., Christian Missionary and Author. 1818-1881.
   Autobiog. prefixed to "Modern Judaism" (London, 1843): *J. W.*, March 4, 1881.
1099. MARQUES, ABRAHAM RODRIGUES. D. 1689.
   Ascamot of Portuguese Cong., p. 91.
1100. MARSDEN, ISAAC M., Communal Worker. 1808-1884.
   J. C. and *J. W.*, Aug. 8, 1884.
1101. MARX, KARL, Socialist and Economist. 1818-1883.
   Times, March 17, 1883.
1102. MEDINA, SOLOMON DE, Army Contractor. Circa 1711.
   Picciotto: "Anglo-Jewish History," p. 50.
1103. MELDOLA, DAVID, Dayan. 1797-1853.
   Morais, "Eminent Israelites," p. 233. *H. O.*, April 15, 1853.
1103a. MELDOLA, ELIEZER, Physician. 1810-1877.
   J. C., Dec. 28, 1877.
1104. MELDOLA, RAPHAEL, Chacham. 1754-1828.
   European Magazine, Oct., 1828: Morais, "Eminent Israelites," pp. 230-233: Cat., p. 52 (Portrait : Barlin, pinx.; Lopez, sculp.)
1105. MENASSEH BEN ISRAEL, Founder of the Anglo-Jewish Community. 1604-1657.
   Pocock (*see* No. 240) : Kayserling (*see* No. 238) : Wolf (*see* No. 239).
1106. MENDES, ABRAHAM, Thief Taker. Circa 1718.
   "Chronicles of Crime."
1107. MENDES, ANDREA, Court Chamberlain. Circa 1665.
   Lindo, "Jews of Spain and Portugal."
1108. MENDES, FERNANDO, Physician. D. 1724.
   Barbosa Machado : Munk, "Coll. of Phys.," i. p. 434 : Lindo, "Jews of Spain and Portugal": Cat., p. 48 : (Portrait, in "Stadium Apollinare," by F. M.).

1109. MENDEZ, MOSES, Banker and Poet. D. 1758.
European Magazine, Oct. 1792 (Portrait) : Rose, "Biog. Dict." : Allibone, " Crit. Dict." : *J. W.*, Feb. 14, 1873 : Cat., p. 50.

1110. MENDOZA, DANIEL, Pugilist. 1763-1836.
" Memoirs," by himself (*see* No. 822) : Egan, "Boxiana " (Portrait) : " Pugilistica " (Portrait : Robinson, pinx., Gardner, etch., 1789).

1112. MERCADO, DAVID RAPHAEL DE, Founder of Barbadoes Sugar Industry. Circa 1655.
State Papers, Colonial Series.

1113. MERTON, LOUIS, Financier. 1840-1874.
Times, Jan. 20, 1874 : *J. C.*, Jan. 23, 1874.

1114. MESQUITA, MOSES GOMES DE, Chacham. 1688-1751.
Cat., p. 49 (Portrait : Da Silva pinx. ; Faber, sculp., 1752).

1115. MOCATO, MOSES, Merchant and Author. Circa 1677.
Graetz, " Geschichte," x., Note i., p. xiii. : *Leisure Hour*, July, 1886.

1116. MOCATTA, ABRAHAM, Communal Worker. 1797-1880.
J. C. and *J. W.*, April 30, 1880.

1118. MOCATTA, DAVID, Architect. 1806-1882.
J. C., 1882.

1119. MOCATTA, ISAAC LINDO, Theological Writer. 1818-1879.
J. C., Nov. 21, 1879.

1120. MOCATTA, MOSES, Author. 1768-1857.
J. C.. Oct. 2, 1857.

1121. MOMBACH, JULIUS (ISRAEL) LAZARUS, Musician and Composer. 1813-1880.
J. C. and *J. W.*, Feb. 13, 1880 : Portrait prefixed to Synagogue Music.

1122. MONTEFIORE, ABRAHAM, Stockbroker. 1788-1824.
" Life of Sir M. Montefiore," (*see* No. 839), pp. 13, 15, 18, 25.

1123. MONTEFIORE, CHARLOTTE, Authoress. D. 1854.
Kayserling, "Judische Frauen," pp. 275-276 : *J. C.*, July 14, 1854.

1124. MONTEFIORE, HORATIO, Communal Worker. 1798-1867.
Cat , p. 61.

1125. MONTEFIORE, JACOB ISAAC LEVI, Australian merchant and Politician, 1819-1885.
J. W., Jan. 30 and Feb. 6, 1885.

1126. MONTEFIORE, JACOB MAYER, Commercial worker. 1816-1880.
J. C. and *J. W.*, Oct. 15, 1880.

1127. MONTEFIORE, JOSHUA, Lawyer, Soldier, and Journalist. 1752-1843.
>   Drake, "Dict. Amer. Biog."; Wolf, "Life of Sir M. Montefiore" (*see* No. 839), pp. 7-11 : *J. W.* (Supp.), Oct. 31, 1884.

1128. MONTEFIORE, JUDITH, LADY, Philanthropist. 1784-1862.
>   Kayserling, "Jüdische Frauen," pp. 272-275, 308 : Wolf, "Life of Sir M. Montefiore" (*see* No. 839), pp. 189-212 : *J. C.*, Oct. 3, 1862: Morais, "Eminent Israelites," 240-242 : Portrait, *Graphic*, 1885 : Lady Montefiore's Diaries [privately printed].

1129. MONTEFIORE, LEONARD, Author. 1863-1879.
>   Memoir in "Remains" : *Athenæum*, Sept. 13, 1879 : *Examiner*, Sept. 13, 1879 : *Women's Union Journal*, Nov. '79 : *J. C.* and *J. W.*, Sept. 12, 1879.

1130. MONTEFIORE, SIR MOSES, Bart., Philanthropist, 1784-1885.
>   Biographies by J. G. (*see* No. 828), Racah (*see* No. 838), Davis (*see* No. 837), Wolf (*see* No. 839), Anon. (*see* No. 840), Weston (*see* No. 841), Kohn Zekek (*see* No. 835) : *Times* and other newspapers at the time of the Centenary and death : "Eminent Jews of the Times," No. 1 : (Portrait) : Morais, "Eminent Israelites," pp. 236-240 : "Reminiscences of Sir M. M. (by P. B. Benny, ex-private secretary to Sir M.) in *J. W.* July and August, 1885 (Portraits : Richmond, pinx. ; Anon., sc. ; E. L. Montefiore, etch., etc.) : Cat., p. 59 : *Illustrated London News*, 1884 : *Graphic*, 1884-1885.

1131. MONTEFIORE, NATHANIEL, Communal worker. 1819-1883.
>   *J. C.* and *J. W.*, March 30, 1883.

1132. MOREIRA, JACOB RODRIGUES, Teacher and Author. Circa 1773.
>   *J. C.*, Dec. 19, 1884.

1133. MOSES, ABRAHAM LYON, Philanthropist. 1775-1854.
>   *Heb. Obs.* and *J. C.*, March 3, 1854.

1134. MOSES, HENRY, Philanthropist. 1791-1875.
>   *J. C.*, Dec. 10, 1875.

1135. MOSES, J. HENRY, Philanthropist. 1805-1875.
>   *J. C.*, Aug. 13, 1875.

1136. MOSS, ——, Actor.
>   "Thespian Dict." : Clarke Russel, "Representative Actors."

1137. MOZLEY, M. L., Turkish Vice-Consul at Liverpool. 1760-1845.
>   *Voice of Jacob*, June 6, 1845.

1138. MYERS, JOSEPH HART, Physician. 1758-1823.
>   Munk, "Roll of Coll. Phys.," ii. p. 323.

1139. MYERS, MOSES, Chief Rabbi of New Syn. D. 1814.
>   Cat. p. 54.

1140. NATHAN, BARON (BARNETT), Dramatic and Musical *Entrepreneur.* D. 1856.
J. C., Jan 23, 1857.

1141. NATHAN, DAVID, New Zealand Colonist and Merchant. 1816-1886.
New Zealand Herald, Sept. 13, 1886.

1142. NATHAN, ISAAC, Musician. 1792-1864.
Brown, "Dict. Mus.": "Australian Dict. of Dates":
J. C., March 25, 1864 : Cat., p. 60.

1143. NATHAN, M. N., Preacher. 1807-1883.
J. C. and *J. W.*, May 18, 1883, and *J. W.*, May 25 and July 13, 1883 : *Athenæum*, May 26, 1883.

1144. NEUBERG, JOSEPH, Secretary to Carlyle. 1806-1867.
Macmillan's Mag., Aug. 1884, pp. 280-297.

1145. NEWMAN, ALFRED ALVAREZ, Metal Worker and Art Collector. 1851-1887.
Times, Jan. 27, 1887 : *Norwich Argus*, Jan. 27, 1887 :
J. C., and *J. W.*, Jan. 28, 1887 : Cat., pp. 67, 68-77.

1146. NEWMAN, SELIG, Hebraist and Teacher. 1788-1871.
Morais, "Eminent Israelites," pp. 252-255.

1147. NEUMEGEN, LEOPOLD, Schoolmaster. 1787-1875.
J. C., April 16, 1875.

1148. NIETO, DAVID, Chacham. 1654-1728.
Wolf, "Bibliotheca Hebræa," iii. pp. 20 and 809 :
Kayserling, "Juden in Portugal," pp. 325-326 : Barbosa Machado : Cat., p. 48. (Portrait : McArdell, sc.)

1150. NORDEN, JOSHUA D., Field Commandant in Kaffir war. D. 1846.
J. C., July 24, 1846.

1151. NUNEZ, SAMUEL, Marrano Physician. Circa 1733.
J. C., April 30, 1852, March 21, 1862.

1152. OPPENHEIM, MORRIS SIMEON, Lawyer. D. 1882.
J. C. and *J. W.*, Jan. 5, 1883.

1153. OPPENHEIM, SIMEON, Communal Worker. 1798-1874.
J. C., Oct. 30, 1874.

1154. ORNSTIEN, ABRAHAM, Minister of Kimberley (S. A.) Congregation. 1863-1885.
J. C. and *J. W.*, July 17, 1885.

1155. PALGRAVE, SIR FRANCIS COHEN, Historian. 1788-1861.
"Encyc. Brit." (9th edit.) : *Times*, July 10, 1861.

1156. PARDO, DAVID, Chazan. D. 1717.
Steinschneider, "Biblioth. Bodl." II., 884 : De Castro, "Auswahl von Grabsteinen," Part I.: Fränkel's *Monatschrift*, viii. p. 386.

1157. PARDO, JOSEPH, Chazan and Author. D. 1677.
De Castro, " Auswahl von Grabsteinen," Part I. : Fränkel's *Monatsschrift*, viii. p. 387.

1158. PARISH-ALVARS, ELIAS, Harpist and Composer. 1816-1849.
Brown, " Dict. Mus." : Fetis, " Biog. Univ. des Mus.'

PEDAZZUR, GEMALIEL B. *See* GEMALIEL.

PEREIRA, EPHRAIM LOPEZ. *See* AGUILAR.

1159. PEREIRA, JONATHAN, Medical Writer. 1804-1853.
Times, Jan. 24, 1853.

1160. PEREIRA, MARIA NUNEZ, Marrano Beauty. Circa 1590.
Kayserling, " Judischen Frauen," pp. 97-8 : " Sephardim," p. 167 *et seq.*

PEREIRA, MOSES (DIEGO) LOPEZ. *See* AGUILAR.

PHAIBUL, URI. *See* HART, AARON.

1161. PHILLIPS, HON. GEORGE LYON, Jamaica Politician. 1811-
1887.
Falmouth Gazette (Jamaica), Dec. 31, 1885 : *J. C.*, Feb.
4, 1887 : *J. W.*, Jan. 28, 1887.

PHILLIPS, HERSCHELL. *See* FILIPOWSKI.

1162. PHILLIPS, SAMUEL, Journalist. 1815-1854.
Times, Oct. 17, 1853 : Didot, " Nouv. Biog. Gen."

1163. PICCIOTTO, MOSES HAIM, Communal Worker. 1806-1879.
J. C. and *J. W.*, Oct. 24, 1879.

1164. PIMENTEL, SARA DE FONSECA PINA Y, Poetess. Circa
1720.
Kayserling, " Juden in Portugal."

1165. PINTO, ISAAC DE, Author. 1715-1787.
Didot, " Nouvelle Biog. Gen." (gives further sources).

1166. PINTO, THOMAS, Violinist. D. 1773.
Brown, " Dict. Mus."

1167. POLACK, ISAAC, Chazan. Circa 1770.
Cat., p. 56 (Portrait : Leslie, pinx. ; Newman, sculp.,
1799).

1168. PRAG, JACOB, Professor of Hebrew and Preacher. 1816-
1882.
J. W., Jan. 6, 1882.

1169. RABBAN, JOSEPH. Founder of the Beni Israel Community.
Circa 490 C.E.
Graetz, " Geschichte," iv. pp. 405-407.

1170. RANGER, MORRIS, Financier. D. 1887.
Liverpool Daily Post, April 19, 1887 : *J. C.* and *J. W.*,
April 22, 1887.

1171. RAPHAEL, MARK, Hebraist and Controversialist. Circa 1532.
Pocock. (*See* No. 207 a)

1172. RAPHALL, MORRIS JACOB, Preacher and Author. 1798-1868.
    Morais, "Eminent Israelites": *J. C.*, July 17, 1868.
1173. RAUSUK, SAMSON, Hebrew Poet. 1793-1877.
    J. C., Sept. 14, 1877.
1174. REBELLO, DAVID ALVES, Merchant and Numismatist. D. 1797.
    The Bazaar, Jan. 9, 1884: Picciotto, "Anglo-Jewish History," p. 230.
    REY, JACOB. *See* KING, JOHN.
1176. RICARDO, DAVID, Economist and Politician. 1772-1823.
    Memoir (See No. 824): Bagehot, "Economic Studies."
1177. RINTEL, MOSES, Clergyman. 1823-1880.
    J. C., July 9, 1880, and July 30, 1880: Heaton, "Australian Dict. of Dates."
1178. ROTHSCHILD, SIR ANTHONY, Financier and Communal Worker. 1810-1876.
    Times, Jan. 5, 10, and 11, 1876: *J. C.* and *J. W.*, Jan. 7, 1886.
1179. ROTHSCHILD, BARONESS CHARLOTTE DE, Philanthropist. 1836-1884.
    J. C. and *J. W.*, March 14, 1884.
1180. ROTHSCHILD, BARONESS HANNAH DE, Communal Worker. 1782-1850.
    J. C., Sept. 13, 1850.
1182. ROTHSCHILD, BARONESS JULIANA DE. D. 1877.
    J. C. and *J. W.*, March 16, 1877.
1183. ROTHSCHILD, BARON LIONEL DE, Financier and Politician. 1808-1879.
    Times, June 4, 5, 7, 9, 12, and 20, 1879; *J. C.*, June 5, 1879; *J. W.*, June 5 and 6 (special No.), 1879.
1184. ROTHSCHILD, L. M., Philanthropist. 1809-1884.
    J. C. and *J. W.*, Nov. 7, 1884: *J. W.*, Nov. 14, 1884.
1185. ROTHSCHILD, BARON MAYER DE, Financier and Sportsman. 1818-1874.
    Times, Feb. 7, 11, and 12, 1874; *J. C.* and *J. W.*, Feb. 13, 1874.
1186. ROTHSCHILD, BARON NATHAN MAYER, Financier. 1777-1836.
    J. C., Oct. 2, 1874; *J. W.*, April 5, 1878, "Jewish Talisman;" Treskow, "Biographische Notizen über N. M. Rothschild"; Reeves, "The Rothschilds" (1887); "Haus Rothschild" (1837); Ehrentheil, "Familienbuch" (1880).
1187. ROTHSCHILD, BARON NATHANIEL DE. D. 1870.
    Times, Feb. 21 and 22, 1870.
1190. SALOM, MORDECHAI, Chazan. 1754-1818.
    Cat., p. 52.

1191. SALOMONS, ANNETTE A., Authoress. D. 1879.
    J. C. and *J. W.*, April 18, 1879.
1192. SALOMONS, SIR DAVID, Lord Mayor and Politician. 1797-1873.
    Reports of Institution of Civil Engineers, vol. xxxviii. :
    J. C., Nov. 16, 1855, July 25, 1873 : *J. W.*, July 25, 1873.
1194. SALOMONS, LEVI, Financier. 1774-1843.
    Voice of Jacob, Feb. 3, 1843.
1195. SALVADOR, JOSEPH, Philanthropist. Circa 1753.
    Picciotto, "Anglo-Jewish History," pp. 162-163.
1196. SAMUDA, ISAAC DE SEQUERA, Physician. Circa 1721.
    Munk, "Coll. Phys.," ii. p. 73.
1197. SAMUDA, JACOB, Civil Engineer. 1811-1844.
    Voice of Jacob, Nov. 29, 1844.
1198. SAMUDA, JOSEPH D'AGUILAR, Ship-builder and Politician. 1813-1885.
    Times, April 29, 1885: *J. C.*, May 1, 1885 : *J.W.*, May 1 and 22, 1885 : *Celebrities of the Day*, July, 1881.
    SAMUEL B. ISRAEL. *See* SOEIRO.
1199. SAMUEL, BARON DENIS DE, Financier. 1782-1860.
    J. C., Aug. 24 and Oct. 12, 1860.
200. SAMUEL, MOSES, Author. 1795-1860.
    J. C., April 27, 1860.
1201. SAMUEL. MOSES, Financier. 1742-1839.
    Heb. Obs., Aug. 18, 1854.
1202. SAMUEL, SAMPSON. 1804-1868.
    J. C., Nov. 13 and 20, 1868 : *J. R.*, Nov 20, 1868.
1203. SAMUEL, SYDNEY MONTAGU, Author. 1848-1884.
    Times, June 28, 1884 : *J. C.* and *J. W.*, June 27, 1884.
1204. SARMENTO, JACOB DE CASTRO, Physician. 1692-1762.
    Barbosa Machado : Munk, "Roll Coll. Phys.": "Biographie Universelle": Kayserling, "Jüdischen Aerzte," vii. 392 ; viii. 161 : Cat., p. 49 (Portrait ; Pine, pinx. ; Houston, sculp.).
1205. SASPORTAS, JACOB, Chacham. 1618-1698.
    Wolf, "Biblio. Heb.," I., p. 619; III., p. 532 : Graetz, "Geschichte," Note 2 : Cat., p. 48 (Portrait : Van Gunst, sculp.).
1206. SASSOON, DAVID, Indian Philanthropist. 1792-1864.
    Bombay Gazette, Dec. 28, 1864.
1207. SASSOON, SASSOON DAVID. 1832-1867.
    J. C., July 19, 1867.
1208. SCHIFF, TEVLI (DAVID), Chief Rabbi. D. 1792.
    Horowitz, "Frankfurter Rabbinen," iv., pp. 18-22 : Cat., p. 51.

1209. SCHLESINGER, BARTHOLD, Surgeon. 1853-1874.
     J. C. July 31, 1874.
1211. SCHOMBERG, ISAAC, Physician. D. 1780.
     Munk, "Coll. Phys.": Chalmers, Biog. Dict.": *European Mag.*, Mar. 1803. (Portrait : Hudson, pinxt.; Sherlock, sc.)
1212. SCHOMBERG, MEYER LÖW, Physician. D. 1761.
     Munk, "Coll. Phys.": Carmoly, "Medicins Juifs," p. 200.
1213. SCHOMBERG, RALPH, Physician and Author. 1714-1792.
     Munk, "Roll of Coll. Phys.": Chalmers, "Biog. Dict.": Nichols, Lit. Anec., iii. 28, 30 : " Ralph Schomberg" [by Arthur Schomberg], Oxford, 1874, pp. 12. (Portrait ; Gainsborough, pinx. (bought in 1862 for Nat. Gal.) ; Fry, sculp.).
1214. SCHONENBERG, FRANZ VAN, Diplomatist. D. 1717.
     Koenen. "Joden in Nederland" : Van der Aa, "Dutch Biog. Dict.": Kayserling, "Feiertag in Madrid," p. 9.
1215. SCOTT, CHARLES ALEXANDER, Garibaldian and Author, 1803-1867.
     J. C., May 3 and 10, 1867.
1216. SEMON, CHARLES, Philanthropist, 1814-1877.
     Bradford Observer, July, 1877 : *J. C.*, July 27, 1877 : *J. W.*, Aug. 10. 1877.
1217. SEQUERA, ISAAC HENRIQUES, Physician, 1738-1816.
     Munk, "Coll. Phys ," ii. p. 245.
1218. SERRA, ISAAC GOMES, Philanthropist. D. 1818.
     Picciotto, "Anglo-Jewish History," pp. 342, 343.
1219. SICHEL, EDWARD FERDINAND, Australian Merchant. D. 1884.
     Melbourne Argus: J. W., April 11, 1884.
1220. SILBER, A. M., Merchant and Inventor. D. 1887.
     J. C. and *J. W.*, May 20, 1887.
1221. SILVA, JOSHUA DA, Chacham. D. 1679.
     Wolf, "Biblio. Heb.", iii 345 : Kayserling, "Juden in Portugal," pp. 324, 325.
1223. SLOMAN, HENRY, Actor, 1793-1873.
     J. C., Aug. 22, 1873.
1224. SOEIRA, SAMUEL ABARBANEL, Son and Colleague of Menasseh b. Israel, 1625-1657.
     Pocock (*see* No. 240) : Kayserling (*see* No. 239) : Wolf (*see* No. 239).
1225. SOLA, ABRAHAM DE, Chazan and Ab Beth Din. B. 1700.
     Life of D. A. de Sola (*see* No. 829), p. 5.
1226. SOLA, ABRAHAM DE, Clergyman and Professor of Hebrew, 1825-1882.
     J. W., June 23, 1882. "Cyc. Amer. Biog."

L

1227. SOLA, DAVID AARON DE, Preacher and Author, 1796-1860.
Life by A. de Sola (*see* No. 829) : Morais, "Eminent
Israelites."

1229. SOLA, ISAAC DE, Preacher. 1674-1734.
" Life of D. A. de Sola " (*see* No. 829), pp. 3, 4.

1230. SOLA, SAMUEL DE. 1839-1866.
J. C., Sept. 14, 1866.

1231. SOLOMON, ABRAHAM, Artist. 1824-1862.
J. C., Dec. 26, 1862, Jan. 2 and 16, 1863.

1232. SOLOMON, HENRY NAPHTALI, Elocutionist and Hebraist.
1796-1881.
J. C. and *J. W.*, Nov. 18, 1881, and *J. W.*, Dec. 9, 1881.

1233. SOLOMON, MYER, Founder of St. Albans Place Synagogue.
Cat., p. 58.

1234. SOLOMON, SAMUEL, Quack. D. 1818.
Watt, "Biblio. Brit." : Cat., p. 58 : (Portrait : Steel,
pinx. ; Ridley, sculp.)

1235. SOUSA, ANTONIO DE, Portuguese Ambassador in England.
Circa 1643.
Barbosa Machado ; Wolf (*see* No. 239).

1236. STERN, DAVID, VISCOUNT DE, Banker. D. 1877.
J. C., Jan. 26, 1877.

1237. STERN, HENRY ABRAHAM, Christian Missionary. D. 1885.
Biog. by A. A. Isaacs.

1237a. STERN, BARON HERMANN DE, Financier. 1815-1887.
J. C. and *J. W.*, Oct. 21, 1887.
Times, Oct. 21, 1887.

1238. STRAUSS, GUSTAVE LOUIS MAURICE, Author. 1807-1887.
Athenæum, Sept. 17, 1887.

1239. STROUSBERG, BETHEL HENRY, Railway Contractor. 1823-
1884.
Memoirs : *J. W.*, June 6, 1884.

1240. SUASSO, ISAAC (ANTONIO) LOPEZ, Baron Avernes de Gras.
1693-1775.
Koenen, "Joden in Nederland," p. 208 : Graetz, "Geschichte," x.. p. 328.

1242. SUTRO, SIGISMUND, Physician. 1815-1886.
J. C., Feb. 26, 1886.

1243. SYMONS, BARON LYON DE, Communal Worker. Circa 1800.
J. C., May 11, 1860.

1243a. SYMONS, SAMUEL LYON DE, Communal Worker. D. 1860.
J. C., May 11, 1860.

1243b. TANG, ABRAHAM, Author. Circa 1773.
J. C., Dec. 19, 1884.

1244. TEMPLO, JACOB JEHUDA LEON (ARYEH), Author and Designer. 1603-1672.
Graetz, "Geschichte," x., pp. 24, 200, 201 : Picciotto, "Anglo-Jewish Hist.," p. 45.

1245. THEODORES, TOBIAS, Prof of Hebrew. 1808-1886.
J. C. and *J. W.*, April 30, 1816.

1245a. TOLEDO, CHAYIM B. DANIEL DE, Moorish Envoy to London. Circa 1675.
Zunz : "Zur Geschichte," p. 440.
מקוה ישראל, ed. 1692, c. 66.

1246. TREMELLIUS, EMANUEL, Theologian. 1510-1580.
F. Butters: "E. Tremellius, eine Lebenskizze," 1859 : Ath. Cantab., i. 425.

1247. VALLENTINE, ISAAC, Communal Worker. 1792-1868.
Memoir (*see* No. 830).
J. C., July 13, 1860.

1248. VAN OVEN, BARNARD, Physician. 1797-1860.

1249. VAN OVEN, JOSHUA, Surgeon. 1766-1838.
European Magazine, April 1815.

1250. VILLA REAL, ISAAC DA COSTA, Founder of Villareal School. D. 1737.
Ascamot of Portuguese Congregation, p. 93.

1251. WALEY, JACOB, Conveyancer and Professor of Political Economy. 1819-1873.
Times, June 23, 1873 : *J. C.* and *J. W.*, June 27, 1873.

1252. WALEY, SIMON WALEY, Musician. 1827-1876.
Impartial (Boulogne), Jan. 21, 1876 : *J. C.*, Jan. 7 and 14, 1876.

1254. WASSERZUG, H., Chazan and Composer. D. 1882.
J. C. and *J. W.*, Sept. 1, 1882.

1255. WOLFF, JOSEPH, Traveller and Christian Missionary. 1795-1862.
Times, May 7, 1862 : "Travels and Adventures " (1862) (Portrait).

1256. WORMS, MAURICE BENEDICT DE, Financier. 1805-1867.
J. C., June 14, 1867.

1257. WORMS, BARON SOLOMON DE, Financier, 1801-1882.
J. C. and *J. W.*, Oct. 27, 1882.

1259. XIMENES, SIR MORIS, Financier. B. 1762.
Picciotto, " Anglo-Jewish Sketches," p. 303.

1261. ZEDNER, JOSEPH, Hebraist, 1804-1871.
J. C., Oct. 20, 1871 : *J. C.* March 21, 1873 (by M. Steinschneider).

1262. ZIMMERMAN, GODFREY. B. 1788.
Autobiography (*see* No. 826).

(1.) PERIODICALS.

1266. HEBREW INTELLIGENCER, monthly, No. 1, Jan. 1, 1823, London.   Single page, large folio, price 6d.
No names of publishers, editors, or promoters.

1267. גלעד   THE HEBREW REVIEW AND MAGAZINE OF RABBINICAL LITERATURE, edited by Morris J. Raphall.   No. 1, Oct. 3, 1834, London.   16 pp., weekly.

1268. קול יעקב, VOICE OF JACOB (edited by Jacob Franklin), London.   No. 1, Sept., 1841, 4to., 8 pp., fortnightly; Sept. 24, 1847, fol., fortnightly; last number Sept. 1, 1848.

1270. VOICE OF JACOB, Gibraltar.   Started early in 1882.

1271. VOICE OF JACOB, Sydney.   No. 1, May 27, 1842; last number Sept. 5, 1842.

1272. ESPERANZA ISRAELITICO, Gibraltar.   Started in 1843.

1273. THE FIRST FRUITS OF THE WEST.—A Monthly Periodical devoted exclusively to the Jewish Religion and Literature, published in Jamaica under the editorship of the Rev. M. N. Nathan and Lewis Ashenheim, M.A.   No. 1, Feb. 1844.
[In the No. for July, 1844, there is a reference to " the Prospectus of a Jewish Monthly Magazine, to be published in London under the editorship of Mr. Theodores." It does not appear that the magazine ever saw the light.]

1269. ספר זכרון, THE JEWISH CHRONICLE.   Edited by the Rev. Dr. Meldola and Mr. M. Angel.   No. 1, November 12th, 1841.
[Issued with this series " צמח דוד," " Hebrew Rabbinical and Biblical Dictionary "; also " Hagadah for Passover." The latter was withdrawn after the second number and the former not completed.]
London.   Weekly, 4to., price 2d.   Series ended April 23rd, 1841. Issued subsequently in 8vo. form.

ספר זכרון, THE JEWISH CHRONICLE (New Series) AND WORKING MAN'S FRIEND.   Proprietor and

Editor, Joseph Mitchell. No. 1, October 18, 1844. Fortnightly, 4to., price 2d.

June 27, 1845, title altered to ספר זכרון, THE JEWISH CHRONICLE. Weekly from July 9, 1847.

Oct. 11, 1850, enlarged to folio (8 pages), price 3d.

August 18, 1854, edited by M. H. Bresslau.

December 22, 1854, title altered to THE JEWISH CHRONICLE AND HEBREW OBSERVER, enlarged.

January 12, 1855, edited by Dr. A. Benisch until 1869.

1868 enlarged to grt. folio, and a penny edition issued together with the 3rd edition.

April 2, 1869 title altered to ספר זכרון, THE JEWISH CHRONICLE. Price 2d. Edited by Michael Henry.

June 18, 1875, editorship resumed by Dr. A. Benisch till his death, July 31, 1878.

1274. SABBATH LEAVES. Started in June, 1845. London.

1275. בוס ישועות, THE CUP OF SALVATION.—Prospectus of a Monthly Jewish Orthodox Magazine under the above title, edited by the Rev. D. M. Isaacs and Moses Samuel of Liverpool (August, 1845).

Pamphlet of 18 pages, explaining the views and principles of the editors, being an appeal to the Jewish nation.

1276. בוס ישועות CUP OF SALVATION.—Jewish Orthodox Magazine, edited by Rev. D. M. Isaacs and Moses Samuel. Monthly, 8vo., 48 pp. Liverpool. No. 1, March, 1846.

1277. ספר האסיף עם לוח לשנת תר"ה. THE ANNUAL HEBREW MAGAZINE, edited by Herschell Filipowski. London, 1847.

In Heb. and Eng., with Meldola's לוח.

1278. ספר מאספים, THE ANGLO - JEWISH MAGAZINE. No. 1, Oct. 1, 1848. London.

Continuation of VOICE OF JACOB, published monthly.

1279. הצופה, HEBREW OBSERVER. Edited by A. Benisch. No. 1, Jan. 7, 1853. Fol. London.

1280. JEWISH SABBATH JOURNAL. Edited by Mrs. Hartog. Sm. 8vo., 16 pp., weekly. London. No. 1, Feb. 22, 1855. Last No. June 28, 1855.

1281. המאסף. HEBREW REVIEW. Second series. Edited by M. H. Breslau. Weekly, 8vo., 16 pp. London. No. 1, Oct. 21, 1859.

1282. מורה, THE GUIDE. A Monthly Magazine devoted to the diffusion of Knowledge in Jewish Literature. Edited by Raphael d'C. Lewin, Head Master of the Hebrew National Institution. Published by Michael de Cordova, Kingston, Jamaica. No. 1, July, 1865.

1283. כנסת ישראל, THE HEBREW NATIONAL. Edited by H. Filipowski. Weekly, 8vo., 16 pp. No. 1, Feb. 15, 1867. London.
   Words "Jew" and "Jewish" excluded from all articles, "Hebrew" being substituted.

1284. JEWISH RECORD. Weekly. Fol., 8 pp., with occasional supplements. Published by John Edward Morse and edited by L. B. Abrahams. No. 1, June 5, 1868, London; J. E. M. and Asher I. Myers, publishers, Oct. 23, 1868; enlarged (still 8 pp.), Jan. 29, 1869; published by J. E. M. alone, Nov. 5, 1869; discontinued Oct. 6, 1871.

1285. AUSTRALIAN ISRAELITE. Melbourne, Victoria.
   See *Jewish Chronicle*, Aug. 1, 1871.

1286. JEWISH WORLD. No. 1, Feb. 14, 1873. London. Weekly. Price 1d. Gr. Fol. 4 cols. 8 pp. Published by S. H. Valentine. New Series: enlarged to 5 cols. per page. Aug. 13, 1880.

1287. THE JEWISH SCHOOLFELLOW. Pub. by Jewish Schoolboys of Adelaide, South Australia in 1873.

1288. NORTHWICK COLLEGE TIMES. 4to., 4 pp. No. 1, Oct. 24, 1873. London.
   Written and printed by pupils of the Rev. A. P. Mendes, Northwick College School.

1289. פרה. THE JEWISH GAZETTE. Calcutta, 1874.
Marathi in Hebrew characters, weekly. Title as above in English.

1290. THE JEWS' COLLEGE JOURNAL. Edited by Delissa Joseph. No. 1, April, 1875; last No., Oct., 1875. First 5 Nos. 4 pp. 4to., sixth 8 pp. 8vo.

1291. THE DIALECTIC, a Jewish Monthly. Melbourne, May, 1875.

1292. JEWISH TIMES. London, 1876. Weekly.

1293. אור אמת, THE LIGHT OF TRUTH; published in 1877; discontinued in 1882. Marathi in Hebrew characters. Bombay.
Organ of the Beni Israel Community of Bombay.

1294. הכרם, HAKEREM. Edited by Naphtali Levi; published by Abrahams and Distillator. London. Fol., 4 pp., weekly. No. 1, Aug. 29, 1878. Hebrew.

1295. לאנדאנער איזראעליט, LONDON ISRAELITE. Edited by Naphtali Levi; published by Abrahams and Distillator. London. Folio, 4 pp. No. 1, Aug. 29, 1878. Weekly. Judeo-German in Hebrew characters.

1296. ירושלם, JERUSALEM. Edited by H. Guedalla. No. 1, April 13, 1882. Gr. fol., 20 pp. London.
[No more published.]

1297. PURIM.—A new fashioned Annual for an old fashioned Feast. Published by S. H. Valentine, *Jewish World* Office. 8vo., 108 pp. London. No. 1, 1883.
[No more published.]

1298. THE LIVERPOOL JEWISH MAGAZINE. Weekly. Edited and published by James M. Nucompton, Liverpool. No. 1, August 1, 1883. Price 1½d. 8vo., 16 pp. and cover.
[Only one number issued. Some copies were entitled THE LIVERPOOL JEWISH MONTHLY MAGAZINE AND TEACHERS' ADVERTISER.]

1299. JEWISH HERALD. Melbourne, 1882.

1300. דער פוילישער אידעל, THE POLISH YIDEL. Edited
by Boris Winestone (?). Published by Rabbino-
wicz and Werber. London. Large 4to., 4 pp.,
weekly. No. 1, July 25, 1884. Transformed into
דיא צוקונפט (See No. 1301) on November 7th, 1884.
Judeo-German in Hebrew characters.

1301. דיא צוקונפט, "DIE ZUKUNFT" (The Future).
Edited by Boris Winestone (?) ; published by Rab-
binowicz and Werber. London. Large 4to., 8 pp.
No. 1 (No. 16), November 7, 1884, weekly. Judeo-
German in Hebrew characters   Price 1d.
[Continuation of דער פוילישער אידיל.]

1302. השולמית, THE HASHULAMIT. Edited, printed
and published by Judah Leep Bril. London. Gr.
fol., 4 pp., weekly. No. 1 (Judeo-German in Hebrew characters).

1303. THE BEVIS MARKS GAZETTE. By H. Guedalla.
No. 1, February 1886. Large folio, 5 pp. London.
[Started to resist the projected demolition of the Bevis
Marks Synagogue. Two issues of No. 1 were published,
viz., on Feb. 15 and Feb. 17. The publication then
ceased.]

1304. הלבנון, THE LEBANON. Edited, printed, and published by J. J. Leep Bril. London. Large 4to.,
8 pp. Weekly. No. 1, June 1886. Hebrew.
Price 2d.
[Started in Jerusalem in 1862, and resumed successfully
in Paris, Mayence, and London.]

1305. JEWISH RECORD. Manchester, 1887.

(K.) ALMANACS.

1311. ABENDANA, J.—The Jewish Kalendar, containing account of their Fasts and Festivals for the
year 5452. 32mo. Oxford.   1692.
[Also published for 1693, '94, '95, '96 and '99.]

1312. D. NIETO.—בינה לעתים, Calendar for the years
5478-5560. Hebrew and Spanish. 1717.

1313. A. ALEXANDER.—Almanack for Jewish Commer-
cial Travellers, with names of English Towns in
Hebrew Letters, giving details of Coaches, Market
Days, &c. 1782.

1313a. A New Calendar for the years 5551-5600. 12mo.
1791.
[Printed by permission of the gentlemen of the Mahamad.]

1314. MOSES MELDOLA.—A New Almanack for the year
5568 A.M. 12mo. 1807.

1315. לוח של חמשת אלפים תקע״נ לבריאת עולם, 12mo.
1812.

1316. לוח של שנת חמשת אלפים תקצ״ו לבריאת עולם,
Hebrew and English Almanack for year 5596, corresponding with 1835-6. 1835.

1317. Hebrew and English Almanac for the years 1837-
1840, with the Jewish Charitable Institutions.
1836-9.

1318. לוח על . . . תקצח, תקצט, תר . . . תרא, תרב, תרד, תרה,
תרן, רחת, תרט, תרי, תריא, . . . Hebrew and English
Almanack. 16mo., Lond. 1837-51.

1319. שני לוחות. Hebrew and English Almanack.
16mo., [Lond.] [1839-1864.]

1320. E. H. LINDO.—A Jewish Calendar for sixty-four
years: to which are added Tables for continuing the
Calendar to A.M. 6000—2240 C.E., and a Chronological Table forming a summary of Jewish history. 1838.
[Some copies have an additional half-sheet carrying on
the chronological table to 1860.]

1320a. H. BARNETT.—Almanack. 1841.

1320b. H. FILIPOWSKY. — Prospectus to Chronology.
Liverpool. 1844.
[Twelve valuable tables for calculating Hebrew dates.]

1321. VALLENTINE, ISAAC —לוח, Hebrew and English
Almanack for the years A.M. 5604 and 5605.
Continued to the present day.

1322. DE LARA.—Illuminated Hebrew Calendar for 5606. Printed in gold and twelve different colours, from an original design by Mr. de Lara.

Dedicated to Sir Moses Montefiore. *Voice of Jacob* of October 10, 1845, says that Mr de Lara presented a copy to the Queen personally "on Friday last."

1323. Hebrew and English Almanac for the year 5608 —1847-48. Carefully revised and corrected by the Chief Rabbi, the Rev. Dr. Adler, and the Rev. D. Meldola, London.   1847.

1324. DE LARA.—Illuminated Hebrew and English Calendar for 5608.

Dedicated to Sir Anthony de Rothschild. Printed in nine colours and gold, with a tablet representing "King Solomon's Judgment," "typical of the fitness of Jews to exercise legislative functions in honour of the recent return of Baron de Rothschild as a Member of Parliament for the City of London."

1324a. PH. MOSS.—Calendar, English and Hebrew.

1853.

1324b. J. MADDEN.—Almanac, 5615-16.   1855.

1324a. H. FILIPOWSKI.—Hebrew and Roman Almanac from the year 1 C.E. to perpetuity.   1872.

1325. ABRAHAMS.—לוח. Commenced in 1872-3.

1326. M. H. MYERS.—Jewish Calendar and Diary. Compiled by Rev. M. H. Myers. London. 1876.

Annually since 1876.

(L.) COMMUNAL ORGANISATION.

NOTE.—Where no bibliographical references are given the only information known to the Editors is contained in "The Jewish Directory," edited by A. I. Myers. (London, 1873.)

LONDON.

For historical and descriptive accounts of the London community as a whole, see—Picciotto, "Sketches of Anglo-Jewish History"

(No. 303) ; *Examiner*, 1880 ; *Langham Magazine*, 1876 ; Weale, "Handbook to London," pp. 531-7 ; *Jewish World*, Jan. 9, 1880, "The Community as it was," [by Rev. A. L. Green] ; Myers, "Jewish Directory" (1873); J. Jacobs, "Studies in Jewish Statistics" (*Jewish. Chronicle*, 1883) ; Wolf, "Resettlement," &c. (See No. 239.)

1331. ECCLESIASTICAL AUTHORITIES.

Jewish World, Dec. 19, 1879, "The English Rabbinate" [by Rev. A. L. Green]: *Jewish World*, July 22, 1887, "Chachamin of Bevis Marks" [by Lucien Wolf] ; for biographies of individual Rabbis, see Section H., "Miscellanea Biographica."

"Laws and Regulations for all the Synagogues ק״ק אשכנזים in the British Empire." London. 8vo., 23 pp. 1847.

[A model code circulated by the Chief Rabbi for the guidance of the congregations under his charge.]

SYNAGOGUES.

1332. SPANISH AND PORTUGUESE SYNAGOGUE. Founded circa 1640.

History in Picciotto, "Sketches" (No. 303,) *Jewish World*, May 6, 1887.

Laws, 1819, 1831 (Portug.), 1858, 1872 (Eng.) ; amendments undated.

Extract from a scheme submitted to Elders by Mahamad for dealing with freehold property of congregation in city. [Appended is report of solicitors on title deeds and other documents containing some details of history.]

Report to the Elders of the proceedings of the Spanish and Portuguese Jews' Congregation on the occasion of the centenary of Sir Moses Montefiore, Bart. 8vo., 12 pp. 1884.

Lavadores Society [History, *Jewish Chronicle*, Jan. 24, 1879] Reports.

1333. UNITED SYNAGOGUE. Incorporated by Act of Parliament dated 14th July, 1870, 33 and 34 Vic. ch. cxvi. (No. 609.)

History [by A. Asher, M.D.] in Introduction to "Bye laws of the Constituent Synagogues" (1881).

Articles of a new treaty agreed on by the Sub-Committees of the Great, Hambro', and New Synagogues. A.M. 5594 and 5595. 8vo., 11 pp.

Union of the Three Conjoint Synagogues. Report of the Delegates, 1867.

Address of the Wardens of the three City Synagogues, setting forth the reasons for Union. 1868.

Union of the Synagogues. Scheme as finally settled by Council. April, 1869. 8vo., 31 pp.

Alterations and Modifications of the Scheme to the United Synagogue Act. n.d.

Union of the Synagogues. Scheme, which, having been passed by Parliament, received the Royal Assent, July 14, 1870.

United Synagogue Act and Deed of Foundation and Trust, with Scheme as modified. May 24, 1880. 4to., 25 and 4 pp.

Charitable bequests and trusts administered under the direction of the United Synagogue, arranged according to the season of the year at which the dividends are to be distributed. 8vo., 7 pp. 1871.

Bye-laws of the Constituent Synagogues. 8vo., 77 pp. 1881.

Standing Orders of Procedure at Meetings of the Council of the United Synagogue adopted at a meeting of the Council held on June 27, 5631—1871. 8vo., 15 pp.

Accounts and estimates annually since foundation.

Special reports : Abolition of Offerings : Abolition of Privileged Membership : Almshouses : Amalgamation with New Constituent Synagogues : Appointment of a Dayan : Appointment of a Delegate Chief Rabbi : Burial of the Poor : Establishment of a Beth Hamidrash : Extension of Bayswater Synagogue : Financial Regulations : Hasty Interments : Hospital, Asylum, and Prison Visitation : Life Insurance of Officials : Modifications of the Ritual : Motza Distribution : Maintenance of Jewish Children in Reformatory Schools : Pensions to Ministers : Proposed Amalgamation with Oxford Synagogue : Purchase of Land for Cemeteries : Relations with Board of Deputies, Board of Guardians, Schechita Board : Relief of the Poor : Spiritual Condition of the Jewish Poor : Synagogue Accommodation in the Suburbs : Synagogue Choirs : Training of Jewish Ministers.

Burial Society : Laws, 1872.

1334. GREAT SYNAGOGUE.—Founded 1692. Now a Constituent of the United Synagogue.

History in Picciotto " Sketches " (No. 303). U. S. Bye Laws, p. xxx. ; *Jewish World*, May 20, 1887 ; Microcosm of London (illustrated).

Laws : 1771, 1791, 1808, 1810 (Judeo-Germ.) ; 1827 (Hebr. and Eng.) ; 1863 (Eng.)

Burial Society Laws : 1810, 1863.

Institution for relief of decayed members of Great Synagogue. Laws : 1842.

1335. HAMBRO' SYNAGOGUE.—Founded 1726.   Now a Constituent of the United Synagogue.

Historical Notes in U. S. Bye Laws, p. xxx. ; *Jewish Chronicle*, April 22, 1887 ; *Jewish World*, June 3, 1887.
Laws: 1795, 1797 (Judeo-Germ.), 1845 (Eng.), Amendments 1797 (Judeo-Germ.).
Burial Society Laws, 1797.

1336. NEW SYNAGOGUE.—Founded 1760.   Now a Constituent of the United Synagogue.

History in Picciotto "Sketches" (No. 303); U. S. Bye Laws, p. xxxi. ; *Civil Engineer*, I 339 ; *Illustrated London News*, V. 389 ; *Mirror*, Jan. 5 and 12 1839 ; *Jewish World*, June 3, 1887 ; "London Interiors" (illustrated) ; Abraham's "Curiosities" (see No. 566), p. 85.
Laws: 1851.

1337. WESTERN SYNAGOGUE.—Founded 1774.

Historical Notes in *Jewish Chronicle*, Oct. 2, 1857 ; Report Books of the Vestry of St. James's, Westminster.
Laws: 1833, 1842.
Address to members by a member of the Committee 1841.

1338. MAIDEN LANE SYNAGOGUE.—Founded 1815.

1339. WEST LONDON SYNAGOGUE OF BRITISH JEWS. Founded 1841.

History in Picciotto "Sketches" (No. 303) ; *Builder*, 1867, xiv. 499 ; *Illustrated London News*, 1870.
Laws: 1870, 1871, 1874.

1340. CENTRAL SYNAGOGUE.—Founded as branch of Great Synagogue 1855.   Now a Constituent of the United Synagogue.

History in U. S. Bye Laws, p. xxxi. ; Description (illustrated) in *Builder*, 1869, xxvii. 887 ; *Illustrated London News*.
List of donations in aid of Building Fund of Central Synagogue. 8vo., pp. 11, 1870.

1341. BAYSWATER SYNAGOGUE.—Founded 1863.   Now a Constituent of the United Synagogue.

History in U. S. Bye Laws, p. xxxii. ; "Bayswater Guide"; *Illustrated London News*, Feb. 21, 1863 (illustrated).
Laws: 1863.

1342. BOROUGH NEW SYNAGOGUE.—A Constituent of the United Synagogue.

History in U. S. Bye Laws, p. xxxiii.; Description (illustrated), in *Illustrated London News*, May 4, 1867.
Laws : 1868.

1343. NORTH LONDON SYNAGOGUE.—Founded 1868.
Now a Constituent of the United Synagogue.
History in U. S. Bye Laws, p. xxxiii.; Description (illus-
trated), in *Illustrated London News*, Oct. 3, 1868.
Report of Provisional Committee appointed to promote
the building of a Synagogue in Islington, 1863.
Laws : 1869.

1344. DALSTON SYNAGOGUE —Founded 1876. Now a
Constituent of the United Synagogue.
See No. 777.

1345. EAST LONDON SYNAGOGUE. — Founded 1863.
Now a Constituent of the United Synagogue.
History in U. S. Bye Laws, p. xxxiv.

1346. ST. JOHN'S WOOD SYNAGOGUE.
A Constituent of the United Synagogue.
History in U. S. Bye Laws, pp. xxxiii.-iv.

1347. NEW WEST END SYNAGOGUE.
A Constituent of the United Synagogue.
Hist. in U. S. Bye Laws, pp. xxxiv.-v.
Descriptions (illustrated) in *Building News*, 1877, xxxiii.
28; 1878, p. 779.

1348. HACKNEY SYNAGOGUE.

MINOR SYNAGOGUES AND HEBRAS.

Historical notices appeared in *Jewish Chronicle*, Nov. 17,
1876, and Aug. 3, 1877.

1349. GERMAN (now SPITAL SQUARE) SYNAGOGUE.—
Founded 1858.
Laws, 1880.
Burial Society Laws.

1350. SANDY'S ROW SYNAGOGUE : SOCIETY, "KINDNESS
AND TRUTH."—Founded 1851.
Laws, 1867, 1879.

1351. PRESCOTT STREET SYNAGOGUE.—Founded 1748.

1352. SCARBOROUGH STREET SYNAGOGUE. — Founded
1792.

1353. PRINCES STREET SYNAGOGUE.—Founded 1870.

1354. POLISH SYNAGOGUE.—Founded *circa* 1790.

1355. FASHION STREET SYNAGOGUE.—Founded 1858.

1356. WHITE'S ROW SYNAGOGUE: SOCIETY, "SOUL OF MAN." Founded 1860.

1357. SOCIETY, "LOVERS OF PEACE."—Founded 1863.

CEMETERIES.

1358. SPANISH AND PORTUGUESE, Mile End Road. Founded 1657. (Closed.)
Jewish Chronicle, Nov. 26, Dec. 3 and 10, 1880.
Lysons, "Environs of London."

1359. SPANISH AND PORTUGUESE, Mile End Road.
Jewish World, Nov. 5, 1880.
Lysons, "Environs of London."

·1360. UNITED SYNAGOGUE. Willesden.
Thornbury, "Greater London."

1361. GREAT SYNAGOGUE. Alderney Street, Mile End, E. (Closed.)
Lysons, "Environs of London."

1362. GREAT SYNAGOGUE. North [now Brady] Street, Mile End New Town, E. (Closed.)

1363. GREAT SYNAGOGUE. West Ham, E.

1364. HAMBRO' SYNAGOGUE. Hoxton Street, Hoxton, N. (Closed.)
Lysons, "Environs of London."

1365. HAMBRO' SYNAGOGUE. Grove Street, Hackney, E. (Closed.)

1366. NEW SYNAGOGUE, North [now Brady] Street, Mile End New Town, E. (Closed.)

1367. WESTERN SYNAGOGUE, Brompton. (Closed.)

1368. WESTERN SYNAGOGUE, Edmonton.

1369. MAIDEN LANE SYNAGOGUE, Bancroft Road, E.

1370. WEST LONDON SYNAGOGUE, Balls Pond, N.

SCHOOLS.

1371. "GATES OF HOPE" SCHOOLS.—Founded 1664.
Picciotto "Sketches," pp. 41, 154; Laws of Spanish and Portuguese Congregation, pp. 95, 97.

1372. SPANISH AND PORTUGUESE VILLAREAL SCHOOL.—
Founded 1730.
Picciotto " Sketches," p. 75 ; Laws of Spanish and Portuguese Congregation, p. 93.

1373. WESTMINSTER JEWS' FREE SCHOOL.— Founded 1811

ארשת שפתים אשר בשר במקהלות אחד מהצעירים מתלמידי
חברת תלמוד תורה   בוועסטמינסטער ביום
הועד   תרייח
s. sh. fol. 1856.
Reports.

1374. JEWS' FREE SCHOOL.—Founded 1817.
History, *Jewish Chronicle*, Feb. 16, 1883.
Reports annually.
" Isaac Cohen " : Prize Essays by R. Benjamin (1871) ;
R. Harris (1872) ; A. Levy (1873).

1375. SPANISH AND PORTUGUESE NATIONAL AND IN-
FANT SCHOOL.—Founded 1839.

1376. JEWS' INFANT SCHOOLS.—Founded 1841.
Address on the opening of the School, 14th Sept., 1841,
with a list of subscribers. 8vo., 16 pp. 1841.
Reports annually.

1377. WEST METROPOLITAN JEWISH SCHOOL (now JEW-
ISH HIGH SCHOOL FOR GIRLS).—Founded 1845.
Reports annually.

1378. JEWS' COLLEGE.—Founded 1852.
History, by M. H. Picciotto, in " Report on Training of
Jewish Ministers," presented to Council of United Synagogue, 1877.
Reports annually.

1379. STEPNEY JEWISH SCHOOLS.—Founded 1865.
Reports annually.

1380. BAYSWATER JEWISH SCHOOL.—Founded 1866.
Reports annually.

1381. BOROUGH JEWISH SCHOOLS.—Founded 1867.
Reports annually.

1382. Code of Standards of Examination in Hebrew
and Religion issued by the Chief Rabbi, 1885.

CHARITABLE INSTITUTIONS.

1383. SPANISH AND PORTUGUESE ORPHAN SOCIETY.—
Founded 1703.
Laws, 1828, 1863.

J. Dias : A Lecture illustrative of the present condition and comparative merits of the Spanish and Portuguese Jews Clothing Society, 1831.

1384. ALMSHOUSES OF SPANISH AND PORTUGUESE CONGREGATION.—Founded 1703.

1385. SOCIETY FOR GRANTING MARRIAGE PORTIONS TO FATHERLESS GIRLS OF THE SPANISH AND PORTUGUESE CONGREGATION.—Founded 1720.
Laws, 1840.
[Preceded by "A short Account of the Society."]

1386. HONEN DALIM, MENACHEM ABELIM, HEBRAT YEOTMOT, AND HEBRAT MOALIM.—Founded 1724.

1387. SOCIETY FOR INITIATING THE POOR INTO THE COVENANT OF ABRAHAM.—Founded 1745.
Laws, 1848, 1856, 1874, 1886.

1388. BETH HOLIM HOSPITAL.—Founded 1747.
History in *Jewish Chronicle*, Feb. 25, 1876.

1389. SPANISH AND PORTUGUESE LOAN SOCIETY.—Founded 1749.

1390. BREAD, MEAT, AND COAL CHARITY.—Founded 1780.
History in *Jewish Chronicle*, July 21, 1876.
[Lucien Wolf] "The 'Meshebat Naphesh,' 5540-5640. Early History and Anecdotes" [Reprinted from *Jewish World*]. 12mo. 11 pp. 1879.
Laws, 1797.
Centennial Report, 1879.

1391. HOLY LAND RELIEF FUND.—Founded 1805.

1392. JEWS' HOSPITAL (Founded 1808) AND ORPHAN ASYLUM (Founded 1831). Amalgamated 1876.
History of Hospital, *Jewish Chronicle*, Dec. 31, 1875 ; of Orphan Asylum, in "Memoir of Isaac Valentine" (see No. 830), *Jewish Chronicle*, October 30, 1868, and Jan. 14, 1876 ; *Jewish Record*, Nov. 13, 1868.
Laws (Hospital), 1808.
Reports (Hospital) annually to 1876.
   „   (Orphan Asylum) annually to 1876.
   „   (Amalgamation) 1878, 1879, 1880, 1881, 1882, 1883, 1884.
See No. 771.

1393. BARROW'S ALMSHOUSES.—Founded 1816.

M

1394. INSTITUTION FOR RELIEVING THE INDIGENT BLIND.
Founded 1819.
List of Life-Governors and Annual Subscribers.   (15 pp.)
1878.

1395. MONTEFIORE ALMSHOUSES.—Founded 1823.
Wolf: "Life of Sir M. Montefiore" (see No. 839),
pp. 43-44.

1396. PHILANTHROPIC SOCIETY FOR RELIEVING DIS-
TRESSED WIDOWS.—Founded 1825.
Reports annually.

1397. SOCIETY FOR RELIEVING THE AGED NEEDY.—
Founded 1829.
History in *Jewish Chronicle*, Oct. 6, 1876.
Reports (containing also Laws, Lists of Officers, &c.), 1869,
1877, 1880, 1883.

1398. SOCIETY FOR CHEERING THE NEEDY AT FESTIVALS.
Founded 1829.

1399. BOARD OF GUARDIANS (SPANISH AND PORTUGUESE).
Founded 1837.   Reconstituted 1878.
History in Report for 1879.
Laws : 1878.
Reports annually since 1879.

1400. LYON MOSES ALMSHOUSES.—Founded 1838.

1401. SURREY JEWISH PHILANTHROPIC SOCIETY. —
1840.

1402. HAND-IN-HAND ASYLUM (Founded 1840) AND
WIDOWS' HOME (Founded 1843) INSTITUTION.
Now amalgamated.
History in *Jewish Chronicle*, April 14, 1876.
Reports (Hand-in-Hand). ⎫
   „   (Widows).   ⎬ Annually.
   „   (Amalgamated).   ⎭

1403. JEWISH LADIES' WEST END CHARITY.—Founded
1842.

1404. "INDEPENDENT FRIENDS" BREAD AND COAL
SOCIETY.—Founded 1843.

1405. "SIR PAUL PINDAR" BENEVOLENT SOCIETY.—
Founded 1844.
Reports (containing also Laws, Lists of Officers, &c.),
1859, 1873.

1406. JEWISH LADIES' BENEVOLENT LOAN SOCIETY.—
Founded 1844.
Reports annually since 1868.

1406a. JEWISH LYING-IN CHARITY.
Laws, 1845.

1407. JOEL EMANUEL'S ALMSHOUSES.—Founded 1849.

1408. MARRIAGE PORTION SOCIETY.—Founded 1850.
Laws, 1858, 1871.

1408a. JEWS' EMIGRATION SOCIETY.—Founded 1853.
Reports annually.
Copies of Letters addressed to the Commissioners of Im-
migration of New York, and to the United Hebrew Charities
of New York, 1884.
Copy of Letters written by request to the Alliance
Israélite of Paris, and to the Trustees of the Mansion House
Fund for the relief of the Russo-Jewish refugees, asking for
a money grant to the Jewish Emigrants' Aid Society and
Labour Bureau of New York, 1884.
Extracts from Letters of American Jews on the Immigra-
tion Question, 1884.

1409. SOUP KITCHEN FOR JEWISH POOR.—Founded 1853.
History in *Jewish Chronicle*, July 21, 1876.

1410. BOARD OF GUARDIANS, ETC.—Founded 1859.
History in *Jewish Chronicle*, Aug. 18 and Sept. 29, 1876;
also in Twenty-fifth Report (1884); *Our Time*, May, 1881.
Lionel L. Cohen : Scheme for the Better Management of
all the Poor, &c. 1859.
Jewish Poor in London : *Jewish Chronicle*, April 20 and
27 and May 4, 1860.
Foreign Poor in London : by J. Jacobs, *Jewish Chronicle*,
March 9, 1883.
Reports : 1860 (contains historical account of London
Jewish poor since 1690) and annually.

1411. EXCELSIOR RELIEF FUND.—Founded 1860.
Reports : annually since 1862.

1412. SALOMONS ALMSHOUSES.—Founded 1862.

1413. JACOB HENRY MOSES' ALMSHOUSES.—Founded
1862.

1414. JEWS' DEAF AND DUMB HOME.—Founded 1865.
History in *Jewish Chronicle*, Jan. 26, 1876.
[Sir] Henry A. Isaacs : " Sounds versus Signs. A brief
comparison of the two systems now in use for the education
of deaf mutes." 1865.
Reports annually.

164   BIBLIOTHECA ANGLO-JUDAICA.

1415. CITY OF LONDON BENEVOLENT SOCIETY FOR
ASSISTING WIDOWS IN DISTRESS.—Founded 1867.
Annual Statements since 1868.

1416. SABBATH MEALS SOCIETY.—Founded 1868.
Laws, 1881.
Balance-sheets annually.

1417. PENNY DINNERS SOCIETY.—Founded 1869.

1418. JEWISH CONVALESCENT HOME.—Founded 1869.
History in *Jewish Chronicle*, March 17, 1876.
Reports, annually since 1873.

1419. EAST LONDON (formerly STEPNEY) JEWISH BENE-
VOLENT SOCIETY.—Founded 1869.
Laws, 1870, 1879.

1420. HELPING HAND PENSION SOCIETY.—Founded 1870.
Laws, 1877. [Introduction gives History of Society.]

1421. CONVALESCENT HOME FOR INFANTS.—Founded
1870.

1422. JEWISH HOME (formerly JEWISH WORKHOUSE).—
Founded 1871.
History in *Jewish Chronicle*, Feb. 3 and April 14, 1871;
and April 14, 1876.
Reports annually since 1872.

1423. CITY OF LONDON BENEVOLENT SOCIETY. —
Founded 1871.

1424. JEWISH LADIES' ASSOCIATION FOR PREVENTIVE
AND RESCUE WORK.—Founded 1884.
Reports 1885, 1886.

1425. POOR JEWS' TEMPORARY SHELTER.—Founded 1885.
History in *Jewish World*, 1885, and First Report.
Laws, 1885.
Report 1885-6.

1425a. CHARITY FOR THE RELIEF OF THE AGED DES-
TITUTE.

1425b. FIVE SHILLING SABBATH CHARITY.

1425c. "GOOD INTENT" BENEVOLENT SOCIETY.

1425d. LADIES' BENEVOLENT INSTITUTION.

1425e. PACIFICO ALMSHOUSES.

1425f. PASSOVER RELIEF FUND.

1426. JEWISH WARDS IN GENERAL HOSPITALS.
Jewish Chronicle, Feb. 11, 1876.

FRIENDLY SOCIETIES.

1427. "Path of Peace."—Founded 1782.

1428. "Path of Righteousness."—Founded *circa* 1790.
Laws (revised), 1862.

1429 "Loyal Independent Lodge of Good Fellows."
Founded 1810.

1430. "Tent of Righteousness" Friendly Society.
Founded 1812.
Laws (revised and amended), 1886.

1431. "Path of Rectitude."—Founded 1816.

1432. Loyal United Lodge "Sons of Israel."—
Founded 1820.

1433. Society "Charity escapeth an evil Death."—
Founded 1830.

1434. Jewish National Friendly Motza Association.—Founded 1840.

1435. Foreign United Brothers Benefit Society.—
Founded 1854.
Laws, 1878.

1436. "Sisterhood Society."—Founded 1856.

1437. "United Brethren."—Founded 1856.

1438. "Holy Calling and Support of Jerusalem"
Friendly Society.—Founded 1858.

1439. Jewish Mutual "Birmingham" Benefit Society.—Founded 1862.

1440. Ancient Order of Foresters—
Court "Sons of Abraham." Founded 1863.
Court "Sons of Israel."—Founded 1863.
Court "Shield of David."—Founded 1865.

1441. Jewish Females' Confined Mourning Society.
Founded 1870.
Rules, 1877.

1442. Spanish and Portuguese Provident Burial
Society.—Founded 1872.

1443. Metropolitan Jewish Confined Mourning
and Burial Society.—Founded 1874.
Rules, 1874.

1443a. Jewish Medical Aid Society.

166 BIBLIOTHECA ANGLO-JUDAICA.

1443b. JEWISH MUTUAL BENEFIT FUND.

1443c. "PURSUERS OF PEACE."

1443d. "RIGHTEOUS PATH."

1443e. "SOCIAL UNION."

MISCELLANEOUS.

1444. BOARD OF DEPUTIES. – Founded 1745.
Constitution 1855 ; amended 1883.
Reports to 1874, half-yearly and afterwards annually.
Appeal on behalf of the famishing Jews in the Holy Land.
16 pp. London. 1854.
Morocco Mission : Letters from Sir Moses Montefiore,
Bart., to J. M. Montefiore, Esq. 40 pp. London. 1864.
Roumanian Mission : Report of Sir Moses Montefiore,
1867.
Translation of a Letter addressed by Sir Moses Monte-
fiore, Bart., ... to the Jewish Congregations of the
Holy Land. 82 pp. London. 1874.
Palestine. Report by S. Montagu, 1875.
Report on Morocco Mission by M. H. Picciotto.
Reports : Parliamentary Grants to Schools, 1852 ; Persian
Famine Relief Fund, 1873 ; Mission to Holy Land by Sir
M. Montefiore, 1866.

1445. ANGLO-JEWISH ASSOCIATION.—Founded 1871.
Laws, 1880.
Reports annually since 1872.
Trial of Jews at Buseo, Roumania, 1872.
Jews of Roumania, by I. Davis, 1872.
Public Meeting at Mansion House (Russian Jews), 1882.
Notes of information obtained at Bucharest by D. F.
Schloss, 1886. See also 568, 593.
Education in the East, by Dr. M. Allatini ; translated by
J. Picciotto.
Memorial to Shah, Persian and English, 1873.

1446. ROUMANIAN COMMITTEE.—Founded 1872.
Address to the Jews of Great Britain, 1872.
Report, 1875.

1447. TURKISH SUFFERERS FUND.—Established 1877.
Appeal, 1877.

1448. MANSION HOUSE FUND FOR THE RELIEF OF THE
PERSECUTED JEWS OF RUSSIA.—Founded 1882.
Report 1886.
See Nos. 578, 579, and 590.

1449. VISITATION COMMITTEE.—Founded 1886.
Rules for the guidance of Ministers and others visiting the
Jewish Poor. 4to., 4 pp. 1886.

1450. BOARD FOR THE AFFAIRS OF SCHECHITAH.—
Founded 1805.
Statements [giving Statistics of Animals slaughtered] half-
yearly.
The Communicability to Man of Diseases from Animals
used as Food. By Dr. H. Behrend, 1881. [Reprinted from
the *Jewish Chronicle*, and issued by the Board.]

1451. HESHAIM COLLEGE.—Founded 1664.
History in *Jewish Chronicle*, Dec. 10, 1875.

1452. BETH HAMIDRASH.—Founded *circa* 1700.
History in *Jewish Chronicle*, Dec. 24, 1875.
A. Neubauer: Catalogue of the Hebrew MSS. in the
Jews' College, London. 8vo., pp. 64. Oxford, 1886.
[Privately printed.]

1453. ASSOCIATION FOR CIRCULATING STANDARD WORKS.
See *Voice of Jacob*, Nov. 25, 1842.

1454. ASSOCIATION FOR THE PROMOTION OF LITERATURE
AFFECTING JEWISH INTERESTS.
See *Voice of Jacob*, Dec. 23, 1842; and Jan. 6, 1843.

1455. JEWS AND GENERAL LITERARY AND SCIENTIFIC
INSTITUTION.
Catalogue of the Library, pp. 66. London, 1847.
Addenda to Catalogue, pp. 7. London, 1849.
Syllabus each Session.

1456. HEBREW ANTIQUARIAN SOCIETY.
See *Jewish Chronicle*, May 9, 1851.

1457. JEWISH ASSOCIATION FOR THE DIFFUSION OF
RELIGIOUS KNOWLEDGE.—Founded 1860.
Constitution, n. d.
Reports annually since 1861.
Sabbath Readings.
Tracts.

1458. SOCIETY OF HEBREW LITERATURE. — Founded
1870.
See *Jewish Record*, July 8, 1870. See Nos. 2010, 2011,
2011*a*, 5022.

1461. JEWISH VOLUNTEER CORPS.
See *Jewish Chronicle*, May 3, 1861.

1462. NETHERLANDS CHORAL SOCIETY.—Founded 1869.

1463. JEWISH WORKING MEN'S CLUB.—Founded 1875.

1463*a*. PROVINCIAL JEWISH MINISTERS' FUND.

1464. FOUR PER CENT. INDUSTRIAL DWELLINGS COMPANY.
Prospectus, 1886.
Reports Annually.

PROVINCIAL.

1465. BATH—
Synagogue.

1466. BELFAST—
Synagogue. Founded 1872.

1467. BIRMINGHAM—
History of Community in *Jewish World*, June 15, 22, 29, July 15,
20, 27, and Aug, 3, 1877.
Synagogue. Founded *circa* 1680.
See Nos. 1580 and 1581.
Laws, 1872.
Reports annually since 1853.
Hebrew National Schools. Founded 1840.
Reports.
Hebrew Board of Guardians. Founded 1870.
Reports annually since 1871.
Hebrew Benevolent Educational Society.
Hebrew Philanthropic Society. Founded 1828.
Provident Co-operative Matza Association. Founded
1870.
Loyal Independent United Israelites Benefit Society.
Founded 1853.
Ladies' Benevolent Society.
Court "Jacob's Pride" of Ancient Order of Foresters.
Laws, 1874.
Hebrew Young Men's Literary and Debating Society.
Report, 1878.

1468. BRADFORD—
Synagogue.

1469. BRIGHTON—
Synagogue. Founded 1823.
See Nos. 1582 and 1583.
Laws.
Schools. Founded 1871.
Reports.
Hebrew Philanthropic Society.
Reports.

1470. BRISTOL—
Synagogue.
See No. 1584.
Hebrew Ladies' Benevolent Society.

1471. CANTERBURY—
Synagogue. Founded *circa* 1760.

1472. CARDIFF—
Synagogue. Founded 1840.

1473. CHATHAM—
    Synagogue. Founded *circa* 1760.
1474. CHELTENHAM—
    Synagogue. Founded 1837.
    See No. 1585.
1475. COVENTRY—
    Synagogue. Founded 1850.
1476. DOVER—
    Synagogue. Founded 1862.
    See No. 1586.
    Jewish Ladies' Philanthropic Society.
1477. DUBLIN—
    Synagogue. Founded 1822.
    Philanthropic Society.
    Ladies' Society.
1478. EDINBURGH—
    History of Community in *Jewish World*, April 13, 1883.
    Synagogue.
    Laws,
1479. EXETER—
    Synagogue. Founded 1764.
1480. FALMOUTH—
    Synagogue.
1481. GLASGOW—
    History of the Community by James Brown. (See No. 296.)
    Synagogue.
    See No. 1587.
    Hebrew School.
    Philanthropic Society.
1482. HANLEY—
    Synagogue. Founded 1872.
1483. WEST HARTLEPOOL—
    Synagogue.
    School.
1484. HULL—
    Synagogue.
    Hebrew Schools.
    Hebrew Board of Guardians. Founded 1880.
    Reports annually since 1881.
    Jewish Soup Kitchen. Founded 1872.
1485. LEEDS—
    Synagogue. Founded 1840.
    Board of Guardians.
    Reports annually from 1878.
    Society for the Relief of the Sick. Founded 1872.
    Ladies' Lying-in Society. Founded 1872.
    "Social Union" Benefit Society. Founded 1854.

1486. LEICESTER—
Synagogue.

1487. LIVERPOOL—
History of Community in *Jewish World*, Aug. 10, 17, 24, and 31, 1877.
Synagogue (Seel Street). Founded 1780.
Laws, 1818.
Synagogue (Hope Place). Founded 1842.
See No. 1590.
Hebrews' Educational Institution and Endowed Schools.
Founded 1840.
Reports.
Hebrew Philanthropic Society. Founded 1811.
Board of Guardians.
Reports annually since 1877.
Society for Visiting and Aiding the Sick.
Jewish Ladies' Benevolent Institution. Founded 1849.
Report of Committee of Ball, 1877.
Visiting Committees of the Hebrew Congregations of
Manchester and Liverpool.
Report, 1884.
Soup Kitchen for Jewish Boys.
Society or Clothing Boys of the Educational Institution.
Founded 1866.
Hebrews Free Loan Society. Founded 1861.
Jewish Literary and Debating Society.
Reports annually from 1875.
Jewish Choral Society. Founded 1871.

1488. MANCHESTER—
History of Community in *Jewish World*, Sept. 7, 14, 21, Oct. 12,
19, Nov. 2, 9, 16, 23 and 30, 1877.
See Nos. 1644 and 1645.
Synagogue (Great). Founded 1780.
Synagogue (Reform). Founded 1856.
Synagogue (South). Founded 1873.
Synagogue (Portuguese). Founded 1874.
Jews' School. Founded 1838.
Reports annually since 1839.
Talmud Torah Report, 1886.
Board of Guardians. Founded 1867.
Reports annually since 1868.
Hebrew Philanthropic and Loan Society. Founded
1825.
Ladies' Association for Visiting the Jewish Poor.
Reports, 1885, 1886.
Visiting Committee of the Hebrew Congregations of Man-
chester and Liverpool.
Report, 1884.
Hebrew Sisters Charity.
Report, 1872.
Hebrew Sick and Burial Benefit Society. Founded 1860.
Cracow Hebrew Society. Founded 1868.

1489. MERTHYR TYDVIL—
 Synagogue. Founded 1848.
 See No. 1646.

1490. MIDDLESBOROUGH—
 Synagogue.

1491. NEWCASTLE—
 History of Community in *Jewish World*, Dec. 21, 28, 1877, and
  Jan. 4 and 18, 1878.
 Report of Meeting of Members of Old and New Con-
  gregations, 1873.
 Synagogue. Founded 1837.
 See No. 1647.
 Laws.
 Congregational Schools.
 Reports.
 Hebrew Philanthropic Society. Founded 1853.
 Jewish Ladies Benevolent Society. Founded 1872.
 Hebrew "Friend in Need" Society. Founded 1873.
 Hebrew Ancient Sacred Society.
 New Hebrew Friendly Society.

1492. NEWPORT (MON.)—
 Synagogue.
 Benevolent and Loan Society. Founded 1873.

1493. NORWICH—
 Synagogue.

1494. NOTTINGHAM—
 Synagogue.
 Hebrew Philanthropic Society.
 Laws, 1884.

1495. PENZANCE—
 Synagogue.

1496. PLYMOUTH—
 Synagogue. Founded 1762.
 "Jacob Nathan" School. Founded 1868.
 "Hand-in-Hand" Charitable Society. Founded 1861.

1497. PORTSMOUTH—
 Synagogue. Founded 1747.
 History in *Jewish World*, Dec. 3, 1887.
 Laws, 1873.
 Aria College. Founded 1874.
 History in *Jewish Chronicle*, March 22 and 29, 1872.
 Hebrew Educational Classes. Founded 1862.
 Hebrew Benevolent Institution. Founded 1804.
 Ladies' Provident Society. Founded 1770.
 Jewish Almshouses. Founded 1851.

1498. RAMSGATE—
 Synagogue. Founded 1831.

See Wolf, "Life of Sir M. Montefiore " (No. 839), p. 51.
See Nos. 1648 and 1649.
Judith Lady Montefiore Theological College.   Founded
1866.
  Deed of Foundation, 1867.
  Statutes, 1867.

1499. SHEFFIELD—
  Synagogue.   Founded 1850.
  Schools.
  Board of Guardians.   Founded 1885.
    Reports, 1886.
  Jewish Sisters' Benevolent Society.
  Hebrew Benevolent Society.   Founded 1873.
    Laws, 1873.

1500. NORTH SHIELDS—
  Synagogue.

  SOUTH SHIELDS—
  Synagogue.

1501. SOUTHAMPTON—
  Synagogue.   Founded 1865.
  See No. 1650.
  Hebrew Sabbath School.
  Society for the Relief of the Poor.

1502. SUNDERLAND—
  Synagogue.
  See No. 1651.
  School.
  Hebrew Benevolent Society.   Founded 1871.
    Laws, 1873.
  Young Men's Hebrew Benevolent Society.
  Hebrew Benefit Society.

1503. SWANSEA—
  Synagogue.
  See No. 1652.
  Jewish School.

1504. TREDEGAR—
  Synagogue.
  Hebrew Benevolent Society.

1505. WOLVERHAMPTON—
  Synagogue.
  See No. 1653.
  School.
  Hebrew Benevolent Society.

1506. YARMOUTH—
  Synagogue.
  See No. 1654.

COLONIAL.

1507. JAMAICA—
Synagogue (Kingston).
See No. 1589.
Hebrew Benevolent Society (Kingston). Founded 1851.
Laws, 1853, 1862.

1508. INDIA—
Israelite School of the Anglo-Jewish Association (Bombay).
Reports annually from 1880.
Bene Israel Benevolent Society (Bombay).
Reports annually from 1854,
Jewish Boys' and Girls' School (Calcutta).
Reports, 1882, 1883, 1884, 1885.

1509. AUSTRALIA—
"Jews of New South Wales," *Jewish World*, Sept. 5, 1884.
"Jewish Benevolent Societies of Sydney," pp. 40-41, "Charity and Philanthropy," by Rev. S. W. Brooks. Sydney, 1878.
Synagogues (Sydney).
History in *Jewish Chronicle*, Sept. 5, 1873.
Reports, 1845-1878.
See No. 1655.
Synagogue (Melbourne).
See No. 1643.
Laws, 1848.
Reports, 1881, 1882, 1883, 1884, 1885, 1886.
Synagogue (East Melbourne).
Report, 1878.
Hebrew Certified Denominational School (Sydney).
Reports.
Hebrew Philanthropic and Orphan Society (Sydney).
Laws, 1873.

1510. CAPE OF GOOD HOPE—
Synagogue (Cape Town).
Synagogue (Kimberley).
See No. 1588
Jewish Benevolent Society (Cape Town).
Laws, 1878.
Benevolent Society (Griqualand West).
Laws, 1878.

(M.) RITUAL.*

PRAYERBOOKS, &c.

1511. הגדה של פסח. London. 1709.

1512. GAMALIEL BEN PEDAHZUR.—The Book of Religion : Ceremonies and Prayers of the Jews as prac-

* A number of works issued in Marathi by the Beni Israel are catalogued, but without years of publication, in Cat., pp. 46-47.

tised in their Synagogues and Families on all occasions. Translated from the Hebrew by G. b. P., Gent. 2 parts. 8vo.   1738.

1513. I. NIETO.—Orden de las oraciones de Ros-ashanah y Kipur. Nuevamente traduzidas por I. Nieto.   1740.

1514. —— Orden de las Oraciones de Ros Ashanah y Kipur, par E.I.H., H.R., Ishac Nieto, Rab del K.K. de Londres.   1740.

1515. Prayers for Shabbath, Rosh-Hashanah and Kippur, with the Amidah and Musaph of the Moadim, according to the Order of the Spanish and Portuguese Jews. Translated by Isaac Pinto, and for him printed by John Holt in New York.   1766.
[The Mahamad would not allow a translation to be printed in England.]

1517. SOLOMON BEN JUDAH BEN GABIROL.—Keter Malchut .... traduzido por I. Nieto.   1769.

1518. TEPHILLOTH, containing the Forms of Prayers which are publicly used in the Synagogues. From the original. Translated by R. Meyers and A. Alexander. 213 pp.   1770.

1519. A. ALEXANDER.—The הגדה של פסח, containing the Ceremonies and Prayers which are used and read by all families in all houses of the Israelites. Translated by A. Alexander and assistants.   1770.
[Fifth edition in 1808.]

1520. Orden de las oraciones cotidienas .... nuevamente traduzidas. Por I. Nieto.   1771.

1521. A. ALEXANDER.—ספר פתיחה להתפלות, or a Key to part of the Hebrew Liturgy : containing several very remarkable paragraphs worth the reader's notice. Likewise a Chronological Summary of remarkable things relating thereto. 12mo.   1775.

1522. —— Fast Day Prayers, with translation. [Spanish rite.]   1776.

1523. HAGADA.—סדר הגדה לפסח.   1778.
[With Jew-German lettering.]

1524. Liturgies—Spanish Rite.—סדר עבודות כהן
גדול ביום הכפורים 1780.

1525. סדר הושענות. Prayers for Tabernacles. 1780.

1525a. רפואת הנפש. Prayers and Readings for those
who visit the Sick. 1780.

1526. S. Alexander.— Pentateuch and Haphtaroth,
with English translation and Notes. 5 vols., 8vo.
London. 1785.
[Printed by Alexander and Son, No. 11, Church Street,
Spitalfields.]

1527. A. Alexander.—Arvith L'ir Kippur. Service
translated into English. 1787.
[German rite.]

1528. A. Alexander.—Hagadah Translated. 1787.

1529. D. Levi.—Translation of the Pentateuch. 1787.

1530. A. Alexander.—Festival Prayers. [Spanish
rite.] 1788.

1531. —— Daily Prayers, with English Translation.
[Spanish rite.] 1788.

1532. —— Rosh Hashonah Service, translated into
English. [German rite.] 1789.

1533. Isaac Delgado.—A new English translation of
the Pentateuch. 4to. 239 pp. [A.N.]. List of
Subscribers. 1789.
[Dedicated to the Bishop of Salisbury.]

1534. D. H. Schiff. — שירות ותשבחות. Occasional
Prayers. Great Synagogue. 4to. 1790.

1534a. M. Edrehi.—ספר תורת חיים—מאמרי הזוהר ותג"ך
ותפלות. Edited by Moses ben I. Edrehi. 1792.
[Readings for Sabbath Eves, mostly from Zohar.]

1535. D. Levi.—Hagadah, translated 1794.

1535a. D. Levi.—Daily Prayers, translated 1801.

1536. Form and Service of the Hosannas as said at the
Feast of Tabernacles, according to the Custom of
the Polish and German Jews. Translated into
English by A. Alexander. 74 pp. 1807.

1536a. הגדה של פסח כמנהג ספרדים. Orden de la Agada

de Pesah en Hebraico y Español. Traducido por
J. Meldola.   1813.

1537. A. ALEXANDER.—Alexander's interpreting Tephilloth. [German Rite.]   1817.

1538. LEVY ALEXANDER.—A.'s Hebrew Ritual and
Doctrinal Explanation of the whole Ceremonial
Law, oral and traditional, of the Jewish Community in England and Foreign parts. 8vo. London.   1819.

1538a. J. VAN OVEN.—Form of Daily Prayers with
English translation and Preface.   1822.

1539. L. ALEXANDER.—The Holy Bible in Hebrew and
English. 8vo.   A.M. 5584 (1824).

1540. DAVID AARON DE SOLA.—סדר ברכות. The Blessings ; or, Expressions of Praise and Thanksgiving
said by Israelites on various occasions, with an
Interlineary Translation, accompanied with an Ex-
plication of their Source, the Precepts, and דינים
(regulations) attached to them and explanatory
notes. To which is prefixed an Introductory Essay
on the Motives and Duty of Thanksgiving. 8vo.
London.   1829.

1542. L. E. PYKE.—Form   Prayers for Hosanna
Rabba, including the Hosannas, pp. 81.   1830.

1543.—שער התפלה וסדר העבודה . . . revised by J. Levi.
                                                1830.
[Appeared with English translation in 1834.]

1544. H. N. SOLOMON.—Daily Prayers. For the use of
the Jews' Free School.   1830.
[Seventh edition in 1861.]

1545. Hagadah, with D. Levi's translation reprinted by
H. Barnett.   1833.

1545a. סדר תפלת ישראל Daily Prayers (Sabbath and
Festival), with explanatory rules by H. A. Henry.
2 vols.   1836.

1545b. שער התפלה וסדר העבודה . . . . revised by I. L.
Lyon. Hebrew and English.   1836.

1546. סדר תפלות כמנהג ק״ק ספרדים. Forms of Prayer, with an English translation by D. A. de Sola. To which are added Tables, forming a complete Hebrew Almanac from 1836-8. 5 vols. 1836-8.

1547. NATHAN ISAAC VALENTINE. — תפלה קרבן תודה לנשים יולדות. Form of Prayer to be used by ladies when they go to Synagogue after their accouchement. [Translated by H. A. Henry.] 16mo. 1837.

1548. West London Synagogue of British Jews.—Daily Prayers. סדר התפלות. Forms of Prayer used in the West London Synagogue of British Jews, with an English translation. Edited by D. W. Marks (and A. Loewy). 5 vols. Lond. 8vo.
5601-3 [1841-43].
[A second edition of Vol. I. in 1859.]

1548a. West London Synagogue of British Jews.— Hagada for the Night of Passover. Edited by D. W. Marks. 1842.

1549. תפלה. The Daily Prayers, &c. Fourth edition. London, 5602. 8vo. 1842.

1550. HAGADA.—סדר הגדה של פסח לונדון בני ישראל. London. 8vo. 1843.

1551. תפלת נכונה. London, 5608. 8vo. 1848.

1552. REV. B. H. ASCHER.—ספר החיים. Book of Life, in Hebrew and English. London. 1846.
[A second edition appeared in 1861.]

1553. חסד אמת. —Prayers, Instructions, Laws, &c., &c., for the Guidance of those who have to perform the Solemn Duties of רחיצת המת according to the Minhag of the Spanish and Portuguese Jews. London. 1846.

The prayers translated and the whole arranged by Solomon Sequerra. Approved at a meeting of the Society of מקוה ישראל Rohazim רוחצים, held Rosh Hodesh Tebet, 5605. Printed at the expense of Isaac Jalfon, Esq. (Cf. advertisement in *V. of J.*, Jan. 2, 1846.)

1555. RABBI HIRSCH EDELMANN.—הגיון לב Meditation
of the Heart. Hebrew Daily Prayer.   1847.
(Published for the author, Bury Street, St. Mary Axe.)

1556. מחזור מכל השנה, with the Translation of D. Levi.
6 vols. Lond. 8vo.   1850?

1557. M. H. BRESSLAU.—תחנות לבנות ישראל Devotions
of the Daughters of Israel. Edited by M. H. B.,
from the German. Lond.   1852.

1558. MIRIAM WERTHEIMER.—Devotional Exercises for
the Use of Jewish Women on Public and Domestic
Occasions. Translated from the German of Dr.
Wolfgang Wessely. Lond.   1852.

1559. ISRAEL ALBU (from Berlin).—Hours of Devotion.
Lond.   1852.
[Dedicated to the Baroness Lionel de Rothschild.]

1560. תפלה מכל השנה. Hebrew and English. London.
8vo.   1852?

1561. —— Abraham's interlineary Tephillath, &c.
London. 8vo.   1853.

1562. —— תפלה נכונה · · · מוגה ומדויקת היטב ע״פ כמה
ספרי תפלות.—The Daily Prayers . . . Sixth Edition.
Revised and corrected with Emendations and Notes
by H. N. Solomon. Hebrew and English. London,
5614. 8vo.   1854.

1563. —— סדר תפלת ישראל.—Daily Prayers (Sabbath
and Festival Prayers), with explanatory Rules, &c.
2 vols. London. 8vo.   1854.

1564. HESTER ROTHSCHILD.—אמרי לב. Prayers and
Meditations for every situation and occasion in life.
Translated and adapted from the French. London.
1856.
[The profits to be devoted to the Jews' Orphan Asylum.]

1565. חמשה חומשי תורה עם ההפטרות · · · עם תרגום בלשון

אנגליש. The Pentateuch, Haphtorahs, and Sabbath
Morning Service. 5 vols. London. 8vo. 1858.

1566. חמשה חומשי תורה עם ההפטרות וחמש מגילות וסדר
התפלות לשבתות. The Five Books of Moses, with
the best English translation. 5 vols. Fuerth. 8vo.
1859.

1567. ABRAHAM BENISCH.—The Haphtaroth. Translated by A. B. Hebrew and English. 1860.

1568. מחזור למועדי ה'. The Festival Prayers . . . with a
new translation by D. A. De Sola. 6 vols. London.
8vo. 1860.

1569. —— תפלות ישראל Hebrew Prayers . . . with an
improved translation by H. Filipowsky. London.
32mo. 1862.

1570. REV. B. H. ASCHER.—חנכת הבית. Dedication
of the House, adapted for the use of consecrating
Private Dwellings ; to which is added a series of
prayers in English, suitable for private and domestic
devotion, especially adapted for Families and Young
Children. London. 1862.

1571. HAGADA.—סדר הגדה לליל שמורים. Service for the
first nights of Passover . . . with a new English
translation by A. I. MENDES. London. 8vo.
1862.
[Second Edition, "carefully revised and corrected" the
same year.]

1572. שיה יצחק כולל התפלות מכל השנה . . . ונלוה אליו
הרבה דינים מלוקטים מסדור דרך החיים. The Daily
Prayers . . . . with a new translation by A. P.
Mendes. Lond. 8vo. 1864.

1573. ברכות ארוסין ונשואין Marriage Ceremony. Hebrew and English. [London.] 8vo. 1865.

1573a. A. P. MENDES.—Prayers for intermediate days
of Tabernacles, with English translation by A. P. M.
1870.

1574. H. FILIPOWSKI, F.I.A , F.A.S. —תפלות ישראל
Hebrew and English Prayer Book. With an im-
proved translation. 2nd edition. 16mo. 147 pp.
Hebrew and English.   1872.

1575. DR. A. ASHER.—The Jewish Rite of Circumcision, with the Prayers and Laws appertaining
thereto, translated into English, with an introductory
essay by A. Asher. סדר המילה כפי מנהגי בני ספרד
Hebrew and אשכנז ופולין עם כל הדינים הנלוים עליהן
English. Lond. 8vo.   1873.

1576. REV. B. SPIERS and REV. L. GROJEWSKY.—הנדה
של פסח. Hagadah for Passover, containing a revision of the Hebrew text, according to a MS.
written in the year A.M. 5374, by the celebrated
grammarian, Rabbi Shabsi Safer of Premslow; also
a valuable commentary, copied from a MS. of the
well-known Rabbi Jonathan Eybeschuetz . . . . . .
together with . . . . . an English translation of some
illustrative parables, by Rabbi Jacob, Magid of
Dubno. Hebrew and English. 4to. 48 pp. [1887.]

1577. ANON. [BARONESS LIONEL DE ROTHSCHILD].—
Prayers and Meditations for daily use in the house-
holds of Israelites. Lond.   1884?

1578. [A. L. COHEN]—Prayers. Heb. and Eng. 12mo.
38 pp.   1884.
[Privately printed for the use of the author's children.]

ORDERS OF DIVINE SERVICE ON SPECIAL OCCASIONS.

A.—*Laying the Foundation, Consecration, Re-opening
of Synagogues, Schools, Hospitals.*

CONSECRATIONS, &C., OF SYNAGOGUES.

1580. Birmingham, New Hebrew Congregation, 1853.
1581. Birmingham New Synagogue, 1856.
1582. Brighton New Central Synagogue, Laying the foundation-
stone, 10 Kislev, 5635.

1583. Brighton New Central Synagogue, Consecration, 23 Ellul, 5635.

1584. Bristol Synagogue, Consecration, 22 Ellul, 5546.

1585. Cheltenham Synagogue Re-opening, 1865.

1586. Dover Synagogue, Consecration, 25 Ab, 5623.

1587. Glasgow New Synagogue, Consecration, 28 Ellul, 5618.

1588. Kimberley Synagogue Consecration, 1876.

1589. Kingston, Jamaica, Synagogue of the Portuguese Jews' Congregation, Renewal of the Dedication, 5602.

1590. Liverpool New Hebrew Congreg. Synagogue, Consecration, 5 Nisan, 5604.

LONDON.

1591. Bayswater Synagogue, Laying the foundation-stone, 5622.

1592. Bayswater Synagogue, Consecration, 14 Ab, 5623.

1593. Bayswater Synagogue Re-opening, 1885.

1594. Bevis Marks Portuguese Synagogue, Commemoration of the Dedication, 5575.

1595. Bevis Marks Portuguese Synagogue, Renewal of Dedication, 27 Ellul, 5603.

1596. Bevis Marks Portuguese Synagogue, Reopening, 23 Ellul, 5619.

1597. Bevis Marks Portuguese Synagogue, Installation of Prof. Artom as Haham, 8 Tebet, 5627.

1598. Borough New Synagogue, Consecration, 2 Nisan, 5627.

1599. Borough New Synagogue, Reopening, 21 Ellul, 5636.

1600. Broad Street Synagogue, Consecration, 28 Iyar, 5627.

1601. Bryanston Street Portuguese Synagogue, Laying the foundation-stone, 11 Nisan, 5620.

1602. Bryanston Street Portuguese Synagogue, Dedication, 8 Nisan, 5621.

1603. Bryanston Street Synagogue, Re-opening, 1865.

1603a. Central Branch Synagogue, Laying the foundation stone, 6 Nisan, 5629.

1604. Central Branch Synagogue, Consecration, 6 Nisan, 5630.

1605. Cutler Street Polish Synagogue, Consecration, 15 Ellul, 5627.

1606. Dalston Synagogue, Consecration, 22 Tamuz, 5645.

1607. East London Synagogue, Laying the foundation stone, 23 Nisan, 5636.

1608. East London Synagogue, Consecration, 5637.

1609. Great Synagogue, Consecration, 24 Ellul, 5526.

1610. Great Synagogue, Consecration, 11 Nisan, 5550.

1611. Great Synagogue, Consecration, 24 Ellul, 5595.

1612. Great Synagogue, Re-opening, 18 Ellul, 5612.

1613. Great Synagogue, Installation of Chief Rabbi, the Rev. Dr. Nathan Marcus Adler, 4 Tamuz, 5605.

1614. German Synagogue, Spital Square, Consecration, 1886.

1615. Hambro' Synagogue, Re-opening, 1837.

1616. Hambro' Synagogue, Re-opening, 1877.

1617. Hand-in-Hand Asylum Synagogue, Consecration, 1878.

1618. Hope Street Synagogue, Consecration, 1885.

1619. Maiden Lane Synagogue, Re-opening, 14 Adar, 5611.

1620. Maiden Lane Synagogue, Consecration, 19 Ellul, 5618.

1621. Mildmay Park Temperance Synagogue, Consecration, 1886.

1622. New Synagogue, Laying the foundation stone, 5 Iyar, 5597.

1623. New Synagogue, Re-opening, 21 Ellul, 5607.

1624. New Synagogue, Re-opening, 23 Ellul, 5615.

1625. New West End Synagogue, Foundation Stone, 1877.

1626. New West End Synagogue, Consecration, 6 Nisan, 5639.

1627. North London Synagogue, Laying the foundation stone, 27 Kislev, 5628.

1628. North London Synagogue, Consecration, 6 Nisan, 5628.

1629. North London Synagogue, Re-opening, 15 Ellul, 5633.

1630. Portland Street Synagogue, Consecration, 10 Nisan, 5615.

1631. St. John's Wood Synagogue, Consecration, 28 Ellul, 5636.

1632. St. John's Wood Synagogue, Laying the foundation stone, 15 Adar, 5642.

1633. St. John's Wood Synagogue, Consecration, 14 Ab, 5642.

1634. Sandy's Row Synagogue Consecration, 1870.

1635. Spencer House Synagogue, 1865.

1636. West London Synagogue of British Jews (Burton Street), Consecration, 1842.

1637. West London Synagogue of British Jews, Re-opening, 1859.

1638. West London Synagogue of British Jews, Laying the foundation stone, 4 Sivan, 5608. [Margaret Street.]

1639. West London Synagogue of British Jews, Consecration, 26 Ellul, 5630. [Margaret Street.]

1639a. Western Synagogue, Consecration, 24 Ellul, 5617.

1640. Western Synagogue, Re-opening, 26 Ellul, 5625.

1641. Western Synagogue, Re-opening, 22 Ellul, 5630.

1642. Wigmore Street Synagogue of the Portuguese Jews, Consecration, 27 Ellul, 5613.

1643. Melbourne Hebrew Congregation, Consecration of Synagogue, 5637.

1644. Manchester Hebrew Congregation, Consecration of Synagogue, 11th March, 5618.

1645. Manchester Synagogue, Re-opening, 1874.

1646. Merthyr Tydvil Synagogue, Consecration, 10 Tamuz, 5637.

1647. Newcastle-on-Tyne Synagogue, Consecration, 1880.

1648. Ramsgate Synagogue, Re-opening and 50th anniversary of the wedding of Sir M. Montefiore and Lady Judith Montefiore, 30 Sivan, 5622.

1649. Ramsgate Synagogue, 53rd Anniversary of Opening, 1886.

1650. Southampton Synagogue, Opening, 1865.

1651. Sunderland Synagogue, Laying the foundation stone, 3 Tamuz, 5621.

1652. Swansea Synagogue, Opening, 1859.

1653. Wolverhampton Synagogue, Consecration, 14 Ellul, 5619.

1654. Yarmouth Synagogue, Opening, 1842.

1655. Sydney Great Synagogue, Consecration, 1878.

Special Occasions.

1656. Public religious examination of children, Bayswater Synagogue, 13 Sivan, 5626.

1657. Prayer for the Ceremony of Religious Majority, by Dr. Artom, 5627.

1658. Confirmation, West London Synagogue, 1872, 1875, &c.

1659. Presentation of Sepher Torah, Bevis Marks, 1851.

1660. Presentation of Sepher Torah, Bryanston Street, 1881.

1661. Service on Presentation of a Sefer-torah, Great Synagogue, 5579.

1662. Service on Presentation of a Sefer-torah, Bevis Marks Synagogue, 19 Iyar, 5620.

1663. Service on a Presentation of a Sefar-torah, Bevis Marks Synagogue, 11 Nisan, 5611.

1664. Service on a Presentation of a Sefer-torah, Bryanston Street Synagogue, 23 Ellul, 5625.

1665. Presentation of Sepher Torah, Sandy's Row, 1883.

1666. Order of Service on the occasion of making collections for the "Metropolitan Hospital Sunday Fund," 1874.

1667. Hospital Fund, Spanish and Portuguese, 1874.

1668. Medical Charities Fund, Leeds, 1886.

1669. Prayer in the Spanish and Portuguese Synagogue on behalf of the oppressed Jews of Russia, 29 Shebet, 5642.

OPENINGS, &C., OF INSTITUTIONS.

1670. Beth Hamidrash Consecration, 1876.
1671. Psalms and Ode, at the re-opening of the Gates of Hope School, 1859.
1672. Bayswater Jewish Schools, Opening, 1879.
1673. Opening of the new premises of Jews' College, June 27, 1881.
1674. Jews' Convalescent Home, Opening, Heshvan 1, 5630.
1675. Jews' Convalescent Home, Consecration of the New Wing for Children, May 16, 5635.
1676. Jews' Hospital, Consecration of Synagogue, 23 Adar, 5578.
1677. Jews' Hospital, Prayer on the Aniversary.
1678. Jews' Hospital, Laying the foundation stone, 28 Sivan, 5621.
1679. Jews' Deaf and Dumb Home, Consecration, 22 Tebet, 5627.
1680. Jews' Free School, Consecration and Examination, Jan. 13, 5582.
1681. Jews' Free School, Consecration, 28 Iyar, 5626.
1682. Jews' Free School, Consecration of new buildings, 1883.
1683. Westminster Jews' Free School, Consecration, June 20, 5618.
1684. Jews' Infant School, Consecration, 14 Sept. 5601.
1685. Jews' Infant School, opening of the New School, July 23, 5618.
1686. Jews' Infant School, Consecration of extension, 1885.
1687. Jews' Orphan Asylum, opening of the New School, April 15, 5626.
1688. Prayer for the use of Jewish patients. Supplied by the United Synagogue.
1689. Great Ealing School, Consecration, Iyar 14, 5640.
1690. Western Synagogue Cemetery, Edmonton, Opening, 1884.

B.—*On Occasions of General Distress and of General Rejoicing.*

1691. Prayer in the Synagogue at Barbados, on the Anniversary of the great calamity, 2 Ellul, 5591.
1692. Prayer on the day of general humiliation and thanksgiving for protection during the earthquake, 29 Adar, 5603.
1693. Prayer for General Fast, 1757.
1694. Day of Humiliation for Famine, West London Synagogue, 1847.

1695. Day of Humiliation, Bevis Marks, 1847.

1696. Prayer for General Fast, 1854 (Spanish and Portuguese).

1697. Prayer during the Severe Visitation raging in Europe; to be used in German Synagogue, 5592.

1698. Prayer during the Severe Visitation raging in Europe; to be used in Spanish and Portuguese Jews' Synagogue, 5592.

1699. Thanksgiving for abundant harvest, West London Synagogue, 5603.

1700. Service, Thanksgiving for abundant harvest, October 17, 5608.

1701. Thanksgiving for cessation of Cholera, West London Synagogue, 1849.

1702. Thanksgiving for abundant Harvest, 1854.

1703. Thanksgiving for abundant Harvest, West London Synagogue, 1847, 1854.

1704. Prayer on account of the prevailing Cholera.

1705. Service, Thanksgiving for the cessation of the Cholera, in Duke's Place Synagogue and Bevis Marks Synagogue, November 15, 5610.

1706. Service, Thanksgiving for the cessation of the Cholera, in other synagogues, Nov. 15, 5610.

1707. Thanksgiving for abundant harvest, Spanish and Portuguese Synagogue, October 7, 5615.

1708. Thanksgiving for abundant harvest, Ashkenazim, October 7, 5615.

1710. Prayer for relief from the cattle plague, 5626.

1711. Thanksgiving for relief from the cattle plague, November 24, 5627.

1712. Prayer against Cattle Plague, West London Synagogue, 1865.

WARS AND BATTLES.

1713. Order of Service, in reference to the American War, December 13, 5537.

1714. Order of Service, on Fast Day, on account of the French Revolution, April 19, 1793.

1715. Order of Service, Thanksgiving for victory, 5559.

1716. Order of Service, on Fast day, on account of the war, 15 Sivan, 5564.

1717. Thanksgiving for Victory, 1805.

1718. Order of Service, Thanksgiving for victory, 14 Kislev, 5566.

1719. Thanksgiving for success of troops in Crimea, 1855.

1720. Order of Service, Thanksgiving for victory in India, 15 Nisan, 5506.

1720a. Prayer for the continuance of Peace, 5608.

1721. Prayer for victory, Ashkenazim, 26 April, 5614.

1722. Prayer for victory, Sephardim, 26 April, 5614.

1723. Prayer for victory, Sephardim, March 21, 5615.

1723a. Prayer for restoration of Peace, West London Synagogue, 1854.

1724. Prayer for success of Army, 1855 (Spanish and Portuguese).

1725. Thanksgiving for capture of Sebastopol, West London Synagogue, 1855.

1726. Thanksgiving for victory, Ashkenazim, Oct. 4, 5616.

1727. Thanksgiving for the restoration of peace, Ashkenazim, May 4, 5616.

1728. Prayer for the restoration of peace, Sephardim, May 4, 5616.

1728a. Prayer for success in Crimean War, West London Synagogue, 1855.

1729. Day for National Prayer, 7th October, 1857.

1730. Prayer for safety of Indian troops, 1857 (Spanish and Portuguese).

1731. Prayer for restoration of Peace in India, West London Synagogue, 1857, 1859.

1732. Prayer for victory, Sephardim, October 7, 5618.

1733. Prayer for victory, West London Synagogue of British Jews, October 7, 5618.

1734. Prayer for victory, Ashkenazim, October 7, 5618.

1735. Thanksgiving for victory, Ashkenazim, April 30, 5619.

1736. Thanksgiving for success in Abyssinia, in Spanish and Portuguese Synagogue, July 4, 5628.

1737. Thanksgiving for success in Egyptian War, 1883.

ROYAL PERSONAGES.

1738. Order of Service on the occasion of the Jubilee of George III., October 25, 1809.

1739. Order of Service on the occasion of the Funeral of Princess Charlotte, 1817.

1740. A dirge chaunted in the Great Synagogue on the day of the funeral of Princess Charlotte, Kislev 10, 1817.

1741. Prayer and Psalms, on the day of the funeral of Queen Charlotte, Kislev 4, 1818.

1742. Prayer and Psalms, on the day of the funeral of King George III., Adar, 5580.

1743. A dirge chaunted in the Great Synagogue on the day of the funeral of George III., 5580.

1744. Prayer for the recovery of King George IV., Sivan 14, 1830.

1745. Order of Service for the day of burial of King William IV., January 5, 5597.

1746. Thanksgiving for safety of Queen from the hand of an Assassin, 1840.

1746a. Thanksgiving for preservation of Her Majesty, 1840 (Spanish and Portuguese).

1747. Prayer for restoration of health of George III., 1788.

1747a. Thanksgiving for George III.'s recovery, Great Synagogue, 1789.

1748. Thanksgiving for the birth of a Prince, 29 Heshvan, 5602, and of a Princess, 3 Kislev, 5601.

1749. Order of Service for the day of burial of the Duke of Sussex, 4 Iyar, 5603.

1750. Masonic form of Service at the Lodges of Joppa and Israel, 4 May, 1843, on the day of burial of the Duke of Sussex.

1751. Thanksgiving for the birth of a Princess, 25 March, 5608.

1752. Thanksgiving for the birth of a Prince, 16 April, 5613.

1753. Thanksgiving for accouchement of Her Majesty, 1840, 1841, 1843, 1846, 1848, 1857.

1754. Form of Service for the day of burial of the Prince Consort, Ashkenazim, 23 December, 5622.

1755. Form of Service for the day of burial of the Prince Consort, Sephardim, 23 December, 5622.

1756. Burial of Prince Consort, West London Synagogue, 1861.

1757. Thanksgiving for the birth of a Prince, January 16, 5624.

1758. Thanksgiving for safety of Duke of Edinburgh, 1868.

1759. Prayer for the recovery of the Prince of Wales, Tebeth, 5632.

1760. Thanksgiving for the recovery of the Prince of Wales, January 27, 5632.

1760a. Jubilee Services, 1887, Ashkenazim, Sephardim, and Beni Israel (in Marathi).

PERSONAL.

1761. Prayer for the safety of Sir Moses Montefiore on his journey to the East, 22 Sivan, 5600.

1762. Thanksgiving on return of Sir Moses Montefiore from the Holy Land, 1846.

1763. Prayer for Sir Moses Montefiore on visit to Holy Land, 1855, 1875.

1764. Thanksgiving for the success of Sir Moses Montefiore on his journey to the East, Adar 15, 5631.

1765. Prayer for the success of Sir Moses Montefiore's mission to Rome, 5619.

1766. Prayer for the success of Sir Moses Montefiore's mission to Morocco, Kislev 10, 5624.

1767. Thanksgiving in the Sephardim Synagogue for the success of Sir Moses Montefiore's mission to Morocco, Nisan 5, 5624.

1768. Thanksgiving in the Ashkenazim Synagogue for the success of Sir Moses Montefiore's mission to Morocco, Nisan 5, 5624.

1769. Prayer for the safety of Sir Moses Montefiore on his journey to Palestine, 5626.

1770. Prayer for the success of Sir Moses Montefiore's mission to Roumania, 24 Tamuz, 5627.

1771. Thanksgiving on the return of Sir Moses Montefiore from Roumania, Ashkenazim, 21 Ellul, 5627.

1772. Thanksgiving on the return of Sir Moses Montefiore from Roumania, Sephardim, 21 Ellul, 5627.

1773. Prayer for the safety of Sir Moses Montefiore on his journey to Russia, July 18, 5632.

1774. Thanksgiving on entry of Sir Moses Montefiore into his 100th year, 1883.

1774a. Prayer and Thanksgiving on Sir Moses Montefiore completing his hundredth year, 26 Oct. 5645.

1775. Service in memory of Sir Moses Montefiore, 4 Ab, 5645.

1776. Funeral of Chief Rabbi, Rev. S. Hirschell, 1842.

1777. Installation of Rev. N. M. Adler as Chief Rabbi, 1845.

(N.) SERMONS.

1778. DA SILVA, R. JOSUA.— Discursas (31) predycoveys que o docto H. H. Yeosua du Sylva pregan na K. K. Sahar a Samaym em Londres. Amsterdam. 1688.

1779. Sermon, Oracion, y Problematico Dialogo, que se hizieron Eula celebridad dela Fundacion dela

Santay pia Hermandad de Saharé *ora'*, *vaavi ieto-mim*. Estampadas en Londres, 5463. 1703. The " Sermon " is by Nieto (D.) ; the " Oracion " by Isaac Henriquez Lopez ; and the " Dialogo " by Moses and Isaac Nieto, sons of the Haham. 32 pp.

1780. Los Triunfas de la Pobreza Panegirico Predicado eula solemnidad dela fundacion de la pia, y Santa Hebra de Bikur Holim. Londres, 5469. 32 pp. 1709. Preached by David Nieto on Sabbath, 17 Iyar, 5469.

1781. En Nombre de el dio Bendito esta Santa Hermandad de Bikur Holim. 1709. Impreso en Londres. Ano 5469. Por David Fernandez. 10 pp.

1782. SARMENTO, JACOB DE CASTRO.— Exemplar de Penitencia, dividido en tres Discursos Predicaveis para o Dia Santo de Kipur. 1724.

1783. ―― Sermao funebre eis deploraveis memorias do muy reverendo e doutissimo Haham Mareun A. R. Doutor David Neto, in signe Theologo eminente Pregador, e cabeça da congrega de Sahar Hassamaym. Londres. 1728.

1784. SAMUDA, DR. ISHAC DE SEQUEYRA. — Sermao funebre da memoria de R. D. Netto. 1728.

1785. MENDEZ, ABRAHAM.—Sermao funebre a la memoria de R. D. Netto. 1728.

1787. NETTO, ISAAC.—A Sermon preached in the Jews' Synagogue on Friday, February 6th, 1756, being the day appointed by authority for a general fast. By I. N., Archsinagogus of the Portuguese Jews' Synagogue. Translated from the Spanish language by the author. (A.N.) 4to., 18 pp. 1756.

1788. BELISARIO, ISAAC MENDES.—Sermon de Exequias por el Falecimiento de fu Magestad el Rey Jorge II. Predicado en 21 Quislev 5521 que corresponde a 29 Noviembre, 1760. 1761.

1789. BELISARIO, ISAAC MENDES. — A Sermon [on

1 Chron. xxix. 27, 28], occasioned by the death of
his late Majesty (George II.), preached in the Synagogue of the Portuguese Jews in London. Translated from the Spanish. London. 8vo.   1761.

1790. JUDAH, MOSES B., OF MINSK. — דמעה שערי
[Funeral Sermon on R. Joseph of Brody, and R.
David ben Loeb of Berlin.] 4to.   1771.

1791. Orden de la oracion . . . en el dia de ayuro . . .
para humillarnos delante del omnipotente Dios, im-
plorando . . . la Divina asistencia a las armas de
su Magestad . . . con el sermon predicado en esse
dia por . . . M. Cohen D'Azevedo.   Hebrew and
Spanish.   1776.
  [Also in Hebrew and English.]

1792. SOLOMON, ISRAEL MESHULLAM.— Sermon on
General Fast and Prayer.   1777.

1793. CROOL, RABBI JOSEPH.—The Service, performed
in the Synagogue of the Jews, Manchester, on the
19th of October, 1803.   Being the day appointed
for a General Fast, consisting of Prayers. a Sermon,
Psalms and Hymns.   Delivered in Hebrew by
R. J. C., and translated by him into English. 8vo.,
32 pp.   Price 6d   [A.N.]   1803.

1794. HIRSCHELL, SOLOMON.—A Sermon delivered on
the day appointed for a General Thanksgiving for
the success of the fleet off Trafalgar.   Arranged
and rendered into English by a Friend.   London.
                                    5565 (1805).
  "A Friend" was Dr. Joshua van Oven.

1795. MELDOLA, RAPHAEL BEN HEZEKIAH —Funeral
Sermon (on Job xiv. 1, 2), delivered at the Spanish
and Portuguese Synagogue, on the day of burial of
Princess Charlotte Augusta, &c.   8vo.   London.
                                        1817.

1796. GOODMAN, RABBI TOBIAS.—The Faith of Israel,
a discourse delivered at the Jews' Synagogue, Seel
Street, Liverpool, on May 2nd, 1819.   Liverpool.
                                        1819.
  [First Sermon preached and published in English.]

1797 MELDOLA, DAVID.—Funeral Sermon (on Numbers, xvi. 16), delivered at the Ancient Synagogue of the Spanish and Portuguese Jews in England, in Memory of R. Meldola, &c. (together with a second discourse on the same subject, and a dirge in Hebrew and English). London. 2 parts. 8vo. 1828.

1798. DE SOLA, DAVID AARON.—A Sermon on the Excellence of the Holy Law, and the Necessity and Importance of Religious Instruction. Delivered in the Portuguese Synagogue, London, on Sabbath Hagadol, Nisan 12, 5591=March 26, 1831. Lond. 1831.

[First English Sermon delivered in the Bevis Marks Synagogue.]

1799. BRANDON, DAVID R.—A Discourse delivered at the Spanish and Portuguese Jews' Synagogue, on the day of the National Fast, Veadar 19, 5592 (March 21, 1832). 1832.

1800. DE SOLA, DAVID AARON.—The Consolation of Jerusalem A Sermon, &c., delivered on Sabbath Nahamu (July 27, 1833.) London. 1833.

1801. A Sermon delivered in the Synagogue, Bevis Marks, on Sabbath *Nahmu* (27 July). By D. A. de Sola. 1833.

1802a. ISAACS, D. M.—Funeral Oration delivered on the Occasion of the Burial of his Most Gracious Majesty, on Saturday night, Tamuz 5, 5597, at the Synagogue, Seel Street, Liverpool. 1837.

1803. HIRSCHEL, SOLOMON.— Address delivered on laying the Foundation Stone of the intended New Synagogue . . . . with a short Account of the Ceremonial. London. 8vo. 1837.

1804. Discourse delivered on 6th Tamuz, 5597—9th

July, 1837, at the Synagogue of the Spanish and
Portuguese Jews, London, on the occasion of the
Demise of his late Majesty, William the Fourth, by
Mr. A. A. Lindo. Pp. 26.   1837.

1805. ISAACS, D. M.—Funeral Sermon on the Death of
Joshua van Oven.   1838.

1806. SALOMON, DR. GOTTHOLD.—Twelve Sermons de-
livered in the New Temple of the Israelites at
Hamburgh. Translated from the German by Anna
Maria Goldsmid. 8vo. Pp. 247.   1839.

1807. LINDO, A. A.—Discourse on the Passover Festival,
delivered at the Synagogue of the Spanish and
Portuguese Jews, London, on the first day of the
Festival, the 15th Nisan, 5599=20th March, 1839 ;
and at the Western Synagogue, Westminster, on the
seventh day of the Festival, 21st Nisan, 5599=
5th April, 1839. 8vo. Pp. 26. Lond.   1839.

1808. BIBAS, J. L.—Sermon on the day of General
Thanksgiving.   1840.

1809. MELDOLA, REV. A.—A Sermon (on Mal. iv. 2),
On the Importance of the Holy Law, with its effect
in promoting Unity and Peace, delivered on the
Sabbath prior to the Festival of Passover, 8th Nisan
(11th April), 5600. London. 8vo. 5600 (1840).

1810. MARKS, REV. D. W.—Discourse delivered at the
Consecration of the West London Synagogue of
British Jews. London.   1842.
Printed at the request of the Committee of Founders.

1811. ——— Discourse delivered in the West London
Synagogue of British Jews, Burton Street, Burton
Crescent, on the day of its Consecration. 27th
January, 1842. 2nd edition.   1842.

1812. LOEWE, DR. L.—Pessák Yoshiyáhoo, a Discourse

delivered in the Spanish and Portuguese Jews' Synagogue in Bevis Marks, on the second day of Passover. 1842.

1813. —— Tephilah ul Shif-youat, a Discourse delivered in the Great Synagogue on the second day of the Pentecost. 1842.

1814. —— A Discourse delivered in the Spanish and Portuguese Synagogue, Bevis Marks, on the day of the Funeral of H.R.H. Prince Augustus Frederick, Duke of Sussex, 4th May, 1843. 1843.

1815. DE LARA, D. E., LL.D.—An Address delivered at the opening of the New Synagogue in Manchester, on Friday the 5th September, 5604. London and Manchester. 1844.

1816. MARKS, REV. D. W.—A Sermon preached on the Festival of Pentecost, 5604, at the West London Synagogue of British Jews. London. 1844.

1817. MELDOLA, REV. DAVID.—A Sermon (on Deut. xxxiii. 36) delivered at the Spanish and Portuguese Jews' Synagogue, &c. London. 8vo. 5605 (1844).

1818. RAPHALL, REV. MORRIS I.—A Lecture delivered at the Consecration of the Synagogue, Hardman Street, Liverpool, March 25, 5604. 1844.
Published in aid of the funds of the Liverpool Hebrew Educational Institution for Boys and Girls.

1819. CARILLON, REV. B. C.—Sermon delivered in aid of the Beth Limud Society. 2nd edition. Jamaica. 1845.

1820. RAPHALL, REV. MORRIS JACOB, M.A.—A Sermon entitled "The Unity of God, the Distinguishing Feature of the Jewish Faith." Yarmouth. 1845.
Republished in London 1849.

1821. ADLER, REV. N. M. (Chief Rabbi).—A Sermon delivered at the Great Synagogue, on the occasion of his installation into office as Chief Rabbi of the

o

United Congregations of Jews of the British Empire, on the 4th Tamuz, 5605 (8th July, 1845). Translated by Barnard Van Oven, Esq., M.D. London.   1845.

1822. MELDOLA, REV. DAVID.—Oration at the Funeral of the lamented Mr. Aguilar.   1845.

> [Mr. Aguilar was father of Grace Aguilar, and a prominent member of the Sephardic Community.]

1823. HENRY, REV. H. A.—Six Discourses on the Principles of the Religious Belief of Israel. London. 8vo.   1846.

1823a. ADLER, REV. N. M. (Chief Rabbi).—Sermon delivered in the Great Synagogue, Duke's Place. on the occasion of the recent General Fast Day, Wednesday, the 24th March, A.M. 5607. London. pp. 15.

> With a prayer in Hebrew and English. Published for the benefit of the sufferers in Ireland and in the Highlands of Scotland.

1824. DE SOLA, REV. D. A. (Minister of the Congregation).—A Sermon delivered at the Spanish and Portuguese Jews' Synagogue, Bevis Marks, on Wednesday, 7th Nissan (24th March), 5607, being the day appointed as a General Fast. London. 1847.

1825. LOEWE, DR. L. — Massa Eliezer. A Discourse delivered in the Great Synagogue at Wilna, Russia, on the occasion of Sir Moses and Lady Montefiore's Patriotic Mission to that most important Community under the sway of the Czar in the year 1846. Wilna.   1847.

1826. ADLER, DR. N. M. (Chief Rabbi).—The Jewish Faith. A Sermon. 8vo.   1848.

1826a. ADLER, DR. N. M. (Chief Rabbi.)—Address delivered by the Rev. the Chief Rabbi, N. M. Adler, Phil. Doc., at the Conversazione of the Jews and General Literary and Scientific Institution, Sussex Hall, on Thursday, Oct. 26, 1848.   1848.

> Single 4to. sheet, printed on one side in two columns.

1827. ADLER, DR. N. M. (Chief Rabbi).—The Bonds of Brotherhood. A Sermon delivered in the Synagogue שער השמים of the Spanish and Portuguese Congregation in London. 8vo. 1849.

1828. ADLER, REV. N. M. (Chief Rabbi).—How can the Blessings of the House of God be attained? A Discourse given at the Consecration of Canterbury Synagogue. 1849.

1829. MELDOLA, DAVID. — דרך אמונה. The Way of Faith, etc. Translated from the Hebrew of Haham Raphael Meldola. 1849.

1829a. MELDOLA, DAVID.—The Divine Judgments imposed; being a discourse (on Deut. xxxii. 39), delivered at the Spanish and Portuguese Jews' Synagogue on the Penitential Sabbath, &c. London. 8vo. 1850.

1830. SCHILLER-SZINESSY, REV. RABBI S. M. (Ph. Dr., F.G.O.S., late of the Synagogue of Eperies in Hungary).—The Olden Religion in the New Year. A Sermon preached before תקיעת שופר in the Birmingham Synagogue on the second day of the Festival of the New Year, 5611 (September 8th, 1850). London. 1850.
Translated by Miss Miriam Nathan.

1831. LEVY, REV. M. B. (Minister of the Brighton Congregation).—A Sermon delivered on the Sabbath הנכה (Dedication), 5611, at the Brighton Synagogue. London. 1850.

1832. DAVIS, ALEXANDER B., Master of the Western Jews' Free School for Boys.—A Sermon on the Mixture of Love, Fear, and Joy, as inspired by the Observances of Judaism, delivered at the Brighton Synagogue on the eighth day of Solemn Assembly, Oct. 19, 5612-1851. London. 1851.

1833. MARKS, REV. D. W.—Sermons preached on various
occasions at the West London Synagogue of British
Jews, Vol. I.   London.   1851.
    Vol. ii. appeared in 1862, vol. iii. in 1884.

1834. The First Ceremony of Confirmation in the
Halliwell Street Synagogue, Manchester, by the
Rev. Dr. S. M. Schiller-Szinessy, local Rabbi.
Manchester.   8vo., 12 pp.   1852.
    [Consists of a Sermon, entitled, "Confirmation—a genuine
Jewish Institution," by Dr. S.-S., Special Addresses to each
of the nine Confirmants, &c.]

1835. KALISCH, DR. MARCUS.—Two Sermons delivered
before the Congregation of the New Synagogue,
Great St. Helens.   London.   1853.
    1. הגיון אמת Our Chief Requirements.
    2. On Predestination and Free Will.

1836. DAVIS, REV. ALEXANDER B.—On Charity; the
first, most beautiful, and chief of the Graces.   A
Sermon delivered on Tuesday, Aug. 7, 1854, at a
Special Service in aid of the Fund for the Relief
of the Famishing Jews of Jerusalem at the Spanish
and Portuguese Synagogue, Kingston, Jamaica.
                                         1854.

1837. ASHER, REV. B. H.—Two Sermons (a) חדש האביב
(b) חץ תשועה לה׳.   1854.

1838. MARKS, REV. D. W.—תורה אור "The Law
is Light."   A course of Four Lectures on the All-
sufficiency of the Law of Moses for the guidance of
the Israelite.   London.   1854.

1839. ADLER, REV. N. M. (Chief Rabbi).—Solomon's
Judgment.   1854.

1840. MENDEZ, REV. A. P.—Sermons.   London.   8vo.
                                         1855.

1841. SCHILLER-SZINESSY, REV. DR. S. M., Rabbi of
Manchester.—Charity: A Sermon preached on
behalf of the "Benevolent Fund" at the Halliwell
Street Synagogue on Sunday, the 5th of Chanuccah,
5616 (Dec. 9, 1855).   Manchester.   1856.

1841*a*. SCHILLER-SZINESSY, REV. DR. S. M.—Harmony and Disharmony between Judaism and Christianity. Two Sermons. Manchester. 8vo. 1859.

1842. GOTTHEIL, G.—Moses *versus* Slavery, being Two Discourses on the Slave Question. Manchester and London. 1861.

1843. RAPHALL, REV. MORRIS JACOB.—Bible View of Slavery. A Discourse. 1862.

1844. Form of Special Service held in the Synagogue, St. Thomas, W. I., on the 7th Dec., 1863, with a Sermon delivered on the occasion by the Rev. M. N. Nathan, in honour of the Memory of the lamented King, Frederick VII., pp. 7. St. Thomas, W. I. 1863.

1845. BAAR, REV. DR. H.—Two Sermons on the Ten Commandments, delivered at the Seel Street Synagogue, Liverpool. 1864.

1846. MENDES, REV. A. P.—In Memoriam Rev. B. Abrahams. 1864.

1847. ADLER, REV. N. M. (Chief Rabbi).—The Morning and Evening Sacrifice. 1865.

1848. ARTOM, REV. PROFESSOR B., Chacham.— The Duties of the Jewish Pastor in the Present Age. 1866.

1849. ADLER, REV. DR. (Chief Rabbi).—The Second Days of the Festivals. A Sermon delivered at the New Synagogue, Great St. Helen's, on the Second Day of Passover, 5628. London. 1868.
Printed by request. See No. 773.

1850. ADLER, REV. DR. HERMANN NATHAN. — נפתולי אלהים. A Course of Sermons on the Biblical Passages adduced by Christian Theologians in support of the Dogmas of their Faith. 8vo. 1869.
Translated into Marathi for the Beni Israel.

1851. EMANUEL, REV. G. J.—Sermon . . . preached on Sabbath, Feb. 10, 5632-1872. Birmingham. 8vo., 9 pp. 1872.

1852. JOSEPH, REV. MORRIS.—Progress. A Sermon delivered in the North London Synagogue. 8vo., 16 pp.   1872.

1853. ARTOM, REV. BENJAMIN (Chief Rabbi of the Spanish and Portuguese Congregations of England). —Sermon preached in several London Synagogues. 1873.

1854. ADLER, REV. DR. HERMANN NATHAN. — Is Judaism a Missionary Faith ? A Sermon preached . . . on the 20th December, 1863. 8vo., 8 pp. 1874.

1855. EMANUEL, REV. G. J.—Sermon delivered on the Seventh Day of Passover.   1876.

1856. ARTOM, REV. DR.—Sermons. Second Edition. 1876.
Sermons on " Cremation," and one delivered at the Consecration of Manchester Sephardi Synagogue, are added.

1857. EMANUEL, REV. G. J., B.A.—Sermon delivered at the Birmingham Synagogue on the Seventh Day of Passover, April 5, 5637. Birmingham. 8vo., 14 pp.   1877.
[Published for the benefit of the Birmingham Hebrew Board of Guardians.]

1858. SIMON, OSWALD JOHN.—The Worship of God. A Sermon. 8vo., 13 pp. London and Ashford. 1880.

1859. EMANUEL, REV. G. J.—Our Jewish Brethren in America.   1882.

1860. WOLFF, REV. PROFESSOR A. A., Ph.D.—The Life and Career of Sir Moses Montefiore. Sermon preached on the occasion of the Hundredth Birthday of Sir M. M. . . . at the Synagogue, Copenhagen. Translated from the Danish by Mrs. A. Simon. 8vo., 11 pp. Copenhagen.   1883.

1861. MYERS, REV. ISIDORE, B.A.—A Sermon in Verse, delivered in the Sandhurst Synagogue on the Jewish New Year, 5643 (Thursday, 14th Sept., 1882). 12 pp. Sandhurst.   1883.

1862. ADLER, REV. DR. H.—The Purpose and Methods
of Charitable Relief. Two Sermons. 8vo., 16 pp.
1884.

1863. ADLER, REV. DR. H. — The Orphan and the
Helpless. A Plea for the Jews' Hospital and Orphan
Asylum. 8vo., 8 pp. 1884.

1864 ADLER, REV. DR. H.—"Remember the Poor."
A Sermon preached in memory of the late Baroness
Lionel de Rothschild at the Central Synagogue.
8vo., 13 pp. 1884.

1865. HIRSHOWITZ, REV. A.—זכרון משה The Memorial
of Moses. A Sermon delivered at the Princes
Street Synagogue on . . . the occasion of Sir
Moses Montefiore, Bart., completing his hundredth
year. Hebrew and English. 8vo., 7 and 9 pp.
1885.

1866. SINGER, REV. S.—The Deaf and the Dumb.—A
Sermon delivered in the New West End Synagogue
on May 30th, 5645-1885. 1885.

1867. ADLER, REV. DR. H.—Hebrew, the language of
our Prayers. A Sermon. 16mo., 15 pp. London.

1868. SALOMON, DR. B. — Address delivered at the Consecration of the New Cemetery of the Manchester
Hebrew Congregation. 1885.

1869. SIMON, OSWALD JOHN.—The Liberty of the Soul.
An unspoken Sermon for the Feast of Passover.
8vo., 7 pp. London. 1885.

1869a. —— Introspection. An unspoken Sermon. 8vo.,
pp. 8. London. 1885.

1870. The Jewish Pulpit. 1886.
[Republication of Sermons issued in connection with the
Jewish Chronicle.]

(o.) THEOLOGY AND BIBLICAL EXEGESIS.

1871. D. NIETO.—Pascologia overo Discorso della Pasca in cui si assegnano le ragioni delle discrepanze

vertenti circa il tempo di celebrar la Pasca tra la
Chiesa Latina, Greca, etc. [?] London.   1702.
[Dedicated "All' Altezza Rever. Franc. Maria Cardinale
di Medici."]

1872. Isaac Abendana.—Discourses of the Ecclesias-
tical and Civil Polity of the Jews. 8vo., 200 pp.
[A.N.]   1706.,
[Second edition in 1709.]

1873. David ben Phinehas Nieto.—מטה דן וכוזרי חלק
שני.—Matteh Dan ... donde se prueva la Verdad
della Dey Mental. Hebrew and Spanish. 4to.
                                               1714.
[See Terni, 1795.]

1874. David ben Phinehas Nieto.—אש דת. Es dat
ò Fuego legal, compuesta en Ydioma Hebraico y traduzido en Romance. Hebrew and Spanish. 169
and 76 pp. (Ilive).   1715.

1875. Daniel Israel Lopez Laguna.—Espejo fiel de
Vidas [Portuguese Translation of the Psalms].
London. 4to.   1720.
    Mem.: Lopez is said to have written a panegyric on
    William and Mary on the occasion of their accession to the
    English throne. (Printed at Amsterdam, 1690.)

1876. Anon. (David Nieto).—Noticias recanditas y
posthumas del procedimiento de las Inquisiciones
de España y Portugal con sus presas. In 2 partes.
Compil. y anod. por un Anonimo. En Villa Franca
(London).   1722.

1877. Jacob de Castro Sarmento.—Extraordinaria
Providencia, que el gran Dios de Ysrael uso con su
escogido pueblo em tiempo de su major aflicion por
medio de Mordehay y Ester contra los protervos in-
tentos del tyrano Aman. Compendiosamente dedu-
zida de la sagrada Escritura en el seguinte Romance. London.   1724.

1878. Joseph ben Ephraim Caro.—Dinim de Sehita
y Bedica colegidos de Sulhan Aruh y traducidos en
idioma Español par A. Mendoza.   1733.

1879. Jacob Sasportas.—אהל יעקב [Rabbinic Responses].   1737.
(Many dated from London, *e.g.*, No. 4, dated Aug., 1664 ; also Nos. 5 and 6, No. 66, addressed to Joshua da Silva, in London, 1673.]

1880. Israel Lyons, Senior.—Observations relating to various parts of Scripture.   Cambridge.   1768.

1881. Jacob ben Eliezer ben Mebr Eisenstadt, of Schidlowitz.—תולדות יעקב [Comments on Biblical and Talmudic Passages].   Publisher W. Tooke. (טוק).   1770.

1882. Mordecai Gumpel (Levisohn).—מאמר התורה והחכמה.   1771.
[Letter on study of Hebrew literature. Reproduced in Meassef.]

1883. Mishnah, translated into English by a primitive Ebrew.   1772.

1884. Moses ben Jehuda, of Minsk.—אבן שהם [על] מאמרי רז"ל ופסוקי תנ"ד] 4to.   1772.

1885. A. Busaglo.—פני מלך. Commentary on אדרות.   1773.

1885a. A. van Oven. דרך איש ישר. Translated from an ancient Indian MS. into Hebrew and English.   1778.

1886. David Levi.—A Succinct Account of the Rites and Ceremonies of the Jews, in which their Religious Principles and Tenets are explained, particularly the Doctines of the Resurrection, Predestination, and Free Will, and the Opinion of Dr. Prideaux concerning these Tenets Refuied.   1782.
[With portrait from "European Magazine."]

1887. Dr. A. Anschel [Worms].—ביאור מספיק על חד גדיא [Commentary on "Chad Gadya" in the Hagada Service.]   1785.

1888. Philo-Veritas.—A Jewish Tract on the Fifty-Third Chapter of Isaiah, written by Dr. Montalto in Portuguese, and Translated from his Manuscript by Philo-Veritas. [A.N.]   1790.

1889. Levi's Discourses to the Nation of the Jews.
Flexneg. 8vo., 3s. 6d. 1790.

1889a. C. J. Asulai. מורה באצבע. 1791.

1890. Eliakim ben Abraham.—עשרה מאמרות.
1794-9.
[Only three of the essays appeared.]

1891. Phineas Samuel.—מדרש פנחם [על מאמרי רבב"ח]
1795.
Explanations of sayings of R. bar bar Hana.

1892. Daniel ben Moses David Terni.—מתנת יד' ס
Notes . . . . ואיזה השגות על קצת דברים שבספר מטה דן
by M. C. Rimini. Florence. 4to. 1795.

1893. David Levi.—Dissertation on the Prophecies,
3 vols. 1796-1800.
[Dedications to David Henriques Jamuna, Samuel Baretta
da Veiga, and Abraham Goldsmid.]

1894. S. M. Ish Yeminy [pseud.]—The Expected Good
End: in 3 parts: I. The Birth of Jacob; II. On
Verses of King Solomon; III. On the Structure of
the Tabernacle. 105 pp. 1800.

1895. R. Joseph Crool (Teacher of the Hebrew Language in the University of Cambridge).—The
Restoration of Israel. 8vo., 94 pp. 1812.

1896. S. Bennett.—The Constancy of Israel, an Unprejudiced Illustration of some of the most Important Texts of the Bible. 8vo., 235 pp. [A.N.]
1812.

1897. Solomon Bennett.—A Discourse on Sacrifices.
1815.

1898. J. King [Rey.]—דרך משה [Dissertation on Book
of Esther, &c.] 1817.

1900. J. King [Rey.]—דרך סלולה [Dissertation on the
Prophecies.] 1819.

1901. H. Bolaffey.—אורח מישור [On a Primeval Lan-
guage]. London. 1820.

1902. H. HURWITZ.—Vindiciæ Hebraicæ, or a defence of the Hebrew Scriptures as a vehicle of revealed Religion, against Mr. Bellamy. 8vo., 270 pp. 1820.

1903. M. H. SIMONSON.—On Joshua x. 12-14. Manchester. 1821.

1904. H. SIMMONDS.—מלחמות האמונה Arguments of Faith, Hebrew and English. 73 and 79 pp. 1823.

1905. PHILIP SARCHI.—An Essay on Hebrew Poetry, Ancient and Modern. 1824.

1906. SOLOMON BENNETT.—The Temple of Ezekiel. London. 4to. 1824.

1907. J. BEN A. SCHNITZLER.—ביאור חדש on Ezekiel xl. to xlix. 4to. 1825.

1907*a*. I. ISSERLES.—Ezekiel xl. explained. 1826.

1908. H. HURWITZ.—Essay on the still existing remains of the Hebrew Sages. 1826.

1909. —— Hebrew Tales, selected and translated. 8vo., 211 pp. 1826.

1910. —— An Introductory Lecture delivered in the University of London, on Tuesday, Nov. 11, 1828 [A.N.] 1828.

1911. Extracts from a work entitled "Elements of Faith," for the use of Jewish Youth, by S. T. Cohen, published in 1815. 1830.

1912. ARTHUR LUMLEY DAVIDS.—Lecture on the Philosophy of the Jews, delivered at the London Tavern to the Society for the Cultivation of Hebrew Literature, December 23, 1830. 8vo., 56 pp. [A.N.] 1833.
[At end reviews of his Turkish Grammar, and a letter to the *Times*, May 6, 1831.

1913. MOSES BEN ISAAC EDREHI.—ספר מעשה נסים. The Book of Miracles, being an important account of the River Sambatyon, &c. 1834.

1914. S. BENNETT.—Critical Remarks on the Authorised Version. 1834.

1915. G. C. BLUMENFELD.—Ecce Homo, im Process mit dem König und dem Priester oder die Selbsterlösung der Menschen, ein Evangelium von Jüngsten Gerichte. London. 1835 (?)

1916. J. VAN OVEN.—Manual of Judaism. 1835.

1917. SOLOMON BENNETT.—דרוש תורני ומהקרי על קדמות‎ וישלמות לשון הקדש‎. A Theological and Critical Treatise on the Primogeniture and Integrity of the Holy Language. 4to. 1835.

1918. B. FRANKLIN.—The Glory of Eternity, relating to the Immortality and Perpetual Peace of the Soul. 8vo., 36 pp., Hebrew and English, and 4 pp. List of Subscribers. [A.N.] 1836.

1919. ISAAC OROBIO.—Israel Defended, Jewish Exposition of Prophecies. 1838.

1920. SELIG NEWMAN.—Emendations of the Authorised Version of the Old Testament. London. 1839.

1921. DAVID AARON DE SOLA.—Prospectus of a New Edition of the Sacred Scriptures, with Notes Critical and Explanatory. 1840.

[Embraces a brief history of former translations. As a literary effort it was considered by Dr. Fürst of sufficient importance to warrant its republication in the " Orient," December 26, 1840.]

1922. REV. MORRIS I. RAPHALL.—מועד ה'‎, The Festival of the Lord, as celebrated by the House of Israel in every part of the World. London. 12mo. 1840.

1923. S. BENNETT.—The Hebrew and English Holy Bible . . . the English version revised by S. B. Part 1, 2 (containing Genesis i.-xli.). London. 8vo. 1841.

[No more published.]

1924. FRANCIS BARHAM.—The Hebrew and English Holy Bible. The Hebrew is reprinted from the text of Heidenheim. The English version compared with the original, and carefully revised by the late Solomon Bennett. The Hebrew text revised and corrected by Mr. H. A. Henry, Head Master of the Jews' Free School, and the work is edited by Francis Barham, Esq. London.   1841.

1925. DAVID AARON DE SOLA, MORRIS J. RAPHALL, and J. L. LINDENTHAL.—ספר תורת ה'. The Sacred Scriptures in Hebrew and English. A new translation, with Notes critical and explanatory. Vol. I., Genesis. London.   1841.
[No further volumes were issued, but a second edition of Genesis without the Hebrew was published in 1843.]

1926. E. H. LINDO.—The Conciliator of R. Menasseh ben Israel; A Reconcilement of the apparent contradictions in Holy Scripture. 2 vols. pp. xxxii.-312; vi.-336. London.   1841.
(Contains a sketch of the life of Menasseh ben Israel, biographical notices of the quoted authorities, and explanatory notes.]

1927. YATES.—Selections from the Old Testament. Liverpool.   1842.

1928. AARON BERACHYAH BEN MOSHEH.—מעבר יבק וקול יעקב [Guide to Devotion].   1842.

1929. DR. L. LOEWE.—Matteh Dan : The Rod of Judgment; being a supplement to the book "Kuzari" . . . by the Rev. David Nieto. . . . Translated from the Hebrew by L. L.   1842.
[The first two conversations.]

1930. DR. EDWARD KLEY.—Catechism of the Mosaic Doctrine. Translated by I. Lutominsky. 8vo. Oxford.   1842.

1931. SOLOMON EZEKIEL.— The Life of Abraham : Lectures delivered before the Penzance Hebrew Society for Promoting the Diffusion of Religious Knowledge. Penzance and London.   1844.

1933. ABRAHAM BEN SHALOM BELAIS.—ספר פרה שושן.
בית לוי דרושים · · · למעלת גודל יראת הרוממות. Biblical Expositions, etc. Hebrew and English. 8vo.
1844.

1934. M. J. RAPHALL, D. A. DE SOLA and I. L. LINDEN-
THAL.—The Sacred Scriptures in Hebrew and
English. A new translation, with notes. Genesis.
8vo.   1844.

1936. GRACE AGUILAR. The Spirit of Judaism. London.

1937. —— The Jewish Faith : Its Spiritual Consolation
Moral Guidance, and Immortal Hope ; with a brief
notice of the reasons for many of its ordinances
and prohibitions. A series of letters answering the
inquiries of youth. 8vo.   pp. xvi.-448. London.
1846.

1937a. GUSTAVE WEIL.—The Bible, Koran, and Talmud.
Translated from the German.   1846.

1939. MENASSEH BEN ISRAEL.—Hope of Israel, translated into English.   1850.

1940. A. BENISCH.—ספר עדות ה'. Jewish School and
Family Bible. Translated by A. B. Hebrew and
English. 4 vols. London. 8vo.   1851-61.

1941. M. H. SIMONSON.—שירת יהושע. Joshua and the
Sun and Moon. London.   1851.

1943. GRACE AGUILAR.—Sabbath Thoughts and Sacred
Communings. Edited by S. Aguilar. London.
8vo.   1853.

1944. ABRAHAM BEN JOSEPH.—שוחט of London, בית
אברהם. Being a complete exposition of the theory
and practice of שחיטה וטרפתת arranged as a commentary on the יורה דעה from chapter 1 to 69.
London.   1853.

1945. BENJAMIN MARCUS.—מקור חיים. Mistranslations
and difficult Passages of the Old Testament Corrected and Explained. Dublin.   1854.

1946. Rev. Dr. Heinrich Jolowicz.— On the Correction of the Text of the Hebrew Scriptures from the Talmud, the Targumim and other Rabbinical Authorities.   8vo, pp. 15.   1855.
[Read before the Anglo-Biblical Institute, 6th March, 1855.]

1947. M. Kalisch.—A Historical and Critical Commentary of the Old Testament, with a New Translation. 3 vols.   3rd vol. (Leviticus) in 2 parts. 1855-1877.
[Exodus appeared first.]

1948. Dr. Ludwig Philippsohn.—The Development of the Religious Idea in Judaism, Christianity, and Mohammedanism.   Translated from the German, with Notes by Anna Maria Goldsmid. xii.-268 pp. London. 8vo.   1855.

1949. B. Cahun.—האמונה יסוד. — Jessod Haamuna : The Thirteen Articles of Faith demonstrated from the Holy Bible.   London, published by Author.

1950. M. H. Simonson.—הפרטי עולם יסוד. The True origin of the Solar System.   Manchester.   1855.
[The author says in an advertisement, "The scientific will stand amazed, astonished and gratified to find the Mosaic narrative of the creation in Genesis corresponding most wonderfully with the Newtonian theory of the world."]

1951. M. H. Bresslau.—שבתות ה' The Sabbaths of the Lord : being Sabbath Meditations on the Pentateuch and on the Haphtorahs.   London. 1858.

1952. Moses Angel.—The Law of Sinai and its Appointed Times.   8vo., 388 pp.   1858.

1952a. J. M. de Sola.—On the Prohibition of Intermarriage with Mamzerim.   Kingston.   1861.

1953. Jacobus (pseud.) —Reflections on the Psalms of David as inspired Compositions, and as indicating the philosophy of the Jewish Faith.   London. Published by S. Solomon, 37, Duke Street, Aldgate.
1863.

1954. ELIAS DAVIS.—A few Words on the Penalty that follows Intemperance and Sin. London.   1870.

1955. HERSCHELL FILIPOWSKI. — Biblical Prophecies, including those relating to the expected Advent of Messiah, as interpreted by the Hebrew Nation, agreeably with the views of Ancient Hebrew Commentators, thoroughly investigated and considerably augmented. London.   1870.

1956. CONSTANCE DE ROTHSCHILD AND ANNIE DE ROTHSCHILD. — History and Literature of the Israelites. 2 vols. London.   1870.

1957. A. ELZAS (Head Master of the Leeds Hebrew School). — The Proverbs of Solomon. Translated from the Hebrew, with Notes critical and explanatory. Leeds and London.   1871.

1958. M. M. KALISCH, Ph. D., M.A · Theology of the Past and the Future. Portrait. 58 pp. Ramsgate.   circ. 1871.

[Reprinted from Part 2 of the Commentary on Leviticus, and published in Thomas Scott's series of " Free Thought " Tracts.]

1959. JAMES SAMUELSON.—Views of the Deity, Traditional and Scientific; a contribution to the study of Theological Science.   1871.

1960. A. ELZAS.—The Book of Job. Translated from the Hebrew Text, with an Introduction and Notes, critical and explanatory.   1872.

1961. I. L. MOCATTA.—Moral Biblical Gleanings.

1963. A. ELZAS.—The Minor Prophets. Translated from the Hebrew Text with an Introduction and a Commentary, Critical, Philological, and Exegetical. Vol. I. Hosea and Joel.   1873.

1964. A. BERNSTEIN.—Origin of the Legends of Abraham, Isaac, and Jacob, critically examined. [Translated by "a German Lady " from the German, and

published in Thomas Scott's series of Free Thought
Tracts.] London. 97 pp.   1874.

1965. H. L. HARRIS.—The Immortality of the Soul.
London.   1874.

1967. DR. A. BENISCH.—Judaism Surveyed: Being a
Sketch of the Rise and Development of Judaism
from Moses to our days, in a series of five Lectures.
London. 146 pp.   1874.

1968. M. M. KALISCH, PH.D, M.A.—Bible Studies.
Part I. The Prophecies of Balaam (Numbers xxii.
to xxiv.), or "The Hebrew and the Heathen."
Part II. The Book of Jonah.   1877.

1969. I. L. MOCATTA.—The Jewish Armoury.   1878.
[Not published.]

1970. REV. JOSEPH KOHN ZEDEK. — מום השכל. A
Series of Discourses, Theological and Homiletic.
London.   1878.

1971. REV. A. L. GREEN.—Judaism in its relation to
Mankind.   1878.
[Privately printed.]

1972. M. KALISCH.—Path and Goal. A Discussion on
the Elements of Civilisation and the Conditions of
Happiness.   1880.

1972a. S. M. SCHILLER-SZINESSY, M.A., Ph D.— הנה
ישכיל עבדי. An Exposition of Isaiah lii. 13, 14,
15, and liii., delivered before the Council of the
Senate in the Law School, on Friday, April 28th,
1882.   1822.
[Printed by request.]

1973. ISRAEL ABRAHAMS, M.A.—The Atonement: A
Clerical Symposium.   1884.
[Contribution from the Jewish standpoint, by I. A.]

1974. DR. FRIEDLANDER. — כתבי הקדש. The Jewish
Family Bible, containing the Pentateuch, the Prophets and the Hagiographs in Hebrew and English.

P

[The Anglican version revised by Dr. F., and published with the sanction of the Chief Rabbi.]   1884.
[Issued in 25 monthly parts.]

1974*a*. Rev. Naphtali Levy. — שני המצות.   Two Commentaries on the Laws bearing upon Duty towards Parents.   Vienna.   1884.

1975. Rev. Dr. Chotzner.—Humour and Irony of the Hebrew Bible.   1885.

1976. Rev. Dr. Hermann Adler.—Immortality : A Clerical Symposium.   1885.
[Contribution from the Jewish standpoint. Pp. 88-109]

1977. Israel Abrahams, M.A.—Inspiration : A Clerical Symposium.   1885.
[Contribution from the Jewish standpoint. Pp. 155-175.]

1978. Anon. [Philip Berger Benny].—Bible Flowers and Flower Lore.   Sm. 8vo., pp. xii.-151.   London.
                                                            1885.
[Reprinted from the *Jewish World*.]

1979. Rev. B. Spiers (Dayan).—דברי חפץ.   Acceptable Words.   Addresses delivered by the Rev. B. S.
                                                            1886.

1980. Rev. Simeon Singer. — Future Probation : A Symposium.   1886.
[Contribution from the Jewish standpoint. Pp. 25-52.]

(P.) RABBINIC SCHOLARSHIP.

1981. T. Goodman.—בחינת עולם, translated into English.   1830 (?)

1981*a*. Joseph ben Joshua the Priest.—The Chronicles of Rabbi Joseph ben Joshua.   Translated by C. H. F. Bialoblotzky.   2 vols.   1835-6.
[Oriental Translation Fund.]

1982. A. Asher.—מסעות.   The Itinerary of Rabbi Benjamin of Tudela.   Translated and edited by A. A.

(Vol. 1. Text Bibliography and Translation. Hebrew and English. Vol. 2. Notes and Essays.) 2 vols. London and Berlin. 12mo.   1840-41.

1983. SELIG NEWMAN.—ספר השרשים. A Hebrew and English Lexicon, containing all the words of the Old Testament, with the Chaldee Words in Daniel, Ezra, and the Targums and the Talmudical Words derived from them. London.   1841.

1984. ABRAHAM BEN RAPHAEL JALPHON.—ספר חיי אברהם
וי"ר בא"ח · · · מרן שלחן על · · · [First edition, Leghorn ; second at] Calcutta.   1844.

1985. ABIGAIL LINDO.—A Hebrew and English and English and Hebrew Dictionary. 8vo.   359 pp. (numbered reverse).   1846.

1986. JOSEPH ZEDNER (of the British Museum).—הוא
פירוש הרא"בע על אסתר מהדורא תנינא על ידי יוסף
צעדנר ויוסף אברהם Abraham aben Ezra's Commentary on the Book of Esther, after another version ; copied from an old MS. in the Harleian Collection, and edited for the first time. London. 1850.

1987. HERSCHELL E. FILIPOWSKI.—מורה נבכים כפי אשר
העתיקו רבי יהודה אלחריזי ז"ל. The Guide for the Perplexed : as translated from the original Arabic of Maimonides by the celebrated Poet, Rabbi Jehuda Al-Charizi.   Illustrated with abundant Critical Notes, as to the correctness of this translation with reference to the old one of Aben Tibbon, by the famous Dr. I. Munk, of the National Library of Paris.   Edited by H. E. F.   London.   1850.

1988. M. H. BRESSLAU (Editor of the "*Jewish Chronicle*").—גנזי אקספרד. Treasures of Oxford. Being compositions by the most eminent ancient Hebrew Writers, faithfully copied from MSS. in the Bodleian Library, Oxford, by Rabbi H. Edelman and Mr. Leopold Dukes, with notes.   Edited and translated by M. H. B.   London.   1850.

212 BIBLIOTHECA ANGLO-JUDAICA.

1989. הא לך ספר מבחר הפנינים · · · לפי כתב יד הנמצא
בבית המדרש דק"ק לונדון עם באור · · · מאתי צבי
פיליפאווסקי (ספר מגלת אנטיוכוס · · · בלשון ארמי
ומתורגם לשון עברי ואנגלי) London, 32mo. 1851.

1990. H. FILOPOWSKI. — ספר העבור. Abraham ben
Chyiah . . . on the mathematical and technical
Chronology of the Hebrews, Nazarites, Mahomet-
tans, etc., from two MSS. Edited by H. F. London. 8vo. 1851.

1991. L. SCHLOSSBERG.—ספר מורה נבכים העתקת ר' יהודה
חריזי. More Nevochim ; translated into Hebrew,
by R. Jehudah Charizi, with Notes by Dr. S. Scheyer.
Edited by L. S. Part I. Bagster & Sons. London. 1851.

[The remaining two parts were published in 1875 and 1879.]

1994. HIRSCH EDELMAN.—דרך טובים. The Path of Great
Men ; being a Collection of Proverbial Instructions to Children by Authors distinguished in Israel
for Wisdom and Learning, viz., Juda ben Saul Aben
Tibbon, for his son Rabbi Samuel Aben Tibbon ;
the illustrious Rabbi Moses Maimonides, for his son
R. Abraham, being their last Will for the Instruction
of Mankind. Also ancient Arabic and Greek proverbs
rendered into Hebrew. Edited from MSS. in the
Harleian Library, Oxford, and accompanied by an
English translation [by M. H. Bresslau]. London.
8vo. 1852.

1995. DR. S. M. SCHILLER-SZINESSY.—Specimens from
unpublished work שערי ציון, "The Gate of Zion,"
comprising Occasional Prayers, Addresses, Bene-
dictions, &c. Part I. London. 1852.

1996. ABRAHAM DE SOLA.—Behemoth Hatemeoth, the
nomenclature of the prohibited animals of Leviticus,
as determined by the most eminent Authorities,
both Jewish and Christian. Montreal. 16 pp. 1853.

1997. HIRSCH EDELMANN.— דברי חפץ מערכה א כוללל
כתבי יד לגדולי ישראל. Part I. London. 8vo. 1853.
[No more published.]

1997a. AZARIAH DE ROSSI.—מצרף לכסף Tentina Argenti
Ed. H. Floipowski. 1854.
[With biography of author by L. Zunz.]

1998. MENACHEM BEN JACOB BEN SARUK.— מחברת מנחם ,
הוא הספר הראשון אשר חובר על שרשי לשון הקדש · · ·
נדפס עתה ראשונה ונוספו בו מקומות המקראות גם פירוש
קצר · · · וחקירות ר' שמואל דוד לוצאטו ור' יששכר בער
בלומענפעלד The first Hebrew and Chaldaic Lexicon . . . . [partly] translated by H. Filopowski.
8vo. Edinburgh. 1854.

1999. H. FILOPOWSKI, L. DUKES and R. KIRCHHEIM.
ספר תשובות דונש בן לברט עם הכרעות רבינו יעקב—
תם · · · והוא חלק שני לכפר מחברת מנהם · · · נדפסו
· · ·עתה ראשונה עם תוכפת הערות· · ·ר' צבי פיליפאווסקי
ר' יהודה ליב דוקעם ור' רפאל קירכהיים Edinburgh.
8vo. 1855.

2000. DR. A. BENISCH.—Travels of Rabbi Petachia
of Ratisbon, who, in the latter end of the Twelfth
Century, visited Poland, Russia, Little Tartary, the
Crimea, Armenia, Assyria, Syria, Holy Land, and
Greece. Translated into English by Dr. B., with
Explanatory Notes by the translator and W. F.
Ainsworth, Esq. London. 1856.
[Hebrew and English on opposite pages.]

2001. M. STEINSCHNEIDER.—Jewish Literature from the
Eighth to the Eighteenth Century, with an intro-
duction on Talmud and Midrash. London. 8vo.
400 pp. 1857.
[Translation of article contributed to Ersch and Grüber's
Encyclopædie.]

2002. HIRSCH FILOPOWSKI.—ונלוו · · · ספר יוחסין השלם
אליו הגהות יעב"ץ · · · כדרו והעריכו לדפוס ר' צבי
פיליפאווכקי 2 parts. Edimburgi. 8vo. 1857.

2003. REV. H. B. ASCHER.—מבחר הפנינים. A choice of
Pearls ; embracing a Collection of Ethical Sen-
tences and Maxims, originally compiled from the
Arabic by Rabbi Solomon Ibn Gabirol, and trans-
lated into Hebrew by Rabbi Jehuda Ibn Tibbon.
London.   8vo., xxiii.-189 pp.   1859.
[Hebrew and English with notes.]

2005. Horæ Talmudicæ.   Rabbi Joshua ben Hanania.
1860 (?)
[Written in English : printed in Berlin.]

2006. ELIAS SOLOWEYCZIK.—Moses Maimonides Yad-
Hachasaka or Mishne Torah, Hilchoth Melachim,
containing Laws concerning Kings and their Wars.
Translated from the Hebrew into English by several
learned writers.   Edited and revised by E. S.
London.   Small 8vo., 47 pp.   1863.

2007. ZEDNER.—Catalogue of the Hebrew Books in the
Library of the British Museum.   1867.

2008. S. RAPPOPORT.—Stories and Sayings translated
from the Talmud.   56 pp.   1869.
[Revised for press by Lady Magnus.]

2009. SOLOMON SEBAG.—מסעי אחד מבני ישראל.   1870.
[Not published.]

2010. M. FRIEDLANDER, Ph. D.—The Commentary of
Ibn Ezra on Isaiah, edited from MSS., and trans-
lated with Notes, Introductions, and Indexes.
London.   2 Vols.   8vo., xxvii.-332 and iv.-407 pp.
1873.
[Vol. I. consists of the Commentary, and Vol. II. of the
Anglican version of Isaiah amended according to the Com-
mentary.   Published by the Society of Hebrew Literature.]

2011. MISCELLANY OF HEBREW LITERATURE.   Vol. 1.
8vo., pp. viii. 228.   London.   1872.
CONTENTS.
1. "The Minister R. Samuel Ibn Nagrela."   Translated
from the German of Dr. Graetz by A. J. K. D.
2. "Specimen of the Biur."   Translated, with Notes, by
Dr. Benisch.

3. "Specimen of the book Cusari." Translated by A. Neubauer.
4. "Chisdai, the son of Isaac." Translated from the German of Dr. Cassel. by A. J. K. D.
5. "Epistle of R. Chisdai to the King of the Cusars." Translated from the German of Zedner by A. J. K. D.
6. "Answer of Joseph, King of the Togarim." Translated from the Hebrew by A. J. K. D.
7. "Selections from Two Letters written by Obadia da Bertinoro. Translated from the Hebrew by A. J. K. D.
8. Zunz "On the Sufferings of the Jews of the Middle Ages." Translated by the Rev. A. Löwy.
9. "Letter of Maimonides to R. Jehudah Ibn Tibbon." Translated from the Hebrew by the Rev. Dr. H. Adler.

2011a. MISCELLANY OF HEBREW LITERATURE. Vol. II., Second Series, 8vo., pp. viii. and 276, and 15 pp. Heb. London. 1877.

CONTENTS.

1. "The Life and Labours of Menasseh ben Israel." Translated from the German of D. M. Kayserling, by the Rev. Dr. F. de Sola Mendes.
2. "The Sons of the Prophets and the Prophetic Schools," by Dr. A. Benisch.
3. "Legends from the Midrash." Translated by Thomas Chenery, M.A.
4. The Hebrew translation of "L'Image du Monde," by A. Neubauer.
5. "Travels in Abyssinia." Translated from the French of J. Halévy, by James Picciotto.
6. Abraham Ibn Ezra's "Short Commentary on Daniel," with an Appendix of the variations of two additional MSS., of his "Commentary on the Canticles after the First Recension," by H. J. Matthews, M.A.

2012. EMANUEL DEUTSCH.—Literary Remains of the late Emanuel Deutsch. With a Brief Memoir. 8vo. xx.-465 pp. 1874.
[Contains nineteen articles, lectures, &c., reprinted from various publications including the famous *Quarterly* article on "The Talmud."]

2013. ADLER (NATHAN MARCUS), Chief Rabbi.—נתינה לגר באור על תרגום אונקלוס 8vo., 5 vols. Wilna. 1874.

2014. ADOLPH NEUBAUER.—Talmudical and Rabbinical

Literature. (In the transactions of the Philological Society, 1875-6.)   1876.

2015. Rev. Albert Löwy.—On a Unique Specimen of the Lishaun ohel Unrain, the Modern Syriac, or Targum Dialect of the Jews in Kurdistan and adjacent Countries, with an account of the People by whom it is spoken.   1875.
[Paper read before the Soc. of Bibl. Archæology, 4th May, 1875, and published in the transactions for June.]

2016. Ad. Neubauer.—Kitâb-al-uzûl, or the Book of Roots, by Abul' Walid Marwan Ibn Janah, otherwise called "Rabbi Jonah," now first edited, with an Appendix containing extracts from other Hebrew-Arabic Dictionaries. Oxford.   1875.

2017. Dr. L. Loewe. — On a Karaite Tombstone, brought from Djuffet Kelea, in the Crimea.   1875.
[Reprinted from the "Transactions" of the Society of Biblical Archæology.]

2018. H. Polano —The Talmud : Selections from the Contents of that Ancient Book, its Commentaries, Teachings, Poetry, and Legends. Also Brief Sketches of the Men who made and commented upon it. Translated from the Original by H. P. London. 8vo., pp. xi.-359.   1876.
[Issued in the "Chandos Classics" Series.]

2019. S. M. Schiller-Szinessy, Ph.D.—Catalogue of Hebrew MSS. preserved in the University Library, Cambridge.   1877.

2019a. Ad. Neubauer, M.A.—The Fifty-third Chapter of Isaiah according to the Jewish Interpreters. 2 vols. Oxford.   1877.

2020. S. M. Schiller-Szinessy.—והמה בכתבים.—Occasional Notices of Hebrew Manuscripts.   1879.

2021. Philip Berger Benny.—The Criminal Code of the Jews, according to the Talmud, Mishna Synhedrion.   1880.
[Reprinted from the *Pall Mall Gazette*.]

2021*a*. S. M. SCHILLER-SZINESSY, M.A., Ph.D.—The First Book of Psalms, according to the Text of the Cambridge MS. Bible. Add. 465, with the longer Commentary of R. David Qimchi; critically edited from nineteen manuscripts and the early édition. Cambridge. 8vo. 1884.

2022. M. FRIEDLANDER, Ph.D.—The "Guide of the Perplexed" of Maimonides. Translated from the Original, and annotated. London. 8vo., 3 vols., pp. lxxx.-370; ix.-226; and xxvii.-327. 1885.
[Published as Vols. XXVIII.-XXX. of the English and Foreign Philosophical Library. The first Vol. was originally issued by the Society of Hebrew Literature (vide 1881). Parts of the Translation were ccntributed by Mr. Joseph Abrahams, Ph.D., and Rev. H. Gollancz.]

2023. REV. DR. CHOTZNER.—זכרונות [Zichronoth; or Reminiscences of a Student of Jewish Theology.] Written in Hebrew Rhymed Prose, and accompanied by an Essay in English on "the Rise and Progress of Hebrew Poetry in Post-biblical Times." London. 8vo., pp. xvi.-84. 1885.

2024. JOSEPH ABRAHAMS, B.A., Ph.D. — The Sources of the Midrash Echa Rabbah : a Critical Investigation. Berlin. 8vo., 61 pp. 1885.

2024*a*. S. M. SCHILLER-SZINESSY, M.A., Ph.D.—משא בערב. Romanelli's Travels in Morocco, towards the end of the Eighteenth Century. With Preface, Notes, and Life of the Author. In two Parts : Hebrew and English. I. Hebrew Text. 1886.
[The English Part has not yet appeared.]

2024*b*. AD. NEUBAUER.—Catalogue of the Hebrew MSS. in the Bodleian Library. 4to. Oxford. 1886.
[Accompanied by a portfolio of Facsimiles.]

2024*c*. S. SCHECHTER.—Aboth de Rabbi Nathan . . . recensiones duas edidit. 4to., pp. xxxvi.-176. 1887.

HEBREW POEMS, &c.

2025. B. BARUCH.—Elegy on the death of Isaac ben David Netto.   1773.

2026. H. FRIEDLÄNDER. — Poem in honour of the Barmitzvah of S. Cohen.   1790.

2026a. M. KÖNIGSBERG. — Poem spoken by Master J. Keyser on his Barmitzvah.   1792.
[A similar poem for S. Keyser, 1794.]

2027. DANIEL BEN RAPHAEL MELDOLA, JUNIOR. — תהלה
לדוד · · · לכבוד החתן אברהם בן יעקב מוקאתה
                                                            1818.

2027a. HYMAN HURWITZ.—The Tears of a Grateful People, a Hebrew Dirge and Hymn, chaunted in the Great Synagogue, St. James's Place, Aldgate, on the Day of the Funeral of his late Most Sacred Majesty, King George III., of blessed memory. 15 pp. Hebrew and English. Price 2s. [A. N.]   1820.

2028. ABRAHAM MELDOLA.—Stanzas in Honour of the Anniversary of the Jews' Hospital.   1821.

2028a. H. HURWITZ.—The Knell, an Elegy on George the Third. From the Hebrew of H. H. by W. Smith. Thurso.   1827.
[Followed by the original Hebrew in English letters.]

2029. REV. DAVID MELDOLA.—קינה. A Dirge in Memory of the late much lamented Rev. Dr. Meldola, Chief Rabbi of the Spanish and Portuguese Jews' Congregation, chaunted by the boys of the Orphan Society, on the evening of the 7th Tammuz, 5588 (18th June, 1828), composed by his son and pupil, David Meldola. [A. N.]   1828.

2030. DR. BENJAMIN FRANKLIN. — אבל כבד.—Elegy on the Death of N. M. Rothschild, with a free Translation from the Hebrew. 4to., 24 pp. [A. N.]
                                                            1836.

2031. Ode, Hebrew and English, spoken at the Anniversary of the Jews' Free School.   1838.

2032. JACOB EICHENBAUM.—שיר, הקרב (A Poem on Chess). 1840.

2033. NATHAN ISAAC VALLENTINE.—מחסות העליון. The Refuge of the Omnipotent . . . who displayed His peculiar protection over Queen Victoria and her illustrious Consort on the event which occurred to them on the 10th of June, A.M. 5600. Hebr. and Eng. 1840.

2034. DAVID BEN RAPHAEL MELDOLA, the Younger — מזמור לתודה · · · על דבר ישע והצלת אחינו ב״י בדמשק Hebrew and English. 8vo. [London.] 1841.

2035. MICHAEL JOSEPHS.—תהלת ישרון. A Hebrew Poem; in Honour of Sir Moses Montefiore, on his Return from his Mission to the East. Translated into English and German. London. 8vo. 1841.

2036. ABRAHAM BEN SHALOM BELAIS.—ספר רוח והצלה. Poem on the safe Delivery of . . . . Queen Victoria of a Princess. Also a New Poem, in honour of Sir Moses Montefiore, &c. 8vo. [1841 ?]

2037. זכר רב. A Lyrical Ode on the Death of the Rev. Dr. Hirschel. Published by A. Abrahams, Houndsditch. London. [? By B. Fränkel.] 1843.

2038. ABRAHAM BEN SHALOM BELAIS.—קינת סופרים. Elegy on the Death of H.R.H. Augustus Frederick, Duke of Sussex. 8vo. 1843.

2039. S. HOGA.—ספר הליכות אורח. Translated from the English of John Bunyan, by S. Hoga. 2 vols. London. 8vo. 1844.

2040. ALEXANDER POPE. — Pope's Universal Prayer, with a Hebrew Translation, by M. Josephs. London. 4to. 1845.

2041. FRANKEL, REV. DR. BENJAMIN (author of the נצח והוד, &c.).—אשרי משכיל. Ashry Masscil. A Poem, in Honour of the Rev. Dr. N. M. Adler, Chief Rabbi of Great Britain, &c. London. 1845.

2042. ABRAHAM BEN SHALOM BELAIS.—קול תודה וקול זמרה
Thanksgiving to Almighty God for the success which
crowned the Mission of Sir Moses Montefiore to
Russia, &c.   Hebrew and English.   8vo.   1846.

2042a. Ode for the Anniversary Meeting of the Jews'
Hospital, held at the London Tavern . . . . and
recited by one of the Girls of the Institution.
(Broad sheet.)   1846.
  [Signed S. S.   These Odes were almost an annual insti-
  tution.]

2043. RABBI ABRAHAM BELAIS (late Treasurer to the
Bey of Tunis, and Chief Rabbi of Nice).—An Ode
in English on the late Election of the Baron Lionel
de Rothschild, M.P., on the success of Sir Moses
Montefiore's recent Mission to France in the affairs
of the Jews of Damascus, and on the liberal-
minded Pope Pius IX., the friend of the Jews.
Also a Prayer in Hebrew and English for the above
distinguished Men, as well as for H.M. the Queen,
H.M. the Queen Dowager, and the Royal Family.
[London.]   1847.

2044. DAVID BEN RAPHAEL MELDOLA, the Younger.—
Epitaph to the Memory of . . . . Abigail, third
Daughter of D. A. Lindo.   Hebrew and English.
8vo. [London.]   1848.

2045. SAMSON RAUSUK.—פורים.   [A Poem.]   Hebrew.
8vo.   1849.

2046. —— שיר.   Dedicated to Master A. Cohen, &c.
Hebrew. 8vo.   1849.

2047. —— בן מאיר יוסף . . . קינה על מות החכם   8vo.
                                               1849.
  [Another by L. Dukes.]

2048. ABRAHAM BEN SHALOM BELAIS.—קינה.   Elegy on
the Death of . . . . Baroness H. de Rothschild.
Hebrew and English. 8vo.   1849.
  [Others by H. Edelman and B. H. Ascher.]

2049. "The Voice of Lament."—A Collection of Elegies and Poems, in Hebrew and English, written on the Death of the late Hananel de Castro, Esq , Member of Deputies of the British Jews, President of the Jewish Literary and Scientific Institution, Sussex Hall, &c.   1849.

2050. SAMSON RAUSUK.—שיר. A Poem. Dedicated to Master M. Adler, &c. Hebrew. 8vo.   1850.

2051. —— שיר ידידות. A. Poem. Composed in honour of the Marriage of H. Solomon, Esq. and S. Adler, &c. Hebrew. 8vo.   1850.

2052. —— שיר ידידות. A Poem, in honour of the nuptials of J. Sebag, &c. Hebrew and English. 16mo.   1851.

2053. —— תפלה למשה. A Hymn, in honour of Master M. Moses, &c. Hebrew. 8vo.   1851.

2054. —— שיר תהלה. A Poem in honour of Master N. H. Adler, &c. Hebrew. 8vo.   1852.

2055. MARCUS HEINRICH BRESSLAU.—רנה ותפלה. "God Speed to Sir Moses and Lady Montefiore." A Poem, written on the occasion of their journey to the Holy Land. Hebrew and English. 8vo.   1855.

2056. —— קול שלום. "A Voice of Welcome to Sir Moses and Lady Montefiore, on their return from the Holy Land. In verse. Hebrew and English. 8vo.   1855.

2057. SAMSON RAUSUK.—שיר ידידות. A Poem, composed in honour of the Nuptials of A. H. Moses, and H. Cohen. Hebrew. 8vo.   1855.

2058. —— שיר ידידות. A Poem, composed in honour of the Nuptials of L. L. Cohen, Esq. Hebrew. 8vo.   1856.

2059. —— שיר ידידות. A Poem, composed in honour of the Nuptials of H. D. Behrend, &c. Hebrew. 8vo.   1857.

2060. SAMSON RAUSUK.—שיר תהלה. A Poem, in honour
of Master A. Keyser, &c. Hebrew. 8vo. 1857.

2061. —— שיר. A Poem, in honour of Master B. and
J. L. Cohen. &c. Hebrew. 8vo. 1858.

2062. —— שיר ידידות. A Poem composed in honour
of the Nuptials of J. Israel, Esq., and M. Adler.
Hebrew. 8vo. 1858.

2063. Jews' Free School. ארשת שפתים מאחד הצעירים
בחברת תלמוד תורה וחנוך ילדים ביום הועד לתקופת
השנה · · · תרי"ט. London. s.sh. fol. 1859.

2064. Westminster Jews' Free School.— . ארשת שפתים
ביום הועד · · · תרי"ט. s.sh. fol. [London.] 1859.

2065. Jews' Free School.—ארשת שפתים · · · לתקופת השנה
תר"ך · · · s. sh. fol. [London.] 1860.
[Almost annually.]

2066. Westminster Jews' Free School.—ארשת שפתים · · ·
ביום הועד · · · תרכ"ג s. sh. fol. [London.] 1863.
[Almost annually.]

2067. SAMSON RAUSUK.—שיר תהלה. Poem commemo-
rative of the successful Mission of Sir Moses Montefiore to the Court of Morocco. Hebrew and
English. 8vo. 1864.

2068. S. SEBAG.—Elegy on B. Abrahams. 1864.

2069. Gates of Hope School.—שיר. An Ode for the
celebration of the Bi-centenary of the Charity School
"The Gates of Hope," etc. Hebrew and English.
16mo. [London.] 1865.

2070. J. GOLDENWASSER.—עלים לתרופה. Leaves for a
Healing; being a Collection in the Hebrew Language, consisting of Original Poems and Translations from Modern Classics, Friendly Correspondence, and Epitaphs. London. 1865.

2071. SAMSON RAUSUK.—שיר. A Poem in honour of
Master A. M. Sebag, etc. Hebrew. 8vo. [1866.]

2072. SAMSON RAUSUK.—קול רנה וישועה. (A Poem in honour of Sir Moses Montefiore, paraphrased by M. Henry.) Hebrew and English. 8vo. [1867.]

2073. —— שיר ידידות. A Poem composed in honour of the Marriage of B. Cohen and L. Merton. 1870.

2074. —— שיר ידידות. A Poem composed in honour of the Marriage of N. Cohen and J. M. Waley. 1873.

(R.) SCHOOLBOOKS.

2075. JEHUDAH STENNETT. — דקדוק מכלול. (Hebrew Grammar.) 1685.

2076. PHILIP LEVI.—דקדוק לשון הקדש. A Compendium of Hebrew Grammar. Oxford. 1705.

2076a. ABRAHAM YAGEL.—לקח טוב. Catechism, Hebrew and English. 1721.

2077. ISRAEL LYONS, Senior. — מורה תלמידים. The Scholar's Instructor. An Hebrew Grammar. Cambridge. 1735.
[A Second and Third edition in 1757 and 1810.]

2078. R. BENJAMIN LEVI.—דעת קדשים. Epitome of Hebrew Grammar. 1773.

2079. D. LEVI.—Lingua Sacra. 3 vols. 1786.

2079a. H. HURWITZ.—Elements of the Hebrew Language. 1807.
[Went through many editions, and was for a long time the standard Hebrew grammar among English Jews.]

2080. S. J. COHEN.—Elements of Truth for the use of Jewish youth of both sexes. 112 pp. 1815.

2081. Jewish Preceptress, by a Daughter of Israel. 1818.

2082. S. NEWMAN.—ספר מלים. English and Hebrew Lexicon. 1832.
[Followed in 1834 by corresponding Hebrew and English Lexicon.]

2083. SELIG NEWMAN.—A Hebrew and English Lexicon.
8vo., 732 pp. and 4 pp. (of mistranslations in A. V.)
[A. N.]   1834.

2084. M. JOSEPH.—מדרש מלים. English and Hebrew
Lexicon.   1834.

2085. J. L. LYON.—Hebrew and English Spelling Book,
12mo., 166 pp.   1837.

2086. HERMANN HEDWIG BERNARD formerly HOWITZ.—
The Guide of the Hebrew Student, containing an
Epitome of Sacred History, together with easy Pas-
sages in pure Biblical Hebrew, &c.   1839.

2086a. M. CAHEN.—Catechism of Religion.   Liverpool.
1840.

2087. SELIG NEWMAN.—תלמוד לשון עברי. A Grammar
of the Hebrew Language with points, together with
a short sketch of the Chaldee Grammar.   London.
1841.

2088. DAVID ASHER (Head Master of the Manchester
Hebrew Association School). — Outlines of the
Jewish Religion, in a series of Questions and Answers, for the use of Schools and Families   Manchester.   1845.

2089. AN AMERICAN JEWESS. — The Teachers' and
Parents' Assistant, or 13 Lessons, conveying to un-
informed minds the first ideas of God and His
attributes. Publisher, Mrs. Joel, 42, Fore Street,
London.   1845.

2090. M. H. and I. H. MYERS.— Twelve Hundred
Questions and Answers on the Bible; intended
principally for the use of Schools and Young Persons. London. 132 pp.   1845.

2092. A. ABRAHAM.—Moral and Religious Tales for the
Young of the Hebrew Faith. sm. 8vo., xvi.-239 pp.
London.   1846.
[Adapted from the French " Les Matinées de Samedi," of
G. Ben Levi.]

2093. A LADY.—מאיר עין בני הנעורים. A Hebrew and English Vocabulary, from a Selection of the Daily Prayers for the use of Schools and young beginners. London. 1848.

Revised by Sabato Morais, and under the sanction of the Rev. D. Meldola.

2094. Practical Instruction in the Hebrew Language. Part I. ; Reading Lessons, with a Literal Translation. London. 1848.

2095. REV. DR. MELDOLA.—דרך אמונה. The Way of Faith : A Moral and Religious Catechism of the Principles of the Jewish Faith. Translated from the Hebrew by the Rev. Dr. Meldola. London. 1848.

[With portrait of Author. It appears that only "Lecture I., Part I." of this work was published.]

2096. REV. B. H. ASCHER.—חנוך נערים. Initiation of Youth : containing the Principles of Judaism, adapted for the Period of Confirmation, arranged in a Catechetical Form. London. 1850

2097. DR. A. BENISCH.—בכורי הלמוד. Being an Hebrew Primer and Progressive Reading Book, with an Interlinear Translation, preparatory to the Study of the Hebrew Scriptures. Compiled by Dr. A. B. London. 1852.

2098. SOLOMON SEBAG.— The Hebrew Primer and Reading Book. London. 1852.

2100. S. SOLOMON.—למודי הקריאה. Hebrew Primer. London. 1853.

2101. ABRAHAM BENISCH.—Scripture History, simply arranged for the use of Jewish children. London. 1854.

2102. M. DAVIDSON.—Moral and Religious Guide ; based on the Principles of Universal Brotherhood. London. 1855.

[Dedicated by permission to Lord John Russell.]

Q

2103. M. H. BRESSLAU.—Hebrew Grammar and Dictionary. London. 2 vols.   1855.

2104. I. REGGIO.—A Guide for the Religious Instruction of Jewish Youth. Translated by M. H. Picciotto. London.   1855.

2105. MIRIAM MENDEZ BELISARIO.—Sabbath Evenings at Home ; or Familiar Conversations on the Jewish Religion, its Spirit, and Observances. 2 parts. Revised by the Rev. D. A. De Sola. London.
1857.

2106. M. H. BRESSLAU.—A Compendious Hebrew Grammar. London.   1857.

2107. M. H. BRESSLAU.—Sabbath Meditations. London.
1857.

2108. MRS. SARAH HARRIS.—Thoughts suggested by Bible Texts. Addressed to my Children. London. 16mo., 209 pp.   1859.

2109. ISRAEL ALBU.—חק לישראל. A Statute unto Israel, containing an Abridged Account of the Religious Duties of the Israelite, &c. Hebrew and English. London (imp. Berlin). 120 pp.   1860.
[Sanctioned by the Rev.˙the Chief Rabbi.]

2110. MORITZ STEINSCHNEIDER.—Reshith Halimud.
1861.
[Hebrew Grammar for the use of Beni Israel. Has a Hebrew translation of " God save the Queen," composed by M. S.]

2111. REV. A. P. MENDEZ (Head Master of the Jews' Hospital).—תורת משה. The Law of Moses; a Catechism of the Jewish Religion. (Jewish School Books, No. 1.) London.   1861.

2112. DR. A. BENISCH. — An Elementary Practical Hebrew Grammar, with copious Exercises from English into Hebrew especially adapted for Jewish Schools. London.   1862.

2113. ANON. [ABRAHAM ABRAHAM].—The Catechism

of Religious and Moral Instruction for Children of the Hebrew Faith. 2nd and enlarged edition.
1863.
[Translation of Cohen's "Jewish Catechism."]

2114. M. KALISCH.—A Hebrew Grammar with Exercises. 2 vols. 1863-65.
[Second vol. contains exceptional forms, with short history of Hebrew Grammar and Lexicography.]

2115. (Jewish Association for Diffusion of Religious Knowledge).—Little Miriam's Bible Stories, by H. N.
1865-66.
Vol. I., Job; Vol. II., Samson; Vol. III., Gideon; Vol. IV., Ruth.

2116. The Way of Truth; or a Mother's Teachings from the Bible. Part I. The Book of Genesis.
1867.

2117. H. N.—Little Miriam's Holiday Stories. 1868.
Vol. I., The Sabbath; Vol. II., Passover.

2118. REV. A. B. DAVIS (Minister of the Congregation, Sydney.)—Questions upon the Principles and Duties of the Jewish Religion, together with Form of Declaration of Faith to be used at the Confirmation Service of Young Ladies of the Sydney Synagogue. Sydney. 1869.

2119. REV. A. B. DAVIS.—Devotions for Children and Jewish Families. Sydney. 1869.

2120. SOLOMON SEBAG.—The Hebrew Primer and Reading Book. 3rd edition, 217 pp. 1871.

2120a. GIUS. LEVI.—Early Lessons. 1869.

2121. Author of Little Miriam's Bible Stories.—First Hebrew Lesson Book. 1871.

2122. A. STONE (pseud.) [I. L. MOCATTA.]—Times and Places in our History. 1872.
[The initials I. L. M. appear on the cover.]

2123. ANNETTE A. SALAMAN.—Footsteps in the Way of Life. 1873.
[Classified Anthology from the Old Test.]

2124. Author of " Little Miriam's Bible Stories."—Sabbath Stories from the Pentateuch.   1873

2125. REV. A. P. MENDES.— Post-Biblical History of the Jews.   1873.
[Jewish School Books, No. 2.]

2126. A. ELZAS.—An Abridgment of Scripture History.

2127. H. N.—The Historical Fasts. Vol. IX. of Little Miriam's Holiday Stories.   1875.

2128. REV. J. STRAUSS, Ph. D.—Rabbi of the Bradford Association. Religion and Morals; a short Catechism for the use of Jewish youth.   1876.

2131. ANNETTE A. SOLOMON.—" Aunt Annette's Stories to Ada." A Series for Jewish Children. 4 vols.   1876.

2133. ELLIS A. DAVIDSON.—The Bible Reader.   1877.

2134. LILLIE HARRIS.—Mama's Fairy Tales. London.   1878.

2135. MRS. HENRY LUCAS.—The Children's Pentateuch, with the Haphtorahs or Portions from the Prophets.   1878.

2136. K. M. [LADY MAGNUS.]—A History of our People since Bible Times, for Jewish Boys and Girls. Part I.   1879.
[An extended edition of this appeared in 1882 under the title " About the Jews since Bible Times."]

2137. N. S. JOSEPH.—Religion, Natural and Revealed : A Series of Progressive Lessons for Jewish Youth. 8vo., xii.-296 pp. London.   1879.
[Published by the Trustees of the Jacob Franklin Fund.]

2138. ADA S. BALLIN and F. L. BALLIN.—A Hebrew Grammar.   1881.

2139. DR. D. CASSEL.—Manual of Jewish History and Literature, preceded by a brief summary of Bible History. Translated from the German by Mrs. Henry Lucas. pp. xvi.-258. London.   1883.

2140. ANON. [BARONESS LIONEL DE ROTHSCHILD.]—
Addresses to Young Children. Series I., 1884;
Series II., 1884. 1884?

2141. L. B. ABRAHAMS.—Manual of Scripture History.
1885.

2142. LADY MAGNUS. — Outlines of Jewish History,
from B.C. 586 to C.E. 1885. Maps. Revised by
M. Friedländer, Ph.D. pp., xxiv.-343. London.
1886.
[Published at the cost of the Trustees of the Jacob Franklin
Fund.]

<hr>

(S.) COOKERY BOOKS.

2143. The Jewish Manual ; or Practical Information in
Jewish or modern Cookery, with a collection of
recipes or hints relating to the Toilet. 8vo. London.
1846.

2144. Aunt Sarah's Cookery Book for a Jewish Kitchen,
Liverpool. 1872.

2145. MRS. J. ATRUTEL.—An easy and economical Book
of Jewish Cookery, upon strictly orthodox principles. 1874.

2146. Aunt Sarah's Economical Cookery. 1877.

<hr>

(T.) SYNAGOGUE MUSIC.

2147. J. BRAHAM and I. NATHAN.—A Selection of
Hebrew Melodies, Ancient and Modern .... The
Poetry by Lord Byron. Fol. 1815.

2148. I. NATHAN.—An Essay on the History and Theory of Music. 4to. 1823.
Pp. 45, 46 specimens of Anglo-Jewish Music.

2149. REV. D. A. DE SOLA and EMANUEL AGUILAR.—The Ancient Melodies of the Liturgy of the Spanish and Portuguese Jews, harmonised by Emanuel Aguilar; preceded by an Historical Essay on the Poets, Poetry, and Melodies of the Sephardic Liturgy, by the Rev. D. A. de Sola. London. 1857.

2150. CHARLES SALAMAN and C. G. VERRINDER.—Music used in the Services of the West London Synagogue of British Jews. Composed, collected, and adapted by C. S.; the ancient melodies harmonized, and the whole arranged with obligato organ accompaniments, and edited by C. G. V. London. 1861
[Mr. Simon Waley collaborated in the work].

2151. C. G. VERRINDER., Mus. Bac. Oxon., Organist of the West London Synagogue.—ישראל נושע ב"ה.
"Israel in Adversity and in Deliverance," a Sacred Cantata. Vocal score, with pianoforte accompaniment in 2 parts. 1862.
[Composed for the degree of Bachelor in Music; performed on the 25th June, 1862, at Oxford.]

2152. M. MARGOLIOUTH.—Sacred Minstrelsy: A Lecture on Biblical and Post-Biblical Hebrew Music. Second Edition. 1863.
P. 34, Example of Jewish Music.

2153. S. F. HEILBRON.—חנוכה (Hanucah).—Hebrew Melody, with Variations. 1872.

2154. REV. M. HAST.—Collection of Sacred Jewish Hymns and Prayers, with Solos and Choruses, and an Accompaniment for Piano or Harmonium. Composed, compiled, and edited by the Rev. M. H., with the co-operation of Prof. Michael Bergson. 1874, &c.

2155. REV. M. HAST & PROF. M. BERGSON.—A Collection of Sacred Jewish Hymns, and Prayers, com-

posed, compiled, and edited by M. H., with the co-
operation of M. B.   1874.

2156. H. GUEDALLA.—Seven Ancient Melodies, har-
  · monised by Mr. E. Aguilar.   Published by H. G.
                                                  1875.
  [Published in aid of the Sir Moses Montefiore Testimonial
  Bazaar.]

2158. A. SAQUI.—Songs of Israel.   1878.

2159. REV. H. WASSERZUG.   ספר שירי מקדש. Synagogue Music, consisting of Chorals, Solos, and
  Adaptations of Old Melodies.   2 vols.   1878.

2160. REV. M. HAST.—The Divine Service.   Vol. 1.
  London.   1879.

2161. D. M. DAVIS.—The Neilah Hymn.   1879.

2162. REV. M. HAST.—" By the Rivers of Babylon."
                                               1879.

2163. D. M. DAVIS.—Psalm XV. to be sung in the
  Synagogues at the Special Service for the celebration of the Centenary of Sir Moses Montefiore,
  Sunday, October 26, 1884.   Music by D. M. D.
  4to., 4 pp.   1884.

2164. DAVID LEWIS.—The Tonic Accents of the Hebrew
  Pentateuch.   1884.

THE END.

WERTHEIMER, LEA & Co., Printers, Circus Place, London Wall.

For EU product safety concerns, contact us at Calle de José Abascal, 56–1°,
28003 Madrid, Spain or eugpsr@cambridge.org.

www.ingramcontent.com/pod-product-compliance
Ingram Content Group UK Ltd.
Pitfield, Milton Keynes, MK11 3LW, UK
UKHW010342140625
459647UK00010B/757